Psalms as Torah

STUDIES *in* THEOLOGICAL INTERPRETATION

Psalms as Torah

Reading Biblical Song Ethically

GORDON J. WENHAM

BakerAcademic
a division of Baker Publishing Group
Grand Rapids, Michigan

Published by Baker Academic
a division of Baker Publishing Group
P.O. Box 6287, Grand Rapids, MI 49516-6287
www.bakeracademic.com

Printed in the United States of America

Library of Congress Cataloging-in-Publication Data

Wenham, Gordon J.
Psalms as Torah : reading biblical song ethically / Gordon J. Wenham.
p. cm. — (Studies in theological interpretation)
Includes bibliographical references (p.) and indexes.
ISBN 978-0-8010-3168-7 (pbk.)
1. Bible. O.T. Psalms—Criticism, interpretation, etc. 2. Ethics in the Bible.
I. Title.
BS1430.6.E8W46 2012
223'.206—dc23 2011042127

Unless otherwise identified, all translations from French, German, and Italian are the author's.

12 13 14 15 16 17 18 7 6 5 4 3 2 1

To St. Mary's Church, Charlton Kings,
a church that sings the psalms

Contents

Series Preface

As a discipline, formal biblical studies is in a period of reassessment and upheaval. Concern with historical origins and the development of the biblical materials has in many places been replaced by an emphasis on the reader and the meanings supplied by present contexts and communities. The Studies in Theological Interpretation series seeks to appreciate the constructive theological contribution made by Scripture when it is read in its canonical richness. Of necessity, this includes historical evaluation while remaining open to renewed inquiry into what is meant by history and historical study in relation to Christian Scripture. This also means that the history of the reception of biblical texts—a discipline frequently neglected or rejected altogether—will receive fresh attention and respect. In sum, the series is dedicated to the pursuit of constructive theological interpretation of the church's inheritance of prophets and apostles in a manner that is open to reconnection with the long history of theological reading in the church. The primary emphasis is on the constructive theological contribution of the biblical texts themselves.

New commentary series have sprung up to address these and similar concerns. It is important to complement this development with brief, focused, and closely argued studies that evaluate the hermeneutical, historical, and theological dimensions of scriptural reading and interpretation for our times. In the light of shifting and often divergent methodologies, the series encourages studies in theological interpretation that model clear and consistent methods in the pursuit of theologically engaging readings.

An earlier day saw the publication of a series of short monographs and compact treatments in the area of biblical theology that went by the name Studies in Biblical Theology. The length and focus of the contributions were salutary features and worthy of emulation. Today, however, we find no consensus regarding the nature of biblical theology, and this is a good reason to explore anew what competent theological reflection on Christian Scripture might look like in our day. To this end, the present series, Studies in Theological Interpretation, is dedicated.

Author Preface

Ten years ago I wrote a book titled *Story as Torah*, which discussed what contribution biblical narratives could make to understanding Old Testament ethics, a topic neglected in many volumes on this subject. Since then, I have noted another scholarly blind spot: the failure to recognize the influence of the psalms on the ethics of both Jews and Christians. I therefore have written this book as a sequel to the earlier volume and termed it *Psalms as Torah*. It aims to demonstrate the importance of the psalms particularly in molding Christian ethics and to offer an initial exploration of the ethics of the psalms.

The literature on the psalms and on ethics is vast, and I make no claim to have mastered it. Doubtless if I had read more widely, I would have nuanced my argument at many points. But I hope that specialists in the Psalter and in ethics will look mercifully on such deficiencies and focus on the main argument. Another matter that I fear may disappoint some readers is the lack of inclusive language. I recognize that I am old-fashioned, often using the generic "he" where others might prefer "they" or "he or she," but it seems to me more elegant English and a closer approximation to Hebrew usage than inclusive alternatives. For the sake of non-Hebraists, I have followed the numbering of chapters and verses from Psalms used in English translations.

Finally, I thank friends, colleagues, and research students whose comments and questions have helped me to formulate my ideas more clearly and, last but not least, the editors of Baker Academic, who prepared the text for publication with great care.

Abbreviations

AB	Anchor Bible
ABD	*Anchor Bible Dictionary*. Edited by D. N. Freedman. 6 vols. New York: Doubleday, 1992
AOTC	Abingdon Old Testament Commentary
ApOTC	Apollos Old Testament Commentary
ATANT	Abhandlungen zur Theologie des Alten und Neuen Testaments
ATD	Das Alte Testament Deutsch
BBB	Bonner biblische Beiträge
BCOTWP	Baker Commentary on the Old Testament Wisdom and Psalms
BCR	Blackwell Companions to Religion
BibJS	Biblical and Judaic Studies
BJS	Brown Judaic Studies
BKAT	Biblischer Kommentar, Altes Testament
BRS	Biblical Resource Series
BZAW	Beihefte zur Zeitschrift für die alttestamentliche Wissenschaft
CahRB	Cahiers de la Revue biblique
CBQMS	Catholic Biblical Quarterly Monograph Series
CBSC	Cambridge Bible for Schools and Colleges
CC	Continental Commentaries

CNTOT	*Commentary on the New Testament Use of the Old Testament*. Edited by G. K. Beale and D. A. Carson. Grand Rapids: Baker Academic, 2007
ESV	English Standard Version
ET	English Translation
EvT	*Evangelische Theologie*
FAT	Forschungen zum Alten Testament
FOTL	Forms of Old Testament Literature
GBS	Grove Biblical Series
HALOT	Koehler, L., W. Baumgartner, and J. J. Stamm, *The Hebrew and Aramaic Lexicon of the Old Testament*. Study edition. Translated and edited under the supervision of M. E. J. Richardson. 2 vols. Leiden: Brill, 2001
HAT	Handbuch zum Alten Testament
HTKAT	Herders theologischer Kommentar zum Alten Testament
IBC	Interpretation: A Bible Commentary for Teaching and Preaching
ICC	International Critical Commentary
JJS	*Journal of Jewish Studies*
JRE	*Journal of Religious Ethics*
JSNTSup	Journal for the Study of the New Testament: Supplement Series
JSOTSup	Journal for the Study of the Old Testament: Supplement Series
JTS	*Journal of Theological Studies*
K&D	Keil, C. F., and F. Delitzsch, *Biblical Commentary on the Old Testament*. Translated by J. Martin et al. 25 vols. Edinburgh, 1875–78. Reprint, Grand Rapids: Eerdmans, 1966–71
KJV	King James Version
LD	Lectio divina
LHBOTS	The Library of Hebrew Bible / Old Testament Studies
LPT	Library of Philosophy and Theology
LXX	Septuagint
MT	Masoretic Text

MTS	Münchener theologische Studien
NCB	New Century Bible
NEB	New English Bible
NICOT	New International Commentary on the Old Testament
NIV	New International Version
NLT	New Living Translation
NRSV	New Revised Standard Version
OTL	Old Testament Library
OTS	Old Testament Studies
PBM	Paternoster Biblical Monographs
RSV	Revised Standard Version
SBLDS	Society of Biblical Literature Dissertation Series
SBT	Studies in Biblical Theology
SSN	Studia semitica neerlandica
SubBi	Subsidia biblica
TDOT	*Theological Dictionary of the Old Testament*. Edited by G. J. Botterweck and H. Ringgren. Translated by J. T. Willis, G. W. Bromiley, and D. E. Green. 15 vols. Grand Rapids: Eerdmans, 1974–2004
THAT	*Theologisches Handwörterbuch zum Alten Testament*. Edited by E. Jenni, with assistance from C. Westermann. 2 vols. Stuttgart: Kaiser, 1971–76
TNTC	Tyndale New Testament Commentaries
TOTC	Tyndale Old Testament Commentaries
TW	Theologische Wissenschaft
UCOP	University of Cambridge Oriental Publications
VTSup	Supplements to Vetus Testamentum
WBC	Word Biblical Commentary
WMANT	Wissenschaftliche Monographien zum Alten und Neuen Testament

Introduction

For most of us, the formation of our ethical principles is largely unconscious. Perhaps we recall a specific occasion when our parents made a fuss about something we did wrong that has stuck with us. But most of what they taught us came from their example and chance remarks; these ideas we just quietly absorbed over many years. In later life we continue to pick up ethical ideas by gradual osmosis from the surrounding culture, our peers, and the mass media. Only if something drastically unconventional is being proposed do we wake up and start to debate its merits.

Similar processes are at work in the sphere of religious ethics. In some churches preachers may boldly denounce selected sins, usually those sins that not too many of their flock will have committed. It would be foolish to upset them if one wants to retain their membership! In other churches ethical instruction may form part of the instruction given to new believers. But I suspect that in the majority of Western churches ethical principles are picked up uncritically from the surrounding secularism, through informal discussion with other churchgoers, or from the liturgy—the prayers, songs, and hymns—that a particular congregation uses.

It is the ethic taught by the liturgy of the Old Testament, the Psalter, that is the focus of this book. The psalms were sung in the first and second temples, and in the subsequent two millennia they have been reused in the prayers of the Jewish synagogue and the Christian church. As we will see, the psalms have much to say about behavior, about what actions please God and what he hates, so that anyone praying them is simultaneously being taught an ethic. Those who use the psalms as prayers are often not aware of this aspect, but I will argue this is one of the most potent forms of ethical indoctrination. It happens in all kinds of worship situations.

Take the Lord's Prayer as an example. Its opening invocation, "Our Father, who art in heaven," clearly teaches some very basic theology about the relationship between God and his people. If they should call him "Father," then they are his children. It is a relationship that involves intimacy, since he is our Father, and also distance, since he is in heaven. But there is also an ethical dimension to calling God "our Father in heaven." In a traditional patriarchal culture the father was an authority figure whose word was law in the family: he had to be obeyed. By saying "our Father," the early church at least was acknowledging divine authority and implicitly submitting to it. Whether the modern worshiper praying the Lord's Prayer intends this is another matter, as perceptions of family and fatherhood have changed drastically in many circles today, but in its original setting early Christians would have been clear about its moral implications.

Even today's worshipers cannot miss the ethical force of the fifth petition: "Forgive us our trespasses, as we forgive those who trespass against us" (Matt. 6:12). This clearly implies that if we want God to forgive us, we must be prepared to forgive others. In the Sermon on the Mount, immediately after giving his model prayer, Jesus underlines the importance of this clause: "For if you forgive others their trespasses, your heavenly Father will also forgive you, but if you do not forgive others their trespasses, neither will your Father forgive your trespasses" (Matt. 6:14–15).

The inclusion of the "as-we-forgive" clause in the petition thus has disturbing implications. If we are unwilling to forgive other people, we should not ask God to forgive us. Forgiveness of others is necessary if we are to receive God's forgiveness. Praying the Lord's Prayer without forgiving others is hypocritical. In this way, the prayer is teaching ethics. In fact, it is making the point more powerfully than does the story of Joseph and his brothers or Jesus's parable about the unforgiving debtor. One can simply hear these stories, perhaps admire them, but one does not have to act on them. But praying a prayer or singing a hymn is different. Prayers and hymns are addressed to God, so hypocrisy toward God is no use. Indeed, it could be counterproductive. A prayer such as "Forgive us our trespasses, as we forgive those who trespass against us" is akin to an oath in court, in that both prayer and oath are addressed to God and, by implication, invite God to act if the speaker is not truthful. We must ask whether it would be better not to pray the Lord's Prayer than to pray it without forgiving those who trespass against us.

The ethical instruction imparted by the Lord's Prayer is not peculiar to it. Many traditional prayers teach ethics. Many of the collects in the *Book of Common Prayer* originated in the fifth century and affirm Augustinian rather than Pelagian principles. For example, the collect for the ninth Sunday after Trinity begins, "Grant to us, Lord, the spirit to think and do always such things as be rightful; that we, who cannot do any thing that is good without thee, may by thee be enabled to live according to thy will." It has been well said that this prayer "expresses as succinctly as possible the whole doctrine of grace."[1]

In churches that do not use set liturgical prayers, the minister typically leads the prayer. In this way, consciously or unconsciously, he sets the agenda for the congregation. By praying for something to be done, he proclaims that he thinks this is important. If he prays for the evangelization of the neighborhood, or for the homeless persons downtown, or for peace in the Middle East, he indicates that he regards these objectives as most important. However, in this sort of prayer there is little pressure to assent to the minister's agenda: a perfunctory "Amen" is all that is required of the rest of the congregation. And of course, hardly anyone will notice if someone not subscribing to the minister's sentiments withholds the "Amen"!

The hymns and songs of apparently liturgy-free churches have much the same role as the prescribed prayers of liturgical worship. Both implicitly and explicitly they teach theology and ethics. Christmas carols, such as "Hark! the Herald Angels Sing" or "O Come, All Ye

1. Massey Hamilton Shepherd Jr., *The Oxford American Prayer Book Commentary*, 200, quoted in L. E. H. Stephens-Hodge, *The Collects, with the Litany and the Occasional Prayers: An Introduction and Exposition* (London: Hodder & Stoughton, 1961), 131.

Faithful," proclaim and explain aspects of the incarnation. "When I Survey the Wondrous Cross" and "There Is a Green Hill Far Away" teach about the meaning of the crucifixion. Hymns such as "For All the Saints" and "Lo, He Comes with Clouds Descending" instruct those who sing them about eschatology. These great hymns often have splendid tunes, which helps them to be remembered and recalled easily in various settings.

But ethical instruction is present in hymns and songs as well. Graham Kendrick's song "The Servant King" has the refrain "This is our God, the Servant King; he calls us now to follow him." George Herbert wrote,

> Teach me, my God and king,
> in all things thee to see
> and what I do in anything
> to do it as for thee.

Many a hymn prays for guidance in the Christian life: "Be thou my guardian and my guide"; "Guide me, O thou great redeemer." Others inculcate Christian virtues: "Blessed are the pure in heart"; "Make me a channel of thy peace"; "O perfect love, all human thought transcending." Some hymns strike a more militant note, urging the singer, "Fight the good fight with all thy might," or "Stand up, stand up for Jesus, ye soldiers of the cross." Thus, the singing of hymns inculcates a variety of Christian truths and ethical principles; indeed, the worshiper is compelled to subscribe to them in the very act of singing. If one objects and refuses to sing a particular line or verse, it may well be noticed! Thus, there is a strong social pressure to conform as well as the theological imperative that we noted above, which is a consequence of a prayer or hymn being addressed to God.

A recent hymnbook whose compilers are not happy with the ethical stance of some older hymns decided either to omit or rewrite them. For example, "Onward Christian soldiers, marching as to war" becomes "Onward Christian pilgrims, Christ will be our light." They comment,

> We were also concerned that the book should use positive and appropriate images, and decided that militarism and triumphalism were, therefore, not appropriate. We recognise that military imagery is used

> in the Bible, but history, including current events, shows only too clearly the misuse to which those images are open. All too often in the Christian and other religions, texts on spiritual warfare are used to justify the self-serving ambitions behind temporal conflicts. Christian "triumph" is the triumph of love which "is not envious or boastful or arrogant" (1 Cor. 13:4): the triumph of the cross.[2]

Now if, as most scholars believe, the psalms were written to be sung in the temple at Jerusalem and later were taken for use in the synagogue and the church, they must give an important window into Old Testament theology and ethics. They must also have exercised a profound influence on both Jewish and Christian thinking ever since. But surprisingly, although the theology of the psalms has been closely analyzed,[3] their ethics have been largely ignored. Recent works on Old Testament ethics concentrate on the Law and the Wisdom literature, less often on the Prophets and Narrative books, but hardly ever on Psalms. For example, Eckart Otto's *Theologische Ethik des Alten Testaments*[4] has thirteen references to Psalms but forty to Proverbs and seventy-eight to Deuteronomy, although the book of Psalms is about three times as long as Proverbs or Deuteronomy. A similar disproportion is noticeable in Cyril S. Rodd, *Glimpses of a Strange Land: Studies in Old Testament Ethics*.[5] R. Norman Whybray, in *The Good Life in the Old Testament*,[6] devotes one out of twenty-nine chapters to Psalms. Christopher J. H. Wright's *Old Testament Ethics for the People of God*[7] has 50 percent more references to Deuteronomy than to Psalms; given the relative length of the two books, comments on Deuteronomy outweigh those on Psalms about four to one. The

2. Foreword to *Hymns Old and New: New Anglican Edition*, comp. Geoffrey Moore et al. (Bury St. Edmunds: Kevin Mayhew, 1996), n.p.

3. For example, Hans-Joachim Kraus, *Theology of the Psalms*, trans. Keith Crim (Minneapolis: Fortress, 1992), as well as many monographs.

4. Eckart Otto, *Theologische Ethik des Alten Testaments*, TW 3, no. 2 (Stuttgart: Kohlhammer, 1994).

5. Cyril S. Rodd, *Glimpses of a Strange Land: Studies in Old Testament Ethics*, OTS (Edinburgh: T&T Clark, 2001).

6. R. Norman Whybray, *The Good Life in the Old Testament* (Edinburgh: T&T Clark, 2002).

7. Christopher J. H. Wright, *Old Testament Ethics for the People of God*, rev. ed. (Leicester, UK: Inter-Varsity, 2004).

collection of essays *Character Ethics and the Old Testament: Moral Dimensions of Scripture*[8] has barely two pages devoted to Psalms.

Stranger still is the neglect of Psalms in the monumental *Blackwell Companion to Christian Ethics*,[9] whose main thrust is that Christian ethics flows out of the liturgy. Although the psalms have been central to traditional Christian worship since New Testament times, there is no recognition in that volume of the contribution that the psalms make to Christian ethical thought.

Two recent works on the place of the psalms in the thought of Augustine and Luther show the importance of the Psalter for their theology and ethics and, by implication, for ours. In *Praise Seeking Understanding: Reading the Psalms with Augustine*,[10] Jason Byassee has as his aim that "we should read the Psalter like St. Augustine"—that is, allegorically and christologically. His book is an analysis of the exegetical methods used by Augustine in *Enarrationes in Psalmos*, the longest patristic commentary on Psalms. Byassee makes a number of observations about the ethical implications of the psalms, but he is mainly concerned with the rationale behind Augustine's interpretative methods.

Brian Bock, in *Singing the Ethos of God: On the Place of Christian Ethics in Scripture*,[11] is concerned to elucidate the relationship between biblical texts and their ethical implications. After surveying modern approaches to biblical ethics, he focuses on the work of Augustine and Luther, both of whom wrote prolifically on the psalms. These theologians recognized the power of the psalms to transform their users when they pray. In his "Preface to the Psalter" Luther commented, "In the other books we are taught by both precept and example what we ought to do. This book not only teaches but also gives the *means and method* by which we may keep the precept and follow the example."[12]

8. M. Daniel Carroll R. and Jacqueline E. Lapsley, eds., *Character Ethics and the Old Testament: Moral Dimensions of Scripture* (Louisville: Westminster John Knox, 2007).

9. Stanley Hauerwas and Samuel Wells, eds., *The Blackwell Companion to Christian Ethics*, BCR (Oxford: Blackwell, 2004).

10. Jason Byassee, *Praise Seeking Understanding: Reading the Psalms with Augustine* (Grand Rapids: Eerdmans, 2007).

11. Brian Bock, *Singing the Ethos of God: On the Place of Christian Ethics in Scripture* (Grand Rapids: Eerdmans, 2007).

12. Quoted in ibid., 170.

Praying the psalms gives us the strength to live the godly life, which they describe. According to Bock, "The essential point that Luther presses on us with increasing insistence is that we must understand how praise makes loving others possible."[13] Bock makes a number of astute observations about the relationship of the psalms and ethics, but he does not bring them into coherent focus.[14]

A short essay by Harry Nasuti, "The Sacramental Function of the Psalms in Contemporary Scholarship and Liturgical Practice,"[15] carries tremendous insight into the way psalms affect and mold those who use them in worship, but its brevity leaves little scope for reflection on the Psalter as a whole.

This book, then, is an attempt to begin to deal with a blind spot in current biblical and theological thinking. I have called it *Psalms as Torah* out of my conviction that the psalms were and are vehicles not only of worship but also of instruction, which is the fundamental meaning of Torah, otherwise rendered "law." From the very first psalm, the Psalter presents itself as a second Torah, divided into five books like the Pentateuch, and it invites its readers to meditate on them day and night, just as Joshua was told to meditate on the law of Moses (Ps. 1:2; Josh. 1:8).

Chapter 1 therefore begins with a review of the uses that Jews and Christians have made of the psalms from pre-Christian times down to the present. They have been incorporated into liturgy in a great variety of ways. This has made them extremely influential, as the frequent explicit quotation of them shows, but their subliminal influence probably has been even more significant.

Chapter 2 deals with the critical approaches to the psalms that have been advocated in the last two centuries. Precritical readers accepted the titles of the psalms as genuine and valid indicators of the circumstances of their composition, but this approach was abandoned in the nineteenth century. Instead, much energy was expended trying

13. Ibid., 232.

14. For further discussion of Bock, see the articles in *European Journal of Theology* 18 (2009): 105–63.

15. Harry Nasuti, "The Sacramental Function of the Psalms in Contemporary Scholarship and Liturgical Practice," in *Psalms and Practice: Worship, Virtue, and Authority*, ed. Stephen Breck Reid (Collegeville, MN: Liturgical Press, 2001), 78–89.

to infer from the content of each psalm when it may have been written. The conclusion often was that a particular psalm was written many years after David, but it was unusual for scholars to agree on how late a particular psalm was.

The mid-twentieth century was dominated by the approach of form criticism. This concluded that the psalms were composed for use in worship, many of them in the preexilic temple. The end of the century saw another turn in scholarship. Though not abandoning form-critical insights, scholarship has turned to examining the final form of the Psalter. It is argued by many that the Psalter is not a collection of random songs put together in no particular order, but rather a deliberately arranged anthology whose sequence is significant and indicative of the editors' concerns. Thus, this canonical approach has far-reaching implications for the interpretation of the psalms. It is particularly germane to a consideration of the impact of the psalms, for very often they are read and prayed in canonical sequence. In examining the ethics of the psalms, I will employ a version of canonical criticism.

Chapter 3 attempts to apply modern insights about the dissemination of sacred texts in antiquity to the Psalter. The classic texts of Mesopotamia, Egypt, and Greece were committed to memory by the educated elite and passed on to the illiterate masses by recitation, often to music, at great national festivals. It has been argued that parts of the Old Testament were similarly recited at the Israelite feasts, so I will explore the possibility that the psalms were used in this way and the suggestion that the Psalter was an anthology to be memorized. I will look at the implications of memorization, oral transmission, and music for the influence of the psalms on biblical ethics.

Chapter 4 examines the nature of the claim made by a prayer on a worshiper. What relationship is presupposed by prayer, and how does this affect what the worshiper says in a prayer? Using insights from reader-response criticism and speech-act theory, I will argue that the claim made on the worshiper by the prayers that he utters is akin to a vow or an oath. Thus, the ethical pull of the psalms is more powerful than that of any other biblical medium, whether it be law, narrative, wisdom, or prophecy.

The next six chapters attempt an outline of the ethics implied and taught by the psalms. Chapter 5 explores how the Psalter views the "law" and the attitude that the righteous should adopt toward it. Chapter 6 compares the teaching of the psalms with that of the laws in the Pentateuch. Among other issues, it compares the Psalter's approach with that of the Ten Commandments, discussing both texts' attitude toward punishment and toward the poor. Chapter 7 explores the Psalter's use of the stories in the Pentateuch and attempts to draw out some of the major ethical lessons that the psalms see in these narratives. Chapter 8 discusses the contrasting characters of the righteous and wicked in the psalms and also the notion of the imitation of God. Chapter 9 looks at one of the chief problems in the Psalter's picture of righteous behavior: the calls for divine intervention to save the besieged from the attacks of the wicked. How far is this compatible with a gospel ethic? This leads to chapter 10, a look at how New Testament writers use the psalms in defining a Christian ethic. After this, I present my conclusion.

1

Jewish and Christian Approaches to the Psalms

We begin a detailed review of the ethics of the psalms by looking for evidence of their use in the Old Testament period. In this chapter it is not my purpose to enter into the critical debates about the date of the psalms or the historical reliability of the narrative accounts of Old Testament worship (some of these issues will surface in the next chapter). Here my concern is simply to record what the canonical texts say about the use of the psalms in Old Testament times. I then will review the use of the psalms in subsequent eras.

The books of Samuel are framed by two psalms, the song of Hannah (1 Sam. 2:1–10) and David's song of deliverance (2 Sam. 22:2–51) (the first is not found in the Psalter, but the second is virtually the same as Ps. 18). There are a number of verbal links between the two songs, which suggests that their location in the books of Samuel is deliberate.[1] It is generally recognized that these two songs encapsulate

1. Especially close and numerous are the connections between Hannah's song and David's psalm. The latter also speaks of "horn," "king," and "anointed" (2 Sam. 22:3, 51), as well as enemies, against whom Yahweh helps (e.g., v. 4). Confessing God as "the rock" and the "only" God (v. 32) also occurs there, as well as the confidence that he will raise the lowly (vv. 17, 28, 49), care for the pious, and punish the evildoer (vv. 22, 26). His

some of the key themes of 1–2 Samuel. But for our purpose, it is not the message of these songs that interests us at the moment, but rather the incidental light that they shed on the use of psalms in worship. It is not clear whether Hannah is viewed as composing her song on the spot or as quoting or adapting some existing song; the close parallels with Psalm 113 have led some commentators to conclude that Hannah's song is an adaptation of that psalm or vice versa.[2] The text simply says, "And Hannah prayed and said" (1 Sam. 2:1).

But what is clear is that her singing accompanied the offering of the sacrifice that she brought in fulfillment of her vow. Scholars may debate whether Hannah actually sang the song recorded in this passage, but its presence here clearly presupposes that it was accepted practice to sing psalms or similar songs to accompany sacrifice. This custom seems to be alluded to in other passages too. Songs and sacrifice accompanied the transfer of the ark to Jerusalem (2 Sam. 6:5, 13–15). In 1 Kings 10:12 it is noted that almug wood was brought from Ophir to make, among other things, "lyres and harps for the singers," who probably were engaged in temple worship.

The books of Chronicles offer many more details about temple worship. According to 1 Chronicles 6:31–32, David appointed the Levites to lead worship in the Jerusalem sanctuary: "These are the men whom David put in charge of the service of song in the house of the LORD after the ark rested there. They ministered with song before the tabernacle of the tent of meeting until Solomon built the house of the LORD in Jerusalem, and they performed their service according to their order." Among the musical Levites named are Heman, Asaph, and Ethan (1 Chron. 6:33, 39, 44; cf. 15:16–17).[3]

Song is first mentioned when the ark was brought from Kiriath-jearim to Jerusalem: "And David and all Israel were rejoicing before God with all their might, with song and lyres and harps and tambourines and cymbals and trumpets" (1 Chron. 13:8). It is not clear what

power as creator and ruler of the world as well as his lordship over death are also sung there with more or less the same concepts as in the song of Hannah (vv. 6, 8, 14, 16). See Walter Dietrich, *Samuel*, BKAT 8 (Neukirchen-Vluyn: Neukirchener Verlag, 2005), 73; David G. Firth, *1 & 2 Samuel*, ApOTC (Nottingham: Apollos, 2009), 515–22.

2. For further discussion, see Dietrich, *Samuel*, 87–94.

3. Heman is said to be the author of Psalm 88, while Psalms 50; 73–83 are ascribed to Asaph, and Psalm 89 to Ethan.

role the Levites were playing in this carnival-like procession, which was cut short by the death of Uzzah (1 Chron. 13:9–14). However, when the transfer was resumed in a much more disciplined manner, the Levites were in charge of transporting the ark and led the accompanying music. First Chronicles 15:15–16 reports, "And the Levites carried the ark of God on their shoulders with the poles, as Moses had commanded according to the word of the Lord. David also commanded the chiefs of the Levites to appoint their brothers as the singers who should play loudly on musical instruments, on harps and lyres and cymbals, to raise sounds of joy." When they arrived in Jerusalem, Chronicles records that David appointed the Levites to sing thanksgivings. The texts sung on this occasion are given in 1 Chronicles 16:8–36, and they correspond to Psalm 105:1–15 (1 Chron. 16:8–22); 96:1–13 (1 Chron. 16:23–33); and 106:47–48 (1 Chron. 16:35–36). Presumably, these are to be understood as just a selection of the psalms used on this great occasion. It is not clear what others may have been used.[4]

When the ark was brought into the newly built temple of Solomon, the singers sang, "For [the Lord] is good, for his steadfast love endures forever" (2 Chron. 5:13). The same refrain rang out after Solomon's prayer at the dedication of the temple (2 Chron. 7:3, 6); it is found in a number of psalms (Pss. 100:5; 106:1; 107:1; 118:1, 29; 136:1). He also used Psalm 132:8–10 on this occasion (2 Chron. 6:41–42).

Some two centuries after Solomon, Hezekiah restored the temple worship. In 2 Chronicles 29:26–30 we are given a vivid picture of the use of music in the temple:

> The Levites stood with the instruments of David, and the priests with the trumpets. Then Hezekiah commanded that the burnt offering be

4. It is noteworthy that none of these psalms is given a title in the Psalter, let alone identified as a psalm of David. It may be that Chronicles understands the title "Of David" in Psalm 103 to apply to the following untitled psalms (Pss. 104–106). It is also interesting that all these psalms come from Book 4 of the Psalter (Pss. 90–106). Does Chronicles imply that all of Book 4 was sung when the ark was installed in Jerusalem? C. F. Keil (*The Books of the Chronicles*, trans. Andrew Harper, K&D [Grand Rapids: Eerdmans, 1966], 211–18) thinks that 1 Chronicles 16:8–36 was originally a Davidic psalm that was subsequently developed into the three separate psalms that we find in the Psalter. But it is more probable to suppose, with A. F. Kirkpatrick (*The Book of Psalms*, CBSC [Cambridge: Cambridge University Press, 1902], 615) and Sara Japhet (*I & II Chronicles*, OTL [London: SCM, 1993], 313), that the Chronicler has brought together three originally independent psalms.

> offered on the altar. And when the burnt offering began, the song to the LORD began also, and the trumpets, accompanied by the instruments of David king of Israel. The whole assembly worshiped, and the singers sang and the trumpeters sounded. All this continued until the burnt offering was finished.
>
> When the offering was finished, the king and all who were present with him bowed themselves and worshiped. And Hezekiah the king and the officials commanded the Levites to sing praises to the LORD with the words of David and of Asaph the seer. And they sang praises with gladness, and they bowed down and worshiped.

This passage indicates that singing accompanied the offering of the sacrifices and continued afterward. It also states that psalms of David and Asaph, "the words of David and of Asaph," were used. The Passover celebrations that soon followed were also marked by song. According to 2 Chronicles 30:21–22, "The people of Israel who were present at Jerusalem kept the Feast of Unleavened Bread seven days with great gladness, and the Levites and the priests praised the LORD day by day, singing with all their might to the LORD. . . . So they ate the food of the festival for seven days, sacrificing peace offerings and giving thanks to the LORD, the God of their fathers."

According to 2 Chronicles 20:21, Jehoshaphat exhorted his army, and then they went into battle with a choir singing, "Give thanks to the LORD, for his steadfast love endures for ever." This refrain introduces a number of psalms (e.g., Pss. 106:1; 107:1; 118:1; 136:1) whose sentiments could be seen as appropriate for a devout army to chant.

The fact that Chronicles was written six centuries after the time of David and that the parallel passages in the books of Samuel barely mention his contribution to temple music prompted Wilhelm de Wette[5] (1806–7) and later Julius Wellhausen[6] (1878) to challenge the reliability of Chronicles. Its testimony is often seen to be a reflection of what the postexilic author thought should have been sung and done in the first temple rather than a reliable witness to what really

5. Wilhelm M. L. de Wette, *Beiträge zur Einleitung in das Alte Testament*, 2 vols. (Halle: Schimmelpfennig, 1806–7).

6. Julius Wellhausen, *Prolegomena to the History of Ancient Israel* (Cleveland: Meridian Books, 1957 [1878]).

happened in the times of the monarchy. But as far as the psalms are concerned, the work of form critics such as Hermann Gunkel and Sigmund Mowinckel has made it much more plausible to suppose that many psalms were originally used in the preexilic temple. As H. G. M. Williamson has observed, "That David should have had a particular interest in the music of the cult, and made arrangements for it, is in itself highly probable. His association with music is known from ancient traditions."[7]

Furthermore, other temples in the ancient Near East had singers attached to them,[8] so it would be surprising if the Jerusalem temple had none. For our purpose, it matters little which critical stance is taken. It is sufficient to recognize that the books of Chronicles and the titles of the psalms point to a conviction that the psalms were used from earliest times in Jerusalem's public worship. Those who reject Chronicles' testimony about the music of the first temple generally suppose that it reflects the practices of the second temple.

The books of Ezra and Nehemiah give us glimpses of worship in the fifth century BC. There were singers who served both in the temple and from time to time elsewhere. Two hundred male and female singers returned from Babylon with the first group (Ezra 2:65).[9] They settled in villages outside Jerusalem (Ezra 2:70; Neh. 12:29) and should have enjoyed, as Levites, a share of the tithes (Neh. 11:23; 13:10). They traced their office back to the time of David (Neh. 12:46). Their first duties are described in Ezra 3:10–11:

> And when the builders laid the foundation of the temple of the LORD, the priests in their vestments came forward with trumpets, and the Levites, the sons of Asaph, with cymbals, to praise the LORD, according to the directions of David king of Israel. And they sang responsively, praising and giving thanks to the LORD,
>
> "For he is good,
> for his steadfast love endures forever toward Israel."

7. H. G. M. Williamson, *I & II Chronicles*, NCB (Grand Rapids: Eerdmans, 1982), 73.

8. Sigmund Mowinckel, *The Psalms in Israel's Worship*, trans. D. R. Ap-Thomas, 2 vols. in 1, BRS (Grand Rapids: Eerdmans, 2004), 2:80.

9. The 245 reported in Nehemiah 7:67 probably is a textual error. See H. G. M. Williamson, *Ezra, Nehemiah*, WBC 16 (Waco: Word, 1985), 28.

> And all the people shouted with a great shout when they praised the LORD, because the foundation of the house of the LORD was laid.

We have noted that this psalm fragment is used several times in Chronicles, so it seems likely that "here it is intended to be illustrative of the type of psalms of praise that would have been used on such an occasion."[10]

At the completion of the temple there is no mention of what the Levites sang; it is noted only that "they set . . . the Levites in their divisions" (Ezra 6:18). But when the fortification of Jerusalem was complete, two choirs with accompanying bands processed around the newly rebuilt walls. They set out from the Valley Gate at the southwest of the city. One procession headed north, moving around the city clockwise, while the other headed south and then east, circling the city in a counterclockwise direction. They met in the temple courtyard. Nehemiah 12:40–43 then reports, "So both choirs of those who gave thanks stood in the house of God, and I [Nehemiah] and half of the officials with me. . . . And the singers sang with Jezrahiah as their leader. And they offered great sacrifices that day and rejoiced, for God had made them rejoice with great joy; the women and children also rejoiced. And the joy of Jerusalem was heard far away." We are not told the text of the thanksgiving songs, but it seems likely that selected psalms were used. These were sung by the professional singers, but there is a hint that the people, "women and children," joined in.

I will argue later that the present shape of the Psalter suggests that it was a book designed to be memorized. It is therefore intriguing that commentators have noticed close parallels between some of the psalms and the prayers in Nehemiah. Nehemiah 4:4–5 is Nehemiah's prayer against Sanballat and his allies. "The whole prayer is reminiscent of such Psalms as 44, 74 and 79."[11] Even more striking is the national confession in Nehemiah 9. This "is often compared with Psalm 106 precisely because both passages use historical recollection as a vehicle for confession and as a ground on which to base an appeal for mercy."[12]

10. Ibid., 48.

11. Ibid., 217.

12. Ibid., 307. Klaus-Dietrich Schunck (*Nehemia*, BKAT 23 [Neukirchen-Vluyn: Neukirchener Verlag, 2009], 274) observes that the penitential prayer is probably made up of a collection of liturgical texts. Nehemiah 9:5 makes it clear that it opened with a hymn.

Other psalms whose similarity with Nehemiah 9 has been noted include Psalms 38; 51; 105; 130; 135; 136. In some cases the similarity is solely one of penitential tone, but the detailed review of Israel's history in other psalms is sufficiently close to make probable some dependence of Nehemiah 9 on them. If the devout in Israel were already memorizing the psalms, we could readily explain the similarities.

For the use of the psalms in the intertestamental period there are two main sources: the books of Maccabees[13] and the Dead Sea Scrolls from Qumran. In the books of Maccabees we see psalms being used in contexts similar to those described in Chronicles: the rededication of the temple and in or after battle. For example, in the battle against Gorgias, "[Judas] raised the battle cry, with hymns; then he charged against Gorgias's troops" (2 Macc. 12:37). They did the same after defeating Gorgias: "On their return they sang hymns and praises to Heaven—'For he is good, for his mercy endures forever' " (1 Macc. 4:24). At the rededication of the temple in 164 BC they offered sacrifice and sang psalms. "They rose and offered sacrifice, as the law directs, on the new altar of burnt offering that they had built. . . . It was dedicated with songs and harps and lutes and cymbals" (1 Macc. 4:53–54; cf. 2 Macc. 10:7).

The Dead Sea Scrolls are generally believed to have been deposited by the occupants of the Qumran settlement, which was founded by dissident priests from Jerusalem.[14] They held that Jonathan Maccabeus had apostatized by assuming the high priesthood, so they set up their own community dedicated to observing the law strictly. Their community at Qumran operated rather like a monastery, with long hours devoted to study and prayer. Among the biblical texts recovered from the Qumran caves were fragments of thirty-six Psalms manuscripts, which is more than any other biblical book (Deuteronomy [30×] and Isaiah [21×] were the next most copied books).[15] The sheer number of manuscripts shows the importance of the psalms to this

13. Apocrypha quotations are from the NRSV.

14. For a summary of modern scholarly opinion, see John J. Collins, "Dead Sea Scrolls," *ABD* 2:85–101.

15. Daniel C. Harlow, "The Hebrew Bible in the Dead Sea Scrolls," in *Eerdmans Commentary on the Bible*, ed. James D. G. Dunn and John William Rogerson (Grand Rapids: Eerdmans, 2003), 943.

Jewish sect, but we do not know how they used them. Philo (*On The Contemplative Life* 80) mentions that at their banquet on the Feast of Pentecost the president commented on the Scriptures and then rose and chanted a hymn, either of his own making or an old one. Then all the others did the same. An "old hymn" could well have been a psalm. We have seen from Samuel and Chronicles that often sacrifice was accompanied by the singing of psalms. But at Qumran the priests could not offer sacrifice, so one might well surmise that they hung on to the tradition of psalm singing even more ardently. The specifically sectarian scrolls, such as the *Community Rule*, the *War Rule*, and the *Thanksgiving Hymns*,[16] give an insight into their own compositions and show a deep indebtedness to the psalms.[17]

Use of the Psalms in Worship in the Second Temple and the Synagogue

Although it is generally agreed that the psalms were sung in the rebuilt temple in the centuries preceding the fall of Jerusalem in AD 70, it is very difficult to know which psalms were used on which occasion. It is likely that later synagogue practice reflects older temple practice at many points, but in most cases it is impossible to be dogmatic. At one point, though, we can be sure of continuity between temple and later practice. According to the Septuagint (second-century-BC Greek translation),[18] certain psalms were to be sung on different days of the week.[19] This is confirmed by the Mishnah and continues to be the case to the present.

16. For translations, see Geza Vermes, *The Dead Sea Scrolls in English* (Harmondsworth: Penguin Books, 1962).

17. See William L. Holladay, *The Psalms through Three Thousand Years: Prayerbook of a Cloud of Witnesses* (Minneapolis: Fortress, 1993), 106–10.

18. According to Henry B. Swete, "At what time the Greek Psalter assumed its present form there is no evidence to shew, but it is reasonable to suppose that the great Palestinian collections of sacred song did not long remain unknown to the Alexandrian Jews; and even on the hypothesis of certain Psalms being Maccabean, the later books of the Greek Psalter may be assigned to the second half of the second century" (*An Introduction to the Old Testament in Greek* [Cambridge: Cambridge University Press, 1902], 25).

19. Psalm 24 (Sunday), 48 (Monday), 82 (Tuesday), 94 (Wednesday), 81 (Thursday), 93 (Friday), 92 (Saturday). Only the Mishnah states the psalms for Tuesday and Thursday (see tractate *Tamid* 7:4).

Some psalms are used in the daily synagogue services. These include Psalms 6; 20; 25; 30; 134; 145–150, as well as many individual verses from other psalms. On the Sabbath more psalms are used, including, among Ashkenazi Jews, Psalms 19; 29; 34; 90–93; 95–99; 104; 120–136; 145–150.[20] On the great festivals—Passover, Pentecost, and Tabernacles—it is customary to recite Psalms 113–118, the so-called Egyptian Hallel. At the Passover meal Psalms 113–114 are recited before the Seder meal, and Psalms 115–118 after it.

William Holladay has calculated that out of the 150 psalms, 57 are regularly used in worship. He points out that the Jewish liturgy prefers the positive psalms, such as hymns, songs of confidence, wisdom psalms, and hymns of Yahweh's kingship. Despite being the commonest type of psalm, few laments are used in Jewish worship. And none of the messianic psalms (Pss. 2; 72; 110) is regularly used. But he points out that there is a strong tradition of reciting the whole Psalter privately on a monthly, weekly, or even daily basis.[21]

Use of the Psalms in Worship in the Early Church

There are more quotations from Psalms in the New Testament than from any other Old Testament book.[22] But references to their use in worship are more limited. According to Mark, the Last Supper ended this way: "And when they had sung a hymn, they went out to the Mount of Olives" (Mark 14:26 [// Matt. 26:30]). The "hymn" is most likely a reference to the second half of the Hallel, Psalms 115–118, traditionally recited at the Passover Seder. Insofar as the Christian Eucharist is a reenactment of the Last Supper, it may well be that the custom of singing psalms at the Eucharist can be traced back to this occasion. In several passages Paul mentions the practice of singing psalms. In 1 Corinthians 14:26 he says, "When you come together, each one has a psalm [*psalmos*]" (my translation).[23] This is part of his instruction on how the Lord's Supper

20. Holladay, *Psalms*, 142–43. Sephardi Jews use a different selection.

21. Ibid., 144–46.

22. Ibid., 115. There are fifty-five citations of Psalms in the New Testament, and forty-seven from Isaiah, which ranks second.

23. Here many translations render the word *psalmos* as "hymn," but clearly it means "psalm" elsewhere in the New Testament (see Luke 20:42; 24:44; Acts 1:20; Eph. 5:19; Col. 3:16).

should be conducted in an orderly fashion. His admonition in Colossians 3:16 (cf. Eph. 5:19) is more general and seems to encourage the use of the psalms in a wide variety of contexts, perhaps even in prison (cf. Acts 16:25):[24] "Let the word of Christ dwell in you richly, teaching and admonishing one another in all wisdom, singing psalms and hymns and spiritual songs, with thankfulness in your hearts to God."

The importance of the Psalter in the subapostolic period is witnessed by works such as *1 Clement* (ca. AD 96). This contains 172 citations from the Old Testament, of which 49 are from Psalms, mainly used to make a moral appeal.[25]

Similarly, in the second century Justin Martyr and Irenaeus drew heavily on the psalms in their writings. We are unable to track exactly how the psalms were used by Christians in this period, but by the beginning of "the fourth century the memorization of the Psalms by many Christians and their habitual use as songs in worship by all Christians about whom we know were matters of long-standing tradition."[26]

The use of the psalms in Christian devotion was most eloquently advocated by Athanasius, bishop of Alexandria, in his *Letter to Marcellinus*. Athanasius says that he is passing on the wisdom of a "studious old man" with whom he once discussed the psalms, but there is no doubt that Athanasius thoroughly agrees with the old man's ideas. From this letter it is clear that Athanasius primarily sees the psalms as an aid to private prayer. He holds that there is a psalm for every mood and circumstance of life. "Whatever your particular need or trouble, from this same book you can select a form of words to fit it, so that you not merely hear and then pass on, but learn the way to remedy your ill."[27]

> Suppose, then, that you want to declare any one to be blessed; you find the way to do it in Psalm 1, and likewise in 32, 41, 112, 119 and

24. The verb *hymneō* is used in Matthew 26:30; Mark 14:26; Hebrews 2:12 to indicate the singing of psalms. Jesus's two quotations from Psalms in Mark 15:34 (// Matt. 27:46), citing Psalm 22:1, and Luke 23:46, quoting Psalm 31:5, may imply that he was reciting psalms as he hung on the cross.

25. Holladay, *Psalms*, 162.

26. Ibid., 165.

27. Athanasius, "The Letter of St. Athanasius to Marcellinus on the Interpretation of the Psalms," in *On the Incarnation: The Treatise "De Incarnatione Verbi Dei,"* trans. a religious of C.S.M.V., rev. ed. (Crestwood, NY: St. Vladimir's Seminary Press, 1993), 103.

> 128. If you want to rebuke the conspiracy of the Jews against the Saviour, you have Psalm 2. If you are persecuted by your own family and opposed by many, say Psalm 3; and when you would give thanks to God at your affliction's end, sing 4 and 75 and 116. When you see the wicked wanting to ensnare you and you wish your prayer to reach God's ears, then wake up early and sing 5.[28]

> Let each one, therefore, who recites the Psalms have a sure hope that through them God will speedily give ear to those who are in need. For if a man be in trouble when he says them, great comfort will he find in them; if he be tempted or persecuted, he will find himself abler to stand the test and will experience the protection of the Lord.[29]

In this letter Athanasius sees the Psalter primarily as a source for private prayer, but at various points he alludes to its use in public worship. He suggests that Psalm 32, beginning with "Blessed is the one whose transgression is forgiven, whose sin is covered," would be appropriately sung at a baptism. He continues, "Whenever a number of you want to sing together, being all good and upright men, then use the 33rd"[30] ("Shout for joy in the Lord, O you righteous! Praise befits the upright").

Athanasius suggests that certain psalms are appropriate for different days of the week. "Do you want to give thanks on the Lord's Day? Then say the 24th; if on a Monday, then the 95th; and if on a Friday, your words of praise are in the 93rd."[31] The psalm for Wednesday is Psalm 94. He recommends the use of Psalm 100 in evangelism: "When you see the providence and power of God in all things and want to instruct others in His faith and obedience, get them first to say the 100th psalm."[32]

Athanasius speaks of singing the psalms as well as saying them. It appears that he expects Marcellinus not only to know the words of

28. Ibid., 107–8.

29. Ibid., 117.

30. Ibid., 109.

31. Ibid., 112. It is striking that Athanasius recommends singing the same psalms that the Jews do on the same days of the week. This may be due to the LXX titles of the psalms (e.g., Pss. 93; 94), but it could also reflect the continuity of worship patterns from Old Testament times into the early church.

32. Ibid.

the psalms by heart but also to know their tunes. Athanasius argues that singing the psalms is particularly valuable because it leads to total concentration on the words.

> To sing the Psalms demands such concentration of a man's whole being on them that, in doing it his usual disharmony of mind and corresponding bodily confusion is resolved. . . . It is in order that the melody may thus express our inner spiritual harmony, just as the words voice our thoughts, that the Lord Himself has ordained that the Psalms be sung and recited to a chant.
>
> Those who do sing as I have indicated, so that the melody of the words springs naturally from the rhythm of the soul and her own union with the Spirit, they sing with the tongue and with the understanding also, and greatly benefit not themselves alone but also those who want to listen to them.[33]

Athanasius mentioned that certain psalms are suitable for particular days of the week or occasions such as baptism. Preaching about a century later than Athanasius, Augustine often refers to the psalm that has just been sung. It was customary in the weekly celebration of the Eucharist to have three readings from Scripture, one from the Old Testament, one from the Epistles, and one from the Gospels. Between the Old Testament reading and the Epistle, or between the Epistle and the Gospel, a psalm was sung. In Augustine's time the church in Carthage introduced the custom of singing psalms during the distribution of the elements of the Eucharist.

From Augustine's sermons it is clear that the psalm for Christmas day was Psalm 85, and for Good Friday Psalm 22. For the vigil of Easter Eve Psalm 118 was used, and for the Sunday after Easter Psalm 116. For the eve of Pentecost he used Psalm 141, and for the Monday after Pentecost Psalm 2.[34] We cannot be sure how closely other parts of the church followed the pattern described by Augustine in his day. But by the seventh century the custom of using a psalm between the Old Testament reading and the Epistle was the universal pattern of eucharistic worship. It was also customary to sing a psalm

33. Ibid., 114–15.
34. Holladay, *Psalms*, 167–68.

or part of a psalm right at the beginning of the service as the priest entered.[35]

The establishment of monasteries involved the discipline of communal prayer in which the psalms played a central part. It became customary to recite the entire Psalter in the course of the week. The highly influential rule of St. Benedict prescribed which psalms were to be used at which office. Some psalms were prayed every day. For example, at daybreak (Lauds) Psalms 51; 67 were said, and at the last service of the day (Compline) Psalms 4; 91; 134 were used. But all the psalms were recited at least once a week.[36]

It was not just in church and monastery that the psalms were used. Pious laity used them in their prayers too. King Alfred the Great "was frequent in psalm-singing and prayer at the hours both of the day and night,"[37] and he carried with him a book "wherein the daily courses and psalms, and prayers which he had read in his youth were written."[38] In the Middle Ages the Psalter was the only portion of Scripture that the laity was permitted to own.

The advent of printing followed by the Reformation changed this. The reading of Scripture was encouraged, and books became more affordable. In the Reformed churches the psalms had a central place in worship. As a monk, Martin Luther was brought up on the Psalter, and he continued to pray the psalms in Latin long after he had translated the Bible into German.[39] He held that the psalms should be the core of public worship too. "The whole Psalter, Psalm by Psalm, should remain in use, and the entire Scripture, lesson by lesson, should continue to be read to the people."[40] His first hymnbook contained twenty-three hymns, of which six were metrical paraphrases of the psalms.

Use of the psalms, often in metrical form, became even more characteristic of churches in the Calvinist tradition. Martin Bucer, the

35. Ibid., 174–75.

36. Ibid., 175–76.

37. John A. Giles, *Six Old English Chronicles* (London: Bell & Dadly, 1872), 68, quoted in Holladay, *Psalms*, 177.

38. Giles, *Six Old English Chronicles*, 76, quoted in Holladay, *Psalms*, 178.

39. Holladay, *Psalms*, 192.

40. "An Order of Mass for the Church at Wittenberg," in *Luther's Basic Theological Writings* (Minneapolis: Fortress, 1989), 468, quoted in Holladay, *Psalms*, 195.

Strasbourg reformer, had produced a German prayer book that included all the psalms, and John Calvin, while he stayed in Strasbourg, started to produce a French metrical Psalter. Eventually, by 1562, all the psalms had been translated into metrical verse.

In the English-speaking world, collections of metrical psalms were produced by Sternhold and Hopkins (1549) and by Tate and Brady (1696). Compared with the original Hebrew, these metrical psalms are wordy and often unpoetic, but some of them survive in modern hymnbooks—for example, "As Pants the Hart for Cooling Streams" (Ps. 42) and "Through All the Changing Scenes of Life" (Ps. 34). These collections of metrical psalms continued to be used in Presbyterian churches until relatively recently, but the Anglican *Book of Common Prayer* (1662) used Coverdale's fairly literal translation (1539). This provides for the entire Psalter to be prayed over the course of a month at morning and evening prayer. In public worship the psalms can be sung to flexible tunes called "chants."

The Counter-Reformation led to an overhaul of liturgical practice in the Roman Catholic Church, including the use of the psalms. In the course of the year verses from 111 psalms were used in the Mass, but, except on Maundy Thursday and Good Friday, complete psalms were not recited. And of course, worship was conducted in Latin, which few laypeople understood. Consequently, "lay Catholics were then not privy to the excitement experienced by lay Protestants as they heard full psalms in their vernaculars."[41]

However, the clergy fared better. Not only did they learn Latin but also all of them were expected to recite the breviary, which included all the psalms. Some psalms, such as Psalms 51; 95, were prayed nearly every day, but in the course of the week every verse of every psalm was covered. Parish priests prayed privately, but in the monasteries the psalms were sung to Gregorian chant.

Subsequent centuries have seen more use of the psalms among Catholic laity. The Second Vatican Council not only encouraged the use of the local languages instead of Latin but also provided for the greater use of the psalms in the Mass. The custom of the early church has been revived of reciting a psalm or part of a psalm between the

41. Holladay, *Psalms*, 222.

Old Testament reading and the Epistle. On Sundays and Saints' days 79 of the 150 psalms are appointed for use, while at weekday masses 124 psalms have been utilized. At the same time, demands on priests and religious have been reduced, so that most of the Psalter is prayed over a period of a month instead of a week.

Among Protestants, the psalms have continued to be an important part of public worship and private devotion. Two centuries of missionary work and Bible translation have made them available to hundreds of language groups throughout the world. But in the English-speaking world use of the psalms has often languished, as hymns and worship songs with catchy tunes have tended to displace the psalms, which are not so easy to sing. This trend would have appalled the apostolic church and the great reformers, and more recent writers such as Dietrich Bonhoeffer and Walter Brueggemann. While one may hope that this modern failure to appreciate the psalms as vehicles of prayer proves to be a blip, it does not obscure their traditional function, which will form the basis for the ensuing discussion.

2

Critical Approaches to the Psalms

In the preceding chapter I reviewed the use of the psalms in the worship of the church and the synagogue down the centuries. In this chapter I will examine modern theories about the origin of the individual psalms and their collection into the Psalter. This is a most complicated and controversial area with few assured results, and it is not my purpose to enter into the main debates but simply to highlight some of the implications of different approaches for the interpretation of the ethics of the psalms.

For many centuries the titles were taken as definitive for the origin of the psalms. For example, both Jesus and the scribes took it for granted that David was the author of Psalm 110. In Mark 12:36 Jesus says,

> David himself, in the Holy Spirit, declared,
> "The Lord said to my Lord,
> Sit at my right hand,
> until I put your enemies under your feet."

Indeed, it was often assumed that the untitled psalms were also by David. The Talmud suggests that David not only composed many of the psalms but also was responsible for the whole collection. "David wrote the book of Psalms including in it the work of the elders, namely, Adam, Melchizedek, Abraham, Moses, Heman, Yeduthun, Asaph, and the three sons of Korah" (*Baba Batra* 14b).

In other words, David collected the psalms written by these ten elders as well as his own compositions. "According to this view therefore, there were no psalms composed after the time of David. All of the psalms were written either by the ten elders, or by David himself."[1]

This pan-Davidic approach was common among Christians as well as Jews for many centuries. The Reformers, however, adopted a more nuanced approach. While entirely accepting the validity of the psalm titles and exploiting them to the full to understand the message of each psalm, John Calvin recognized that the Psalter as a whole must have been created later; he suggested that Ezra might have compiled the Psalter in its present form.[2] However, in the next couple of centuries this possibility was widely ignored; it was simply assumed that the Psalter was Davidic.

The nineteenth century saw a strong movement to question traditional assumptions about the authorship of biblical books, and the Psalter was not exempt. Not only was the probability of postexilic editing of the book widely accepted but also the authenticity of the titles was questioned. It was argued that the title "Of David" simply represented the earlier collection from which the psalm came, not authorship. S. R. Driver, for example, claimed on the one hand that some of the Davidic psalms were not fresh or original enough "for the founder of Hebrew Psalmody,"[3] and on the other hand that others "express an intensity of devotion, a depth of spiritual insight, and a maturity of theological reflection, beyond what we should expect from David or David's age."[4] A century after Driver we can easily spot the romantic view of progress that underlies his critical judgments, so that it is unnecessary to debate them. However, by the end of the

1. Edward J. Young, *An Introduction to the Old Testament*, 2nd ed. (London: Tyndale, 1960), 313.

2. See Calvin's comments on Psalms 79; 89; 137.

3. S. R. Driver, *An Introduction to the Literature of the Old Testament*, 5th ed. (Edinburgh: T&T Clark, 1894), 352.

4. Ibid., 355.

nineteenth century there was a wide scholarly consensus that the bulk of the psalms were composed after the exile and edited in the Maccabean period.[5] It was also agreed that the psalms were written for use in the second temple and the synagogues when they developed. C. A. Briggs, for example, states, "The Psalms were collected for the purpose of public worship in the synagogues and in the temple, some being appropriate for the latter, but the most of them evidently more suitable for the former."[6]

These nineteenth-century scholars thus recognized the role of the psalms in worship, even if they did not recognize their antiquity. This insight alone would be a sufficient starting point for a study of the ethics of the psalms. But the twentieth century saw a revolution in reading the psalms that connected them much more intimately and vividly with worship, especially worship in the preexilic temple. The scholars most responsible for this revolution were Hermann Gunkel and Sigmund Mowinckel, the pioneers in applying form criticism to the psalms.

Gunkel published his commentary on selected psalms in 1905. In this work he wanted to recover the poetry and religion of ancient Israel, which he felt had been somewhat neglected in other studies of the psalms. He held that the psalms often had been judged by foreign norms, not according to their own particular features. According to Hans-Joachim Kraus, Gunkel's great achievement was his fresh understanding of Hebrew poetry and the attention he drew to the religious character of the psalms.[7]

In later works, his full *Commentary on the Psalms* (1926) and his *Introduction to the Psalms* (1933), Gunkel developed his ideas

5. Julius Wellhausen (in Friedrich Bleek, *Introduction to the Old Testament* [1876], 507) said, "The question is not whether [the Psalter] contains any post-exilic Psalms, but whether it contains any pre-exilic Psalms" (quoted in A. F. Kirkpatrick, *The Book of Psalms*, CBSC [Cambridge: Cambridge University Press, 1902], xxxvii). According to C. A. Briggs (*A Critical and Exegetical Commentary on the Book of Psalms*, ICC [Edinburgh: T&T Clark, 1906], 1:lxxxix–xcii), there are only seven psalms from the early monarchy period, and twenty others that are preexilic. Most of the rest come from the Persian and Greek eras, and eight from the Maccabean era. The final editing was done in the middle of the second century BC.

6. Briggs, *Book of Psalms*, 1:xciii.

7. Hans-Joachim Kraus, *Geschichte der historisch-kritischen Erforschung des Alten Testaments von der Reformation bis zur Gegenwart* (Neukirchen-Vluyn: Verlag der Buchhandlung des Erziehungsvereins, 1956), 321.

further. He said that "the scholar should strive to eavesdrop on the inbuilt natural arrangement of this type of poetry."[8] To this end, he distinguished a number of different *Gattungen* (forms), such as hymns, communal and individual laments, pilgrimage psalms, and wisdom psalms. He insisted on strict criteria being met in the classification of psalms. For example, in order to fit a particular *Gattung*, a psalm as a whole must come from a particular cultic occasion. Through his insistence on discovering the occasion for a psalm in Israel's worship and his focus on the religious sentiments of the psalms, Gunkel came to the conclusion that many of them fit the setting of the preexilic rather than the postexilic temple. This was a major change from the late nineteenth-century critical consensus. It also emphasizes the character of the psalms as prayers.

This trend in psalm studies was continued by a Norwegian scholar, Sigmund Mowinckel. The second volume of his *Psalmenstudien* appeared in 1922, subtitled *The Enthronement Festival of Yahweh and the Origins of Eschatology*. For Mowinckel, the autumn Festival of Tabernacles, when Yahweh was acclaimed as king, is the key to Israel's worship and religious life. Psalms 93–99 were used at this festival, and many others reflect its theology. His mature views are summed up in *The Psalms in Israel's Worship* (1951 [ET 1962]): the psalms "must be viewed and comprehended in their relationship to the congregation's devotional life. The great majority of the psalms which have come down to us do not simply derive . . . from ancient cult poetry—they are real cult psalms composed for and used in the actual services of the temple."[9]

Mowinckel agrees with the view that the psalms were used in the postexilic temple; however, he does not think that most of them were composed with that end in view, but rather that they were integral to worship in the first temple. They were not originally private poems that later were adapted for use as hymns; rather, they accompanied the rites of the first temple from the beginning. The frequent mention of Zion, Jerusalem, the house of Yahweh, the sanctuary, and the altar

8. Hermann Gunkel and Joachim Begrich, *Einleitung in die Psalmen* (1933), 10, quoted in Kraus, *Geschichte*, 322.

9. Sigmund Mowinckel, *The Psalms in Israel's Worship*, trans. D. R. Ap-Thomas, 2 vols. in 1, BRS (Grand Rapids: Eerdmans, 2004), 1:xliii.

attests to their intended use in worship. From Psalms 24; 68; 118; 132, Mowinckel thinks that one can glimpse the sort of procession and drama involved at the annual entry of the ark into Jerusalem for the feast of Yahweh's enthronement. "Psalm 132 is (part of) the text for a dramatically performed procession, where we meet both the reigning king, playing the role of 'David,' and his men who have been searching for Yahweh's holy shrine (the ark) and now are bringing it back to its proper place in the sanctuary of Zion. We hear the song of the priests who carry the shrine, the intercession for the anointed descendant of David referring to the merits of his ancestor."[10]

Mowinckel's approach emphasizes the intimate connection between the psalms and public worship. He does, however, think that some psalms were composed later by pious scribes (e.g., Pss. 1; 34; 37; 78). These were not designed for liturgical use, but he stresses that they were intended to be prayers. He remarks, "These poems are, and must be considered as, *prayers*. Like every real psalm, they address God, even though they often address men as well."[11]

Gunkel and Mowinckel transformed psalm studies. It is not that everybody accepted Mowinckel's ideas about the enthronement festival or agreed upon the *Gattung* of every psalm,[12] but that the form-critical classification of the psalms became fundamental, and the origin of most of them in the temple liturgy was very widely accepted. Different scholars introduced their variations on these themes. Thus, Artur Weiser[13] argued for a covenant-renewal festival instead of an enthronement festival, while Hans-Joachim Kraus[14] preferred a royal Zion festival celebrating the role of the Davidic dynasty in Jerusalem. Claus Westermann[15] argued for a different

10. Ibid., 1:6.

11. Ibid., 2:108.

12. For an overview of different scholarly classifications, see Philip S. Johnston and David G. Firth, eds., *Interpreting the Psalms: Issues and Approaches* (Leicester, UK: Apollos, 2005), 295–300.

13. Artur Weiser, *Die Psalmen*, 6th ed., ATD 14, 15 (Göttingen: Vandenhoeck & Ruprecht, 1963), 20–35.

14. Hans-Joachim Kraus, *Psalmen*, 7th ed., 2 vols. in 1, BKAT 15 (Neukirchen-Vluyn: Neukirchener Verlag, 2003), 60–62, 1057–61.

15. Claus Westermann, *The Praise of God in the Psalms*, trans. Keith Crim (Richmond: John Knox, 1965).

classification of hymns and thanksgivings, while J. H. Eaton[16] saw a much larger place for royal psalms than did many other scholars. But these variations from Gunkel and Mowinckel still presuppose their main themes of classification by form and an original setting of many psalms in preexilic temple worship. These principles are still accepted by advocates of the newest trend in psalm studies: canonical criticism.

But before we examine the approach of the canonical critics on these issues, something should be said about Mowinckel's approach to the growth of the Psalter, as again it was typical of twentieth-century scholarship. Like most commentators, Mowinckel thought that the titles of the psalms attest to the existence of earlier collections of psalms—for example, Psalms of David, of Asaph, of Korah; Songs of Ascent. Some of these collections go back to preexilic times. These subcollections may well have been used by guilds of singers in the temple. They were brought together between about 350 BC and 300 BC by learned scribes, whose voice can be most clearly heard in texts such as Psalms 1; 37; 127. These scribes held that ancient sacred poetry "ought to have its place in the temple service and serve as a pattern for the prayers of the pious, or even be used as models for prayers in the wisdom schools and in the private devotions of the individual."[17] Not only were the psalms model prayers but also, for the scribal editors of the Psalter, they instructed the righteous on how to "become wise and lead a godly life."[18] Although this was much more important to the scribes than the use of the psalms in public worship, the creation of a complete Psalter "resulted in making the collection *the* book of psalms for the temple service."[19] This is shown by the way even wisdom psalms such as Psalm 49 and Psalm 127 have liturgical instructions in their titles.

Canonical criticism focuses on the editing process of the Psalter and the interpretation of the final form of the text. Brevard Childs demonstrated the method in his 1974 commentary on Exodus, and his student Gerald Wilson applied it to the psalms in *The Editing of the*

16. J. H. Eaton, *Kingship and the Psalms*, SBT 32 (London: SCM, 1976).
17. Mowinckel, *Psalms*, 2:204.
18. Ibid., 2:205.
19. Ibid.

Hebrew Psalter (1985).[20] Wilson noted various features in the Psalter that suggested that the work had not grown haphazardly over the centuries, but rather that it had been carefully edited into a coherent anthology.

There are, of course, features suggesting editorial activity that have long been recognized. The Psalter is divided into five books, each ending with a blessing. For example, "Blessed be the Lord, the God of Israel, from everlasting to everlasting! Amen and Amen" (Ps. 41:13), or "Blessed be the Lord forever! Amen and Amen" (Ps. 89:52; cf. 72:18–19; 106:48). The Psalter concludes with a group of psalms that amount to an extended doxology to the whole work (Pss. 146–150).[21] This division of the Psalter into five books brings to mind the Pentateuch and suggests that the Psalter itself should be seen as a kind of law. This impression is enhanced by the opening psalm, which introduces one of the key themes of the Psalter: the difference between the righteous and the wicked. According to Psalm 1:2, one of the characteristics of the former is that "his delight is in the law of the Lord, and on his law he meditates day and night." But Wilson went further. He noted that the next psalm introduces another important theme of the Psalter: the Davidic dynasty and covenant. Psalm 2:6–7 reads,

> "As for me, I have set my King
> on Zion, my holy hill."
> I will tell of the decree:
> The Lord said to me, "You are my Son;
> today I have begotten you."

What is more, psalms on this topic seem to be placed at the seams of the different books (see Pss. 2:7–9; 41:11–12; 72:17; 89:19–37). Books 1 and 2 of the Psalter (Pss. 1–41; 42–72) present a quite optimistic view of these promises of an eternal dynasty, whereas Book 3 closes with Psalm 89, which asks, "Lord, where is your steadfast love of old, which by your faithfulness you swore to David?" (v. 49).

20. Gerald H. Wilson, *The Editing of the Hebrew Psalter*, SBLDS 76 (Chico, CA: Scholars Press, 1985).

21. Ibid., 182–86.

According to Wilson, this question is answered in Book 4 (Pss. 90–106). Often these psalms affirm that "the LORD reigns" (e.g., Pss. 93:1; 97:1).[22] This declaration was regarded by Mowinckel as a response in the enthronement festival. But Wilson sees these enthronement psalms as placed at this point in the Psalter by its editor to reassure postexilic Israel that God is still in control, despite the absence of a Davidic king.

Wilson, while not endorsing the authenticity of the psalm titles, also insisted that they provide insight into how the psalms were understood by the final editor. Thus, the title "A Psalm of David" invites the person praying the psalm to identify with David and the various situations in which he found himself.[23]

Wilson's work focused on the major divisions and features of the Psalter. But these points having been noted, subsequent commentators have explored how each psalm is linked to its neighbor. Although some of the alleged linkages seem somewhat tenuous, others have much more plausibility and significance. For example, Patrick Miller, in an essay titled "The Beginning of the Psalter,"[24] puts the structural insights of Wilson and others into the service of exegetical theology. Psalm 1 and Psalm 2 are often held to come from different redactional layers, though some have argued that the two were originally a single psalm that has been split in two (cf. Pss. 42–43). But whichever diachronic explanation is right, in the present Psalter the two psalms are distinct but closely related verbally, and this needs to be borne in mind as we interpret them.

Psalm 1 sets the agenda for the Psalter by dividing mankind into two categories: the righteous, who keep the law and inherit God's blessing, and the wicked, who suffer destruction. These two groups of people keep reappearing in the subsequent psalms. In the laments the righteous repeatedly cry out to God for deliverance from their oppressors, the wicked. In Psalm 37 we have the most extensive discourse on the relationship of the wicked and the righteous and their two ways

22. Ibid., 215.

23. "The final effect within the Psalter has been to provide a hermeneutical approach to the use of the psalms by the *individual*. As David, so every man!" (ibid., 173).

24. Patrick D. Miller, "The Beginning of the Psalter," in *The Shape and Shaping of the Psalter*, ed. J. Clinton McCann, JSOTSup 159 (Sheffield: JSOT Press, 1993), 83–92.

outside of Psalm 1. In general, the plight of the victim, the *ṣaddîq* ("righteous"), in the face of the wicked is very much to the fore at the beginning of the Psalter and throughout much of Book 1.[25]

Also prominent in Psalm 1 is the joy of studying the Torah and its positive benefits for those who do. This emphasis on obeying the law reappears elsewhere in Book 1 of the Psalter. Psalm 15 and Psalm 24 are entrance liturgies setting out the moral requirements for those who would worship in the temple, while Psalm 19 compares the life-giving power of the Torah to that of the sun. The sentiments of Psalm 1 are echoed in the penultimate psalm of Book 1, Psalm 40: "I delight to do your will, O God; your law is within my heart" (v. 8).

Wilson argued that the titles of the psalms must be taken seriously, whereas most nineteenth- and twentieth-century critics disregarded these titles, holding that nearly all of them were later accretions that, despite their claim, tell us very little about authorship or the contexts in which the psalms originated. Most canonical critics would not claim that the titles give historical information about the psalms' origins, but they do hold that these titles were important for the Psalter's editors, who either knew the psalms with their titles or added the titles themselves. Either way, the titles give an important glimpse into the way the psalms were interpreted. The grouping of psalms by author (David, Asaph, etc.) or by type (e.g., Songs of Ascent) probably reflects the contents of earlier psalm collections from which the present Psalter was compiled. But in the present setting in the canonical Psalter that is not the function of the titles; rather, the heading encourages the reader to understand the following psalm in a particular way.

The Psalter contains several groups of psalms with the title "A Psalm of David." The first of these, the first Davidic psalter, consists of Psalms 3–41. Psalm 3 is headed "A Psalm of David, when he fled from Absalom his son." But this is not the first time David's voice is heard in the Psalter; he is clearly the main speaker in Psalm 2, where he introduces himself as the Lord's anointed. But the keyword linkages between each psalm and the next, as well as the Davidic titles, create the impression that the prayer continues through the

25. Ibid., 85–86.

psalms without interruption, "putting the whole collection under the patronage of David."[26]

Furthermore, when the titles with biographical elements as in Psalms 3; 7; 18; 34; 51; 52; 54; 56; 57; 59; 60; 63; 142 are analyzed, it appears that most of them relate to the period before David became king. These describe his persecution by Saul. Of the three psalms whose titles place them in his reign (Pss. 3; 51; 60), two describe unhappy episodes: his flight from Absalom (Ps. 3) and his adultery with Bathsheba (Ps. 51).

Thus, Jean-Marie Auwers comments,

> The "historical" titles of the Psalter present . . . a David who is not yet in power, whose tears and wanderings are counted in God's great book. This David matches the image of his impoverished people and thus becomes a model for Israel in her humiliation and wandering. The historical titles thus give the reader of the psalms, as a type and model, a particular David, full of humility, trust in Yahweh, and penitence.
>
> Paradoxically, the attribution of the Psalter to David has had the effect of easing the appropriation of the psalms by every pious Israelite, in so far as the son of Jesse has been presented as the model with which everyone ought to identify.[27]

The theological significance of the Davidic titles has been more fully explored by Martin Kleer in *Der liebliche Sänger der Psalmen Israels* (1996). Kleer holds that the title *lĕdāwid* ("By David") in Psalms 3–41 turns Book 1 of the Psalter into a spiritual diary of the praying David.

Most of the biographical headings are found in the second Davidic collection, which includes Psalms 51–72. Kleer notes that these biographical snippets draw not on the portrait of David found in Chronicles, where he is portrayed as the founder of the temple and the organizer of its worship, but rather on the difficult periods in his life mentioned in the books of Samuel but not in Chronicles. "The biographical headings portray David predominantly as the persecuted, betrayed and captured, as the mourning and guilty one."[28] These

26. Jean-Marie Auwers, *La composition littéraire du psautier: Un état de la question*, CahRB 46 (Paris: Gabalda, 2000), 136.

27. Ibid., 151.

28. Martin Kleer, *Der liebliche Sänger der Psalmen Israels: Untersuchungen zu David als Dichter und Beter der Psalmen*, BBB 108 (Bodenheim: Philo, 1996), 116.

psalms exemplify problems that the pious may experience, inviting them "like David to overcome . . . particularly life's crises with the help of his psalms and with God."[29]

Book 2 concludes with Psalm 72, whose title, "To Solomon" or "By Solomon," leads Kleer to take this psalm as a prayer by David for Solomon. Thus, the first two Davidic collections cover episodes from David's life, though not in chronological order. But the great hopes for David's descendants expressed in Psalm 72 apparently were shattered by the fall of Jerusalem and the monarchy, events alluded to in many psalms of Book 3, and most explicitly in Book 3's final psalm, Psalm 89.

However, Books 4 and 5 respond to Psalm 89's lament with the call to trust in the Lord's rule, not in human rulers, "without giving up the hope in the eternity of the Davidic covenant."[30] Kleer holds that in Books 4 and 5 of the Psalter the Davidic psalms must be understood as the psalms of a future David. For example, Psalms 101–104 do not look backward, but rather forward. Psalm 101 envisages a new Davidic king whose prayer (Ps. 102) will lead to the universal recognition of Yahweh (Pss. 102–103).

In Book 5 of the Psalter are two Davidic collections, one placed toward the beginning of the book, and the other toward the end (Pss. 108–110; 138–145). In Psalm 110 Yahweh gives victory over those who were afflicting the new David in Psalms 108–109. Despite oppression, this David maintains his faith in the Lord and praises him before the nations, so the Lord "installs the new David as royal-priestly Messiah and intervenes himself against the enemies."[31]

The second Davidic collection (Pss. 138–145) is the new David's response to the questions and doubts of the exiles (Ps. 137:4). For Psalm 138, this is an opportunity to make the praise of the Lord clear to all the kings of the earth (v. 4), while the last verse of Psalm 145 announces the theme of the concluding Hallel (Pss. 146–150), "Let all flesh bless his holy name forever and ever" (v. 21).

These brief summaries of Wilson and Kleer give a feel for the methods and conclusions of modern canonical critics. Although both

29. Ibid., 118.
30. Ibid., 120.
31. Ibid., 123.

scholars agree on the importance of the Davidic psalms, they disagree about whether the final redactor still looked for a messianic figure (so Kleer) or, instead, supposed that faith in God's rule was a substitute for faith in God's promises to the Davidic dynasty (so Wilson). Two great commentaries on Psalms highlight other differences between canonical critics. The first, by Frank-Lothar Hossfeld and Erich Zenger,[32] covers Psalms 51–150 and appeared in two volumes in 2000 and 2008 (ET 2005 and 2011). The second, by Jean-Luc Vesco, deals with the whole Psalter and was published in 2006.[33]

Zenger set out some principles for a canonical reading of the psalms in an essay published in 1991:[34]

1. Canonical exegesis pays attention to the connections between one psalm and its neighbors.
2. Canonical exegesis pays attention to the position of a psalm within its redactional unit.
3. Canonical exegesis sees the titles of the psalms as an interpretative horizon.
4. Canonical exegesis takes into consideration the connections and repetitions of psalms within the collection.

His commentary puts these principles into practice. He notes the links between adjacent psalms and uses the titles to shed light on the editors' understanding of the psalms. He sees several editorial stages in the creation of the Psalter and aims to clarify the meaning of a psalm at these different stages. Thus, Psalm 51:1–17 was composed in the postexilic era and was expanded even later (see vv. 18–19), when people were looking for a spiritual restoration of Zion. Zenger sees the psalm making different points in the various different contexts that he believes it functioned in. This makes his commentary a strongly

32. Frank-Lothar Hossfeld and Erich Zenger, *Psalmen 51–100*, HTKAT (Freiburg: Herder, 2000); idem, *Psalmen 101–150*, HTKAT (Freiburg: Herder, 2008).

33. Jean-Luc Vesco, *Le psautier de David traduit et commenté*, 2 vols., LD 210, 211 (Paris: Cerf, 2006).

34. Erich Zenger, "Was wird anders bei kanonischer Psalmenauslegung?" in *Ein Gott, eine Offenbarung: Beiträge zur biblischen Exegese, Theologie und Spiritualität*, ed. Friedrich V. Reiterer (Würzburg: Echter, 1991), 397–413.

diachronic one, so that it becomes difficult at times to be sure exactly what canon he is dealing with.

Vesco, by contrast, is much more clearly focused on the final form of the text. He does not deny that the Psalter developed over a period of time, but he holds that many critical reconstructions of this process are highly speculative and that the exegete's task is to deal with the text that we have. "Rather than study the psalms by themselves as so many units independent of each other, we have tried to comment on the Psalter as a book, bringing out the links between the psalms and taking account of the order in which they come."[35]

It is not that Vesco denies that many of the psalms originated in temple worship. He points to the many liturgical directions in the psalm titles, such as "To the choirmaster: with stringed instruments" (Ps. 4) and "To the choirmaster: for the flutes" (Ps. 5), and phrases that may refer to the tunes to which psalms were sung, such as "According to The Sheminith [Octave?]" (Pss. 6; 12), "The Doe of the Dawn" (Ps. 22), "The Dove on Far-Off Terebinths" (Ps. 56), and "Do Not Destroy" (Pss. 57; 58). Other indications within the psalms indicate their liturgical use within the temple. Some suggest choirs singing responsively—for example, Psalm 24, with its question "Who is this King of Glory?" and response "The Lord of hosts," or Psalm 136, with its refrain "For his steadfast love endures forever." Mentions of the offering of sacrifice, of the activities of priests and Levites, and of Jerusalem are other marks of origin in temple worship.[36]

But many of the psalms are prayers that can be used by individuals distressed by illness or enemies. Others have a didactic function, as they reflect on the great problems of life or marvel at creation or the lessons of Israel's history. They express profound spirituality and great humanity. In particular, they emphasize the value of meditation on the law, both day and night. This is not only the message of the first psalm (Ps. 1) and of the longest psalm (Ps. 119); it is alluded to in many others as well (e.g., Pss. 4:4; 16:7; 42:8; 63:6; 77:6; 88:1). "The psalms are as much the fruit of personal prayer as the echo of congregational worship. The blessedness that the Psalter celebrates is

35. Vesco, *Le psautier de David*, 31.
36. Ibid., 25–28.

not so much that of the liturgy as that of meditation."[37] It therefore is likely that these psalms owe their origin to the wisdom writers, who composed them to instruct and encourage the postexilic generation. They combined their compositions with the older ones to form a collection suitable for both public and private prayer and meditation. "One cannot distinguish absolutely the liturgical psalms from the wisdom or didactic poems. . . . Private prayers were adapted for public use; liturgical songs became a personal prayer. . . . Born in the shadow of the temple, the psalms survived its destruction, and have never ceased to be prayed, read, and chanted."[38]

Modern canonical criticism of the psalms thus builds on the insights of earlier form-critical studies of the psalms. In general, there is not a great gulf between Vesco's understanding of the growth of the Psalter and Mowinckel's view. But whereas Mowinckel focused on interpreting each psalm in its original *Sitz im Leben* and ignored its setting in the present Psalter, Vesco's priorities are the reverse: he insists on using the present sequence of the psalms as a tool for unpacking their meaning for the Psalter's compilers. This will be my approach too. But for a study of the ethics of the psalms, it probably is not of great moment whether one adopts a form-critical or a canonical approach, for both agree that throughout their usage the psalms have been a vehicle of prayer both public and private. And it is their use as prayers that makes them different from other parts of the Old Testament and gives their ethical teaching a unique character within Scripture.

37. Ibid., 30.
38. Ibid., 31.

3

The Psalter as an Anthology to Be Memorized

In the last chapter I reviewed the findings of the form critics that most of the psalms originated in Israel's worship. Then I noted the conviction of canonical critics that the Psalter is not a random collection of psalms, but rather a carefully arranged anthology that gives clues as to the editors' intentions from the sequence of psalms and their titles. In this chapter I want to refine the canonical critics' approach by arguing that the Psalter is a sacred text that is intended to be memorized. Here I will be drawing on the insights of David Carr and Paul Griffiths, who, independently, have called for a re-examination of the way sacred texts were viewed and used in antiquity, before the advent of printing. Neither Griffiths nor Carr devotes much attention to the psalms, so I will try to apply their ideas to the Psalter more fully. Then I will review the impact of memorizing texts on the memorizer and, finally, discuss briefly the implications for the worshiper of singing sacred texts.

Sacred Texts in the Ancient Near East

David Carr has drawn together many hints from ancient sources about the relationship between scribes and texts in Mesopotamia in the second and first millennia BC. Like most professions in the ancient world, the scribal profession was essentially a family business in which skills were passed down from father to son. Groups of older scribes may have trained their sons together in scribal schools. The education included learning how to read and write the cuneiform signs and how to draft basic legal documents, but this was only the basic level. Their main goal was the memorization and performance of their classic texts.[1] "These written works used in education were but the tip of a largely oral iceberg. The point of education was not mastery of written texts per se. Rather, these written texts served as crucial media to facilitate the oral learning of Sumerian and the memorization and performance of standard Sumerian and Akkadian works."[2]

Carr cites Victor Hurowitz, who has argued that works such as the *Enuma Elish* and the prologue and epilogue to the Code of Hammurabi were intended to be memorized.[3] There are many indications in the Atrahasis Epic that it was intended to be publicly performed with musical accompaniment.[4]

The main purpose of scribal education, however, was not to produce men who could read cuneiform and recite the classic texts, but rather to pass on Mesopotamian culture. These texts served what Carr terms "enculturation." They presented the ideal of human life as envisaged in Mesopotamia. Education "was focused on the perpetuation of humanity in general, humanity as defined by Sumero-Akkadian culture."[5] Interestingly, "it was the king, not the scribe, who embodied the fullest ideal of humanity."[6] Memorization and recital of these texts thus served to transmit the values of this culture more widely among the people at large and to ensure that future

1. David M. Carr, *Writing on the Tablet of the Heart: Origins of Scripture and Literature* (New York: Oxford University Press, 2005), 21.

2. Ibid., 27.

3. Ibid., 29.

4. Ibid., 28.

5. Ibid., 31.

6. Ibid.

generations followed it. Thus, the main transmission and dissemination of these texts was oral; their written form was not used at recitals, but simply served as a check in the scribal schools that they were memorizing correctly.[7]

Even closer to the biblical world than Mesopotamia was Ugarit, a well-excavated site in northern Syria, whose many texts date from the fourteenth to fifteenth centuries BC. There, scribal education seems to have followed the Mesopotamian model. Scribes learned Ugaritic texts such as the Keret Epic as well as Akkadian texts such as the Atrahasis Epic. Once again, the ultimate aim of scribal education was to inculcate traditional Ugaritic values and loyalty to the king. Finds at other Canaanite sites such as Megiddo and Gezer, as well as the letters from Canaanite kings to the Egyptian pharaoh (the Amarna letters), make it probable that scribal schools on the Mesopotamian model existed in many towns before the arrival of the Israelites.[8]

Egypt was another culture with intimate contacts with Israel. According to the Pentateuch, involvement began with Joseph, appointed vizier of Egypt, and continued with Moses, brought up in Pharaoh's household. The exodus represents a break with Egyptian life and culture, but after the establishment of the monarchy Solomon fostered links with Egypt by marrying Pharaoh's daughter. The book of Proverbs, much of which is ascribed to Solomon, finds close parallels with Egyptian works such as the Wisdom of Amenemope.[9] Whatever the history behind these traditions,[10] they show that the Old Testament is aware of its indebtedness to Egyptian culture.

In Egypt the role of the scribe was similar to that in Mesopotamia and Canaan. As in Mesopotamia, the training of scribes took place in a family context and was focused on memorizing texts. "Egyp-

7. Ibid., 38.

8. Ibid., 54–58.

9. See K. A. Kitchen, *On the Reliability of the Old Testament* (Grand Rapids: Eerdmans, 2003), 134–36.

10. Modern scholarship tends to be skeptical about the historical value of the Pentateuch, but this does not matter for the present discussion. I am concerned here only to establish that the Old Testament writers, whenever they wrote, were aware of their debt to Egypt. For positive assessments of the Egyptian connection, see ibid., 241–372; also James K. Hoffmeier, *Israel in Egypt: The Evidence for the Authenticity of the Exodus Tradition* (New York: Oxford University Press, 1996).

tian teachers appear to have used the technology of writing . . . to ensure the continuity and accuracy of ongoing memorization and oral performance."[11] Carr observes that oral performance often involved chanting or singing the texts: it was recognized that musical accompaniment aided memory.[12] Copying the texts was another aid to memorization, but "the ultimate goal . . . was memorized mastery of the cultural tradition."[13]

Classical Greece had a similar outlook on its great cultural texts. Plato (*Protagoras* 325e–326a) says that when children have learned their letters, "they are furnished with the works of good poets to read as they sit in class, and are made to learn them off by heart: here they meet with many admonitions, many descriptions and praises and eulogies of good men in times past, that the boy in envy may imitate them and yearn to become even as they." In Xenophon's *Symposium* (3.5) Nicoratus claims, "My father, wishing me to become a good man, made me learn the whole of Homer, so that even today I can still recite the Iliad and the Odyssey by heart."

Before the fourth century BC there were two branches of education, *gymnastikē* and *mousikē*. The latter "encompassed all elements that led to memorization and musically accompanied recitation of poetry."[14] But the learning of the poets was only a means of training the elite of Greek society in its cultural values. "The student learned from ancient portrayals of heroes in Homer age-old Greek values such as love of glory, the virtue of cunning, and the preservation of honor."[15] At their dinner parties Greek men were expected to show off their learning by reciting these poems. They were also performed at great festivals, such as the Panhellenic games at Olympia and Nemea. The length of these poems—the Homeric corpus is about as long as the Old Testament—led to the production of more compact anthologies. But according to Plato (*Laws* 810e–811a), these anthologies were not approved by the purists, who wanted comprehensive mastery of the poetic tradition.

11. Carr, *Writing*, 73.
12. Ibid., 72.
13. Ibid., 75.
14. Ibid., 100.
15. Ibid., 101.

Carr's survey of scribal training and practices outside ancient Israel challenges biblical scholars to reconsider their models of the textual transmission of the Old Testament. If Israel's scribes operated like their neighbors did, many of the documentary methods by which Old Testament texts supposedly were created seem most unlikely. For example, it becomes hard to envisage a scribe redacting two different written sources to create a third version. New versions of an old tale or poem would have been produced by drawing on the old, memorized version stored in the mind, not by aggregating two or more tablets. Carr argues convincingly that scribal methods used in Israel were similar to those used in the rest of the ancient world. He discusses at some length the implications of this for the narrative, legal, and wisdom texts of the Old Testament, but he devotes relatively little space to the psalms.

Yet many features of the psalms fit with practices attested elsewhere in the ancient world. They are poetry, of course, which lends itself to memorization and performance. Many ancient poems, from the Atrahasis Epic to the *Iliad*, evidently were meant to be sung or chanted by the performer. And many psalm titles show that they were sung—for example, "For the choirmaster: according to Do Not Destroy" (Ps. 75). The exact interpretation of these titles is problematic, but there is a wide consensus that they contain musical directions. Moreover, the book of Chronicles connects the Levites especially with singing. And as we have seen in other cultures, literary and musical skills tend to go hand in hand. The priestly class is likely to have been one of the most literate. Furthermore, although the psalms are not quite as obviously didactic as the book of Proverbs, they certainly have an instructional element, as is obvious in, for example, Psalm 1 and Psalm 119 (note Ps. 119:99: "I have more understanding than all my teachers, for your testimonies are my meditation" [cf. v. 9]).

Carr argues that the education of scribes was designed to train them in royal values and the national culture. This emphasis is apparent also in the psalms: the emphasis on David and the promises to him are prominent both in the titles and at key places in the book (see chap. 2 above). Psalm 101 outlines the qualities of loyalty and integrity that should characterize those who serve the king. There is also much reflection on the national history in, for example, Psalms 78; 105; 106; 114; 132. The psalms thus offer a more rounded education than do the more narrowly focused books of Proverbs or Ecclesiastes. All these features thus support Carr's general approach to ancient sacred texts. They were intended to be memorized, with a view to being publicly recited for the purpose of inculcating the nation's values.

It is hard to know how many people in Old Testament times were able to read. Carr thinks that literacy did not extend much beyond the scribes, priests, and top royal officials. In the Hellenistic period, he believes, more people learned to read and write. But this does not mean that they relied on written texts for their knowledge of the law and other parts of Scripture. Rather, in the synagogues they learned Scripture by heart, and because they had memorized it, they were able to meditate on it day and night.

Paul Griffiths, in his book *Religious Reading*, argues that this approach continued to be the normal practice with sacred texts until the advent of the printing press. Printing was much cheaper than copying texts by hand, and it was printing that made possible the widespread private ownership of books and encouraged the practice of individuals reading texts silently to themselves. But this certainly was not the picture in the early Christian centuries either in the church or in Buddhist monasteries. In these communities few could read, but most knew large portions of their Scriptures by heart, for learning them was a key part of the catechumenate or novitiate.

Griffiths develops his argument by focusing on the practice of the North African church in the third to fifth centuries and Buddhist monasteries in India in the same era. Among other texts, he examines two Buddhist anthologies from India dating from about AD 100 and AD 700, the *Sutrasamuccaya* and the *Siksasamuccaya*, and two Christian anthologies from North Africa dating from the third and fifth centuries, Cyprian's *Three Books of Testimonies for Quirinus* and Augustine's *A Mirror of Sacred Scripture*. Griffiths characterizes these anthologies as follows: "Formally speaking, an anthology is a work all (or almost all) of whose words are taken from another work or works; it contains a number (typically quite a large number) of extracts or excerpts, each of which has been taken verbatim (or almost so) from some other work; and it uses some device to mark the boundaries of these excerpts."[16] Griffiths points out how both Buddhist and Christian texts conform to this definition.

For example, "The *Ad Quirinum* is about 33,000 words long . . . and contains rather more than 700 excerpts" and "would take about three and a half hours to read aloud."[17]

> [Augustine's] *Speculum* is roughly 60,000 words long. . . . It would take something over six hours to read aloud at a speed of 160 words per minute. It contains a little over 800 excerpts, of very varied lengths. The longest is seven pages . . . , containing almost all of Matthew 5–7; there are a number of very short excerpts . . . ; and there is everything in between. The mean length of an excerpt is about seventy words, but there are few of just that length. Augustine, much more than Cyprian, is happy to give lengthy excerpts interspersed with very brief ones. There is no standard length for an excerpt.
>
> Augustine almost always signals the beginning and end of his excerpts with clarity. . . . The *Speculum* is divided into chapters, each of which contains excerpts from only one book of the Bible.[18]

Similarly, Cyprian identifies his excerpts from the Bible, clearly noting from which book they come. However, whereas Augustine follows the biblical order in his excerpts, Cyprian arranges his excerpts topically.[19]

Griffiths observes similar features in the Buddhist anthologies. For example, the *Siksasamuccaya* contains six thousand verses and would take about eleven hours to recite. "Almost all of it consists of excerpts from other works"; the editor contributed at most 5 percent of the text, mostly "very brief phrases introducing an excerpt and giving the title of the work from which it was taken."[20] There are about 312 excerpts, varying in length from a short sentence to 172 verses, but many of them are about ten lines long. In all, 104 sources

16. Paul J. Griffiths, *Religious Reading: The Place of Reading in the Practice of Religion* (New York: Oxford University Press, 1999), 97.

17. Ibid., 165.

18. Ibid., 169.

19. Ibid., 166–67.

20. Ibid., 133.

are identified by name, some many times (e.g., *Candrapradipasutra* twenty-five times), but most just once or twice.[21]

It takes little reflection to see that the Psalter fits this pattern of anthology. The psalms are discrete units, and the variety of titles has long suggested to commentators that they are drawn from a variety of earlier collections. Many of the titles of the psalms seem to refer to the collections from which they were drawn. Except for Psalm 33, all of the psalms in Psalms 3–41 have the title "Psalm of David" and so have come to be called the "First Davidic Psalter." Another group of psalms ascribed to David is found in Psalms 51–72 (though once again, Pss. 66; 67; 71 are anonymous) and is generally called the "Second Davidic Psalter." Psalm 72 concludes, "The prayers of David, the son of Jesse, are ended" (v. 20). This suggests that the other psalms ascribed to David (Pss. 86; 101; 103; 108–110; 122; 124; 131; 133; 138–145) may have come from a third collection of Davidic psalms. Other named authors include Asaph (Pss. 50; 73–83) and the sons of Korah (Pss. 42–49; 84; 85; 87; 88). Two psalms have Solomon's name attached (Pss. 72; 127). Moses (Ps. 90), Heman (Ps. 88), and Ethan (Ps. 89) each have one psalm ascribed to them.

Other groups of psalms within the Psalter may derive from earlier independent collections. The Songs of Ascent (Pss. 120–134) are the most obvious group, but other groups include the kingship psalms (Pss. 93; 95–99), the Egyptian Hallel (Pss. 113–118), the Great Hallel (Pss. 146–150), and the hallelujah psalms (Pss. 104–106). This would make a total of fourteen different collections that have been used to compile the Psalter, as well as the anonymous psalms that may have been drawn from a variety of other collections. The picture is complicated by the appearance of double titles on some of the psalms: Psalm 122 is called both a "Song of Ascents" and a psalm "Of David," and Psalm 88 is identified as both a "Maskil of Heman" and a "Psalm of the Sons of Korah." But there is no doubt that in its present final form the Psalter appears to be a collection of psalms drawn from earlier collections; in other words, it is an anthology.

The length of the Psalter is comparable to the Buddhist and Christian anthologies that Griffiths cites. The Psalter contains 2,527 verses,

21. Ibid., 133–36.

which, read at 9 verses per minute,[22] would take about four and a half hours to recite. The variation in length of individual psalms is comparable to other anthologies. The number of sources cited is rather less, but there are quite a number of anonymous psalms, which could point to a wider variety of sources than is apparent at first. Thus, the evidence that Griffiths has adduced from India and North Africa seems to support the conclusion of canonical critics that what we have in the Psalter is a carefully organized anthology.

But in discussing these features, Griffiths is arguing for another aspect of the anthology, which at least in the case of the Psalter has been more or less ignored: religious anthologies are meant to be memorized. Griffiths contends that before the advent of printing most sacred works were essentially circulated orally. The cost of manuscripts allowed only very few individuals to own them, but that did not prevent their content from being widely known, as they were taught in monasteries, synagogues, churches, and so on.

Griffiths's observations complement Carr's. His contention that the great classical texts of antiquity were memorized seems well founded. It is obvious that the biblical narratives are paced to be read aloud, not skimmed through silently as we do with modern novels. Recent literary studies of the Bible have made us aware of the brilliance of their narrative techniques. This all fits in with a picture of oral recitation of these texts in the biblical world.

Nevertheless, there are few explicit hints in biblical narratives to aid the would-be reciter of them in the task of memorization. Perhaps it is wrong to look for them. In a culture where the memory was cultivated much more than in our own and where rote learning was standard, a person would have required little help to fix stories in the mind and recall them. The same may well apply to the psalms. Looking for connections between one verse and the next, or one psalm and the next, may have been quite unnecessary for the ancient student.

But when we look at the psalms, we see at least three main features that must have helped somewhat in their memorization: (1) the poetic

22. This is the speed at which Griffiths reckons the Buddhist texts would have been recited. This is quite slow for reading the psalms. Kol Israel (Israel radio) read them unhurriedly at ten verses per minute.

form of the psalms, (2) musical accompaniment, and (3) thematic macrostructures. I will explore these features briefly in turn.

The poetic form of the psalms obviously aids their memorization. Everyone finds poetry easier to remember than prose. Its rhythms and symmetries, repetitions and rhymes, combine to assist the memory. Of course, many of the features of modern Western poetry are not found in classical Hebrew, but there are many devices that help make psalms and other poems easier to remember than prose. Most obvious is the use of parallelism, in which the second line complements the first. Although it is unwise to be dogmatic about Hebrew meter, there are clearly firm constraints on the length of lines, which create expectations about how much should come next. The choice of words too can be constrained by the use of word pairs and key words. Acrostics, whereby each line (Pss. 111–112), each verse (Ps. 34), or every eight verses (Ps. 119) begin with the next letter in the alphabet, are universally recognized as aids to memorization. Other devices such as alliteration, assonance, chiasmus, inclusion, resumptive repetition, staircase parallelism, and refrains support attempts to memorize the psalms. It certainly is open to question how many of these devices would have been consciously recognized by Hebrew poets and those who subsequently recited the psalms, but all of them contribute to making the psalms a bit more catchy and memorable.

Another powerful aid to memory is music. If poetry is more memorable than prose, songs are more memorable than poems. And there is ample evidence in the Bible that the psalms were set to music. The Psalter has many commands and self-exhortations to sing to the Lord (e.g., Pss. 13:6; 95:1). It describes the musical instruments that accompanied the singing (see esp. Ps. 150). For example, Psalm 92:1–3 says,

> It is a good to give thanks to the LORD,
> to sing praises to your name, O Most High;
> to declare your steadfast love in the morning,
> and your faithfulness by night,
> to the music of the lute and the harp,
> to the melody of the lyre.

Then there are the mysterious phrases in the psalm titles, which interpreters generally understand to specify the tune—for example, "According to The Gittith," "According to Muth-labben," "According to The Sheminith." And then there is the even more common *lamnaṣṣēaḥ*, traditionally translated as "To the choirmaster," and the word *selâ*, usually interpreted as marking a pause in the recital of the psalm. The historical books of the Old Testament mention choirs of Levites singing the psalms on various great occasions, such as the dedication of the temple or the walls of the city (2 Chron. 5; Neh. 12). Thus, the evidence is very strong that the psalms were set to music when used in worship in the temple. Were they still sung when they were incorporated into the Psalter to form an aid for private devotion or as a catechismal collection? This seems to me less certain but quite probable. The cantillation marks in the Masoretic Text tell the modern reader how to chant the text. It is not known how old this tradition of cantillation is, but like the Masoretic vowel signs, it presumably reflects a tradition much older than the tenth century AD. And within the Christian tradition the psalms have been sung from New Testament times to the present.

Their poetic form and their setting to music were great aids to the memorization of individual psalms. But another problem is recalling their sequence. How does one remember the order of the psalms? Here recent canonical readings of the Psalter help. The division of the Psalter into five books, imitating the fivefold division of the Torah, strikes any reader immediately. But Gerald Wilson noted that often at the beginning or the end of a book is a psalm dealing with the Davidic covenant (e.g., Pss. 2; 41; 72; 89). Concatenation, in which a term in one psalm is taken up and reused in the next psalm, is very thoroughly explored in Jean-Luc Vesco's commentary.[23] This device helps the reciter to recall the order of the psalms. Then there are thematically grouped psalms, such as Psalms 46–48,

23. Jean-Luc Vesco, *Le psautier de David traduit et commenté*, 2 vols., LD 210, 211 (Paris: Cerf, 2006). For some helpful illustrations, see Norbert Lohfink, *In the Shadow of Your Wings: New Readings of Great Texts from the Bible*, trans. Linda M. Maloney (Collegeville, MN: Liturgical Press, 1999), 79–89. Lohfink notes that Franz Delitzsch's 1860 commentary explored these links, but that they have been neglected by subsequent commentators.

often called the "Hymns of Zion," and Psalms 104–106, which constitute a mini-Pentateuch because they begin with creation, move on to the patriarchs, then the exodus, and eventually end with the settlement. There are also paired psalms, such as Psalms 103–104 and Psalms 111–112.

The titles of the psalms, which, I argued earlier, indicate the collections drawn upon in compiling the Psalter, also may have helped in its memorization. Not only do they serve to group different psalms but also some of the historical allusions enable memorizers to picture the situation in which David supposedly composed a particular psalm. Visualization is a vital tool in memory; thus, to picture David fleeing from Absalom and praying Psalm 3, or kneeling before Nathan as he prayed Psalm 51, makes those psalms easier to remember.

Memorization and Religious Reading

Memorization of these texts goes hand in hand with a religious approach to them. This religious approach to reading, Griffiths argues, is quite distinct from the consumerist approach to literature that characterizes the modern world of the printed book and the internet. Modern writings, whether they be blogs or learned tomes, are ephemeral. They are read, perhaps taken note of, and then discarded. They have no particular authority; different readers will ascribe different worth to the same work. You read what you like, when you like, and accept what you like in what you read. Then you discard it and move on to read something else. In Griffiths's opinion, this characterizes our approach to reading everything, from newspaper articles to academic monographs.

But religious reading is characterized by a quite different approach to works. Religious readers see the work read as an infinite resource. "It is a treasure-house, an ocean, a mine; the deeper religious readers dig, . . . the greater will be their reward."[24] The work read is treated with great reverence. Griffiths says, "For the religious reader, the work read is an object of overpowering delight and great beauty. It can never be discarded because it can never be exhausted. It can only be reread,

24. Griffiths, *Religious Reading*, 41.

with reverence and ecstasy."[25] Psalm 119:97 gives expression to this outlook: "Oh how I love your law! It is my meditation all the day." Buddhists say the same sort of thing about their texts.[26]

Works that are read over and over again tend to be committed to memory. Indeed, Griffiths argues that memorization is highly valued by religious readers. He goes further, maintaining that religious texts often are constructed in a way that aids memorization. For religious readers "the ideally read work is the memorized work, and the ideal mode of rereading is by memorial recall."[27] And as a reader memorizes a text, he becomes textualized; that is, he embodies the work that he has committed to memory. "Ezekiel's eating of the prophetic scroll . . . is a representation of the kind of incorporation and internalization involved in religious reading: the work is ingested, used for nourishment, incorporated: it becomes the basis for rumination and for action. . . . A memorized work (like a lover, a friend, a spouse, a child) has entered into the fabric of its possessor's intellectual and emotional life in a way that makes deep claims upon that life, claims that can only be ignored with effort and deliberation."[28]

Medieval theologians used lively images to describe the relationship between the memorized work and the reciter. Bernard of Clairvaux described the Bible as the wine cellar of the Holy Spirit.[29] Anselm of Canterbury compared Scripture to honeycomb: "Taste the goodness of your Redeemer, burn with love for your Savior. Chew the honeycomb of his words, suck their flavor, which is more pleasing than honey, swallow their health-giving sweetness."[30]

As we have already observed, a memorized text has a peculiarly character-forming effect on the memorizer. The text becomes part of his character; he lives in it and lives it out. According to Griffiths, most sacred ancient texts were expected to be memorized and disseminated this way. If this is so, then learning the psalms by

25. Ibid., 42.
26. Ibid., 43.
27. Ibid., 46.
28. Ibid., 46–47.
29. Ibid., 42, quoting Bernard's thirty-fifth sermon on Song of Songs.
30. Ibid., 43, quoting Anselm, *Opera Omnia*, vol. 3 (trans. from F. S. Schmitt, ed. [Edinburgh, 1946]), 84. Anselm seems to be alluding to Psalm 19:7, 10.

heart could be seen as being much the same as, say, learning the Prophets or the Narrative works of the Old Testament. But there is one more aspect of the psalms that has made them even more influential: their titles show us that they were designed to be sung, not merely recited.

The importance of music in worship and also in secular life is obvious, though it is more rarely commented on. Music aids memorization, of course, but it does more. It moves the emotions and captures the will and imagination of the singers, so that they mean the words they sing.

In his *Letter to Marcellinus* Athanasius wrote,

> Words of this kind should be not merely said, but rendered with melody and song; for there are actually some simple folk among us who . . . think the reason for singing them is just to make them more pleasing to the ear! This is by no means so; Holy Scripture is not designed to tickle the aesthetic palate, and it is rather for the soul's own profit that the Psalms are sung. This is so chiefly for two reasons. In the first place, it is fitting that the sacred writings should praise God in poetry as well as prose, because the freer, less restricted form of verse, in which the Psalms . . . are cast, ensures that by them men should express their love to God with all the strength and power they possess. And secondly, the reason lies in the unifying effect which chanting the Psalms has upon the singer. For to sing the Psalms demands such concentration of a man's whole being on them that, in doing it, his usual disharmony of mind and corresponding bodily confusion is resolved, just as the notes of several flutes are brought by harmony to one effect.[31]

Jews likewise have commented on the value of music in intensifying devotion. Judah he-Hasid, a twelfth-century rabbi, wrote, "Say your prayer in the melody that is most pleasant and sweet in your eyes. Then you shall pray with proper concentration; because the melody will draw your heart after the words that come from your mouth. Supplication in a melody makes the heart weep, and praise

31. Athanasius, "The Letter of St. Athanasius to Marcellinus on the Interpretation of the Psalms," in *On the Incarnation: The Treatise "De Incarnatione Verbi Dei,"* trans. a religious of C.S.M.V., rev. ed. (Crestwood, NY: St. Vladimir's Seminary Press, 1993), 114.

in a melody makes the heart happy. Thus you will be filled with love and joy for Him that sees your heart, and you will bless Him with great love and with joy."[32] In 1538 Martin Luther wrote, "Music is to be praised as second only to the Word of God because by her are all the emotions swayed. Nothing on earth is more mighty to make the sad gay and the gay sad, to hearten the downcast, mellow the overweening, temper the exuberant, or mollify the vengeful. . . . That is why there are so many songs and psalms. This precious gift has been bestowed on men alone to remind them that they are created to praise and magnify the Lord."[33]

More recently, David Ford has commented,

> What does [singing] do with the crucial Christian medium of words? It does with them what praise aims to do with the whole of reality: it takes them up into a transformed, heightened expression, yet without at all taking away their ordinary meaning. Language itself is transcended and its delights and power are intensified, and at the same time those who join in are bound together more strongly. So singing is a model of the way praise can take up ordinary life and transpose it to a higher level without losing what is good in other levels. The social power of music in general (for good or ill) is well known, and it moves at levels and in ways that nothing else can.[34]

Thus, set to music and sung communally, the psalms have even more power than when they are merely recited. But even mere recitation, whether or not that involves memorization, is, I have argued, a more powerful instructor than listening to stories, commands, or wisdom sayings. Listening is passive—indeed, the listener can ignore the message—but recitation and, especially, singing are activities that involve the whole person and cannot be honestly undertaken without real commitment to what is being said or sung. This I will explore in the next chapter.

32. Quoted in Abraham E. Millgram, *Jewish Worship* (Philadelphia: Jewish Publication Society, 1971), 29.

33. Quoted in Roland H. Bainton, *Here I Stand: A Life of Martin Luther* (New York: New American Library, 1955), 268–69.

34. David F. Ford and Daniel W. Hardy, *Living in Praise: Worshipping and Knowing God*, rev. ed. (London: Darton, Longman & Todd, 2005), 19.

Conclusion

In this chapter I have argued that in days of old, memorization of the classic texts of a culture was how the great literary and religious works of antiquity were disseminated. The written text's main purpose was to ensure that the work was correctly memorized by those who would later recite it or sing it to the people. There is evidence that much, if not all, of the Old Testament was treated this way. But it is most obviously the case with the Psalter, which bears many marks of an anthology designed to be memorized and sung. The Psalter's poetic form, musical directions, historical retellings, theological and ethical instructions—all of these suggest that it would have served the purpose of "enculturation" very effectively.

4

The Unique Claims of Prayed Ethics

In the introduction to this book I pointed out that prayer has an impact on ethical thought. For example, when we pray, "Forgive us our trespasses, as we forgive those who trespass against us," we are committing ourselves to forgiving other people. I suggested that what worshipers say in prayer ought to have a profound effect on them because these words are addressed to God, who can evaluate their sincerity and worthiness. If we praise a certain type of behavior in our prayers, we are telling God that this is how we intend to behave. On the other hand, if in prayer we denounce certain acts and pray for God to punish them, we are in effect inviting God to judge us if we do the same. This makes the ethics of liturgy uniquely powerful. It makes a stronger claim on the believer than either law, wisdom, or story, which are simply subject to passive reception: one can listen to a proverb or a story and then take it or leave it, but if you pray ethically, you commit yourself to a path of action.

Chapter 1 reviewed the use of the psalms in Jewish and Christian worship. We saw that the Bible portrays them as being central to the liturgy in Old Testament times, and that they have been the most prayed texts by Jews and Christians from the New Testament era to the present.

Chapter 2 summarized modern critical theories about the origin and use of the Psalter. We saw how form critics created a consensus in the twentieth century that many of the psalms were composed for use in public worship in the first temple. Although the most recent studies have accepted these conclusions, the current critical interest is in the final form of the Psalter and in the implications that the titles and sequence of the psalms have for their interpretation. The Psalter is seen as a well-organized anthology, being at once both the hymnbook of the Second Temple and a text for meditative reflection.

In chapter 3 I offered some fresh reflection on the character of the Psalter based on recent studies of the dissemination of literature in ancient times. Great literary and religious texts were memorized by the educated elite and then transmitted to the masses at important festivals. Anthologies containing extracts from the great works were produced for the less learned to memorize. In North Africa catechumens were expected to learn anthologies of biblical texts as part of their preparation for baptism. One could view the Psalter as an anthology from Old Testament times with a similar didactic purpose. Certainly the effort of memorizing sacred texts would have enhanced their power to educate and inculcate theology and ethics. Finally, I noted that throughout the ages the psalms have been sung, and this too must have empowered their teaching, for what is sung grips the heart and the will, not just the mind. As Augustine (*Sermons* 336) said, "To sing once is to pray twice."

But before plunging into the ethics of the psalms, I want to explore further the issues raised in the introduction about the nature of prayed ethics. What is the claim of prayer on the ethics of the worshiper, and how does this differ from that of other ethical discourse? It seems likely that other biblical texts also were intended to be memorized and passed on to others orally, so it is not merely memorization that makes the ethical teaching of the psalms distinctive. But as I have already intimated, the use of the psalms in worship as hymns and prayers makes their character different from other books of the Old Testament. This has been partially explored by Dorothea Erbele-Küster in her book *Lesen als Akt des Betens*, in which she uses reader-response theory to illuminate the rhetorical situation of praying the psalms. Although she does not explicitly discuss how this affects the status of the psalms for their use in ethics, she takes us some way in that direction. Then I will apply to the psalms the ideas of Donald Evans in *The Logic of Self-Involvement*, in which he uses speech-act theory to clarify the status of worship statements. I will discuss how prayer commits the worshiper to particular attitudes and patterns of behavior and note how this must affect our interpretation of the psalms.

We turn, then, to the work of Dorothea Erbele-Küster in *Lesen als Akt des Betens: Eine Rezeptionsästhetik der Psalmen.*[1] She explores the question of what happens when the psalms are used as prayers. How does the person praying the psalms become involved and experience their significance? She sees praying the psalms as a kind of religious reading akin to Paul Griffiths's understanding of religious reading (see chap. 3 above), a way of reading that needs to be distinguished from the critical distance often adopted by biblical scholarship. But she argues that these two approaches are not mutually exclusive; they can shed light on each other.[2]

She starts her discussion by endorsing the insights of canonical critics who have seen the sequencing of the psalms as significant. Psalm 2 proclaims the triumph of the Davidic house, but this is immediately followed by a collection of psalms headed "By David," many of which relate the trials that dogged his life. Like most canonical critics, she does not assume that the titles are historically reliable, but she argues that they do constrain the uncritical reader to value the psalms they head because they represent the words and experience of Israel's greatest king. Thus, Erbele-Küster thinks that these Davidic titles give the psalms a paradigmatic quality and encourage the later reader to identify with their sentiments.[3]

Erbele-Küster draws attention to other devices in the text that clearly aim to influence the reader's perspective. There are general blessings pronounced: "Blessed is the man who / blessed are all who / blessed is the one who" (Pss. 1:1; 2:12; 84:12). The paradigmatic quality of the lifestyle that is pronounced blessed invites the reader to

1. Dorothea Erbele-Küster, *Lesen als Akt des Betens: Eine Rezeptionsästhetik der Psalmen*, WMANT 87 (Neukirchen-Vluyn: Neukirchener Verlag, 2001).

2. Ibid., 51.

3. Ibid., 68, 109.

identify with it. The prospect of blessing should encourage all to adopt this way of life.

Another device inviting the worshiper to identify with the sentiments of the psalm is the use of the first person. The psalmist often speaks in the first person: "I will bless the LORD at all times" (Ps. 34:1). Someone singing or praying this psalm at a later date is thus invited to do the same. Indeed, the suggestion may well be reformulated as a command to share in the psalmist's experience. Psalm 34 continues, "Oh, taste and see that the LORD is good" (v. 8). There then follows a blessing in the third person on anyone who puts trust in God: "Blessed is the man who takes refuge in him!" (v. 8). The psalm concludes (vv. 11–14, 19) with the general lessons that the psalmist has learned and now wishes future generations to appropriate for themselves:

> Come, O children, listen to me;
> I will teach you the fear of the LORD.
> What man is there who desires life
> and loves many days, that he may see good?
> Keep your tongue from evil
> and your lips from speaking deceit.
> Turn away from evil, and do good;
> seek peace, and pursue it. . . .
> Many are the afflictions of the righteous:
> but the LORD delivers him out of them all.

This switch between first and third person encourages the user of the psalm to identify with the viewpoint of the psalmist.[4] But particularly the use of the first person encourages such identification: "The experience of the I of the psalm embodies a religious ideal whose reality is open to the reader to experience."[5]

On the other hand, the depiction of the wicked is designed to deter the user of the psalms from identifying with them. The temptation to do so is vividly portrayed in Psalm 73:3–5:

> For I was envious of the arrogant
> when I saw the prosperity of the wicked.

4. Ibid., 112.
5. Ibid.

For they have no pangs until death;
their bodies are fat and sleek.
They are not in trouble as others are;
they are not stricken like the rest of mankind.

The psalmist goes on (vv. 17–19) to say that he nearly threw in his lot with them:

. . . until I went into the sanctuary of God;
then I discerned their end.
Truly you set them in slippery places;
you make them fall to ruin.
How they are destroyed in a moment,
swept away utterly by terrors!

He concludes (v. 28) by reaffirming his loyalty to God:

But for me it is good to be near God;
I have made the Lord God my refuge,
that I may tell of all your works.

In many psalms the words of the wicked are quoted. For example, Psalm 10:4, 6, 11:

In the pride of his face the wicked does not seek him;
all his thoughts are, "There is no God."

He says in his heart, "I shall not be moved;
throughout all generations I shall not meet adversity."

He says in his heart, "God has forgotten,
he has hidden his face, he will never see it."

These quotations serve more than one function: they portray the arrogance of the wicked; they provoke God to intervene; and, by bringing the issue into the open, they reassure the user of the psalm that God does care and will protect the vulnerable. Thus, Psalm 10 goes on to declare in verses 17–18,

> O LORD, you hear the desire of the afflicted;
> you will strengthen their heart; you will incline your ear
> to do justice to the fatherless and the oppressed,
> so that man who is of the earth may strike terror no more.

This, then, is another device whereby the one praying the psalms is encouraged to identify with God's point of view and reject that of the wicked.

Another technique that encourages the user of the psalms to adopt the psalmist's standpoint is the use of gaps. Gaps in narrative or poetry are points glided over by the author that the reader has to fill in from personal imagination to make sense of the passage. The terseness of poetry means that there are many gaps, which thereby force the reader to puzzle over the connection between one line and the next. The frequent mood swings in the psalms have long perplexed commentators and require every reciter of them at least to think of a connection between apparently contradictory statements. But more positively, the absence of many details within the psalms gives them a general validity that allows their sentiments to be appropriated by readers in a variety of circumstances. Erbele-Küster thinks that form critics were misguided in being overly concerned about the precise *Sitz im Leben* of each psalm. For example, in lament psalms it does not matter whether the psalmist was facing literal persecution or an illness or was using images of one situation to describe another. The absence of precision opens up a psalm to a broad range of situations and invites readers to make its sentiments their own.[6]

Erbele-Küster's monograph is a very useful examination of how the psalms work as prayers. She illuminates many of the devices whereby those who pray the psalms are led to identify with the righteous psalmist and make his prayers theirs, to identify with his outlook, and make his aspirations their own. Erbele-Küster does not directly apply her conclusions to the issue of the ethics of the psalms, but it is clearer as a result of her work how the later user of the psalms is encouraged to identify with the stance of the psalmist.

Another approach that sheds light on the uniqueness of psalmic ethics draws on the insights of speech-act theory. Speech-act theory was

6. Ibid., 141–80.

developed in the late twentieth century by philosophers of language, such as J. L. Austin and J. R. Searle, and then applied to theology by various scholars, such as Donald Evans and Anthony Thiselton. Unfortunately, there have been no major attempts to use speech-act theory to illuminate the ethics of the psalms, but it seems to me to offer great potential. Andreas Wagner, in a recent collection of essays,[7] makes a number of shrewd observations applying speech-act theory to individual psalms, but he does not use it to illuminate the function of prayer in general.

We have already observed that the psalms differ from other parts of the Bible in that they are meant to be recited or sung as prayers. That is, they are public address to God. The psalm puts powerful words into the worshiper's mouth, as Psalm 5:9–10 shows:

> For there is no truth in their mouth;
>   their inmost self is destruction;
> their throat is an open grave;
>   they flatter with their tongue.
> Make them bear their guilt, O God;
>   let them fall by their own counsels;
> because of the abundance of their transgressions
>   cast them out,
>   for they have rebelled against you.

Here the psalmist is accusing the wicked and summoning God to intervene against them. We have a similar scenario in Psalm 52. Erbele-Küster has aptly described the scenario. These psalms "distribute the roles of the actors as though the 'I' [the worshiper], those standing around (the righteous and wicked), and God stood simultaneously opposite each other."[8] This involvement of the worshiper in expressing assent to these sentiments makes the psalms quite different from the other modes of teaching ethics in the Old Testament. The Old Testament narratives presumably were recited by storytellers within the family or in the tribes, but they rarely make explicit their

7. Andreas Wagner, *Beten und Bekennen: Über Psalmen* (Neukirchen-Vluyn: Neukirchener Verlag, 2008).

8. Erbele-Küster, *Lesen als Akt*, 140.

judgments on the actions that are recited, so the moral of the story might be missed and certainly did not have to be endorsed by the listeners. They could just ignore the point, as I suspect many listening to worthy sermons often do.

The same is true of the laws. We are not sure how they were passed on in Bible times. Few people would have had written copies of the law; some texts suggest that the Levites were involved in teaching the law. In the light of the practice in neighboring cultures, it seems likely that most people's knowledge, if any, came from hearing recitations of the laws at religious festivals. But once again, for the listener the reception of the law was essentially passive. You listened to the law and maybe heard an explanation of it by a preacher, and then it was up to you to keep it or reject it as you saw fit (cf. Neh. 8:1–10). As long as you did not publicly reject or break the law, you would escape censure at least socially. Thus, receiving the ethical teaching of the law or the history books of the Old Testament was basically a silent, passive affair.

But reciting the psalms is quite different. One who prays the psalms is taking these words on his lips and saying them to God in a personal and solemn way. An example is Psalm 7:8–9:

> The Lord judges the peoples;
> judge me, O Lord, according to my righteousness
> and according to the integrity that is in me.
> Oh, let the evil of the wicked come to an end,
> and may you establish the righteous—
> you who test the minds and hearts,
> O righteous God!

The psalmist affirms that God will judge all the peoples, but then he invites God to judge him, despite affirming that God tests the minds and hearts. It is a challenging and disturbing prayer: does every worshiper really want God to test his innermost motives, I wonder? But time and again in the psalms we meet this sort of prayer. The reciter or singer of the psalms is thus involved in giving very active assent to the standards of life implied in the psalms.

The closest analogy in Scripture to this affirmation of standards is found, I think, in Deuteronomy 27. There, in a ceremony to be performed shortly after entry into the promised land, all the tribes stand before the Levites, who then pronounce curses on certain types of (mostly secret) sins. For example,

> "Cursed be the man who makes a carved or cast metal image, . . . and sets it up in secret" (v. 15).
>
> "Cursed be anyone who dishonors his father or his mother" (v. 16).
>
> "Cursed be anyone who misleads a blind man on the road" (v. 18).

And after each curse, "All the people shall say, 'Amen.'" But even saying "Amen" to a curse is, in my view, semipassive when compared with reciting a psalm. When you pray a psalm, you are describing what actions you will take and what you will avoid. It is more like taking an oath or making a vow. Perhaps this is what Psalm 119:106 is hinting at: "I have sworn an oath and confirmed it, to keep your righteous rules."[9]

J. L. Austin pointed out that many remarks are much more than statements about facts, which are either true or false. Promises, for example, change the situation and impose obligations on the speaker and create expectations in the listener. A promise is an example of a speech act. Wedding vows are speech acts too. The key words in a marriage ceremony are spoken publicly and to God. "I, A, take thee, B, to be my wedded wife, to have and to hold from this day forward, for better for worse, for richer for poorer, in sickness and health, to love and to cherish, till death do us part." Then there are words as rings are exchanged: "With this ring I thee wed, with my body I thee worship, and with all my worldly goods I thee endow, in the name of the Father, and of the Son, and of the Holy Ghost."

One trusts that brides and grooms pronounce these words after careful thought beforehand and with complete sincerity on the big

9. Some commentators (e.g., Kraus, Anderson) refer to Friedrich Horst's suggestion ("Der Eid im AT," *EvT* 17 [1957]: 371) that the reference is to a cultic oath sworn when one enters the temple. But this seems unlikely without further evidence of such an oath being used. Gianfranco Ravasi's more general comment seems adequate: "The psalmist solemnly affirms that he has dedicated his whole self to the observance of the 'judgments of thy righteousness'" (*Il libro dei Salmi: Commento e attualizzazione*, Lettura pastorale della Bibbia [Bologna: Edizioni Dehoniane, 1981–85], 3:483).

day. The words themselves transform their status: they become man and wife. Thus, the words are performative.[10] They change the situation. Speech-act philosophers have refined our understanding of illocutionary acts. According to J. R. Searle, some utterances are directives; that is, they ask someone to do something, as in Psalm 69:1 and Psalm 62:8:

> Save me, O God!
> For the waters have come up to my neck.

> Trust in him at all times, O people;
> pour out your heart before him;
> God is a refuge for us. *Selah*.

Other speech acts are commissive; that is, the speaker promises to do something, as in Psalm 39:1:

> I said, "I will guard my ways,
> that I may not sin with my tongue;
> I will guard my mouth with a muzzle,
> so long as the wicked are in my presence."

Yet others are expressive; that is, they express the emotion the speaker feels, as in Psalm 38:9:

> O Lord, all my longing is before you;
> my sighing is not hidden from you.

Other speech acts are declarative; that is, their very utterance effects a change, as in Psalm 2:8:

> Ask of me, and I will make the nations your heritage,
> and the ends of the earth your possession.

Finally, some acts are assertive declaratives; that is, they are assertions carrying the force of a declarative, as in Psalm 97:1:

10. See Paul Ramsey, "Liturgy and Ethics," *JRE* 7, no. 2 (1979): 139–71. Ramsey (pp. 145–46) argues that many liturgical remarks are performative.

> The LORD reigns, let the earth rejoice;
> let the many coastlands be glad!

Searle, whose classification I have just used, points out, "Often we do more than one of these things in the same utterance."[11] Using this categorization of speech acts, I suspect, one could say that praying the psalms involves the worshiper in many commissive speech acts: the psalms as prayers are really a series of vows. This is what sets them apart from other biblical texts with an ethical dimension.

One of the earliest writers to apply speech-act theory to the language of worship was Donald Evans in *The Logic of Self-Involvement*.[12] He does not specifically discuss the language of the psalms, but his more general observations are quite pertinent to the present discussion. Evans does not use the more nuanced analysis of speech acts found in Searle's work; rather, he builds on Austin's simpler understanding of performative acts. He argues that most theological statements from a believer have a stronger or weaker commissive sense. This observation, I believe, aptly describes the situation of those praying the psalms. It is particularly pertinent to a study of the ethics of the psalms.

Evans begins by noting that when God addresses mankind, he makes a commitment, and when mankind addresses God, there is a commitment in response. "Similarly man does not (or does not merely) assert certain facts about God; he addresses God in the activity of worship, committing himself to God and expressing his attitude to God. In so far as God's self-revelation is a self-involving verbal activity ('His Word is claim and promise, gift and demand') and man's religious language is also a self-involving verbal activity ('obedient, thankful confession and prayer'), theology needs an outline of the various ways in which language is self-involving."[13]

11. J. R. Searle, *Expression and Meaning: Studies in the Theory of Speech Acts* (Cambridge: Cambridge University Press, 1979), 29, quoted in Richard S. Briggs, *Words in Action: Speech Act Theory and Biblical Interpretation; Toward a Hermeneutic of Self-Involvement* (Edinburgh: T&T Clark, 2001), 50.

12. Donald M. Evans, *The Logic of Self-Involvement: A Philosophical Study of Everyday Language with Special Reference to the Christian Use of Language about God as a Creator*, LPT (London: SCM, 1963).

13. Ibid., 14.

His book attempts to provide such an analysis of how the language of worship involves the worshiper. He adopts the terminology of J. L. Austin, the founder of speech-act theory, to define the character of worship language. Evans argues that this language falls into two main categories: *commissives*, in which the speaker commits himself to a course of action, and *behabitives*, in which an attitude is expressed. Typical commissives are "promise," "pledge," "accept," "undertake," "engage," "threaten," "swear loyalty," "declare as policy," "take as wife." Behabitives include terms such as "praise," "thank," "apologize," "commend," "blame," "reprimand," "glorify," "worship," "confess," "welcome," "protest," "accuse."[14] Obviously, both commissives and behabitives are found throughout the Psalter.

> But I, through the abundance of your steadfast love,
> will enter your house.
> I will bow down toward your holy temple
> in the fear of you. (Ps. 5:7)

> But let all who take refuge in you rejoice;
> let them ever sing for joy,
> and spread your protection over them,
> that those who love your name may exult in you. (Ps. 5:11)

> I will give to the Lord the thanks due to his righteousness,
> and I will sing praise to the name of the Lord, the Most High. (Ps. 7:17)

> I will give thanks to the Lord with my whole heart;
> I will recount all of your wonderful deeds.
> I will be glad and exult in you;
> I will sing praise to your name, O Most High. (Ps. 9:1–2)

> In the Lord I take refuge;
> how can you say to my soul,
> "Flee like a bird to your mountain?" (Ps. 11:1)

14. Ibid., 29.

Evans says that statements such as "I promise" and "I pledge" "are Commissive performatives, for the speaker *commits* himself in more than a verbal way. They have a 'content,' for the speaker is undertaking to behave in a specified way in the future; for example, he is undertaking to 'return this book tomorrow.'"[15]

God's promises are commissives, as in, for example, Psalm 12:5:

> "Because the poor are plundered, because the needy groan,
> I will now arise," says the LORD;
> "I will place him in the safety for which he longs."

Or Psalm 75:2–3:

> At the set time that I appoint
> I will judge with equity.
> When the earth totters, and all its inhabitants,
> it is I who keep steady its pillars. *Selah.*

Or Psalm 91:14:

> Because he holds fast to me in love, I will deliver him;
> I will protect him, because he knows my name.

These divine commitments evoke a response from human beings. In fact, in many of the psalms, divine promises are quoted by the psalmists in their prayer and praise. Following Austin's terminology, Evans identifies sentiments such as "I thank you," "we praise thee, O Lord," and "I apologize" as behabitives, "since they related the speaker to another person in the context of human *behaviour* and social relations, without being strongly Commissive. The speaker implies that he has certain attitudes in relation to the person whom he addresses, or towards what he is talking about. In saying, 'I thank you,' I imply (but do not report) that I am grateful to you; in saying, 'I apologize for my behaviour,' I imply (but do not report), that I have an unfavourable attitude towards my behaviour. Behabitives imply attitudes."[16] Evans argues that most language about God is either

15. Ibid., 32.
16. Ibid., 34–35.

commissive or behabitive and therefore self-involving. Self-involvement is particularly evident in first-person utterances. "Where *I* report my attitude in the present tense, my utterance is rarely a mere report, equivalent to *your* report of my attitude. It tends to *commit* me to the pattern of behaviour to which I am referring; it has a forward reference to behaviour for which I am the responsible agent, not merely an observer."[17] Many psalms illustrate this.

> Blessed be the Lord,
> for he has wondrously shown his steadfast love to me
> when I was in a besieged city.
> I had said in my alarm,
> "I am cut off from your sight."
> But you heard the voice of my pleas for mercy
> when I cried to you for help. (Ps. 31:21–22)

> I acknowledged my sin to you,
> and I did not cover my iniquity;
> I said, "I will confess my transgressions to the Lord,"
> and you forgave the iniquity of my sin. *Selah.*
> Therefore let everyone who is godly
> offer prayer to you at a time when you may be found;
> surely in the rush of great waters,
> they shall not reach him. (Ps. 32:5–6)

> Oh, magnify the Lord with me,
> and let us exalt his name together!
> I sought the Lord, and he answered me
> and delivered me from all my fears.
> Those who look to him are radiant,
> and their faces shall never be ashamed. (Ps. 34:3–5)

> I waited patiently for the Lord;
> he inclined to me and heard my cry.
> He drew me up from the pit of destruction,
> out of the miry bog,
> and set my feet upon a rock,
> making my steps secure.

17. Ibid., 119.

He put a new song in my mouth,
a song of praise to our God.
Many will see and fear,
and put their trust in the Lord. (Ps. 40:1–3)

Many remarks that on first sight seem to be mere statements of fact, constatives, have clearly performative force within the context of worship. According to the Old Testament, "man in general is created with a role as nature's steward and God's articulate worshipper. In the biblical context, to say, 'God is my Creator' is to acknowledge the *role* which God has assigned."[18] To say "I acknowledge you as my king" or "You are my king" is to express a strong commitment.[19] The so-called enthronement psalms offer many examples of this.

The Lord reigns; he is robed in majesty;
the Lord is robed; he has put on strength as his belt.
Yes, the world is established; it shall never be moved.
(Ps. 93:1)

O Lord, God of vengeance,
O God of vengeance, shine forth! (Ps. 94:1)

For the Lord is a great God,
and a great King above all gods. (Ps. 95:3)

Say among the nations, "The Lord reigns!
Yes, the world is established; it shall never be moved;
he will judge the peoples with equity." (Ps. 96:10)

The Lord reigns, let the earth rejoice;
let the many coastlands be glad! (Ps. 97:1)

The Lord reigns; let the peoples tremble!
He sits enthroned upon the cherubim; let the earth quake!
(Ps. 99:1)

18. Ibid., 155.
19. Ibid., 52–53.

These "Commissives are utterances in which the speaker commits himself to future patterns of more-than-merely-verbal behavior."[20]

Even a remark such as "God is holy" in a song of praise to God is more than a statement of God's attribute of holiness; it expresses a certain sense of awe in the worshiper. In the biblical context, to say "God is glorious" or "God is holy" is to worship God; it is to express an attitude. As an expression of attitude, the utterance is both performative and expressive: "The words are used performatively to perform an act of praise and to commit oneself to various attitudes of supreme and exclusive devotion to God."[21]

Andreas Wagner makes a similar point. In the Old Testament, he says, "every confession of faith in Yahweh carries with it obligations. What is expressed in the sentence following Deuteronomy 6:4 may be implied in all confessions of faith in Yahweh."[22] Deuteronomy 6:4 says, "Hear, O Israel: The LORD our God, the LORD is one." It continues in verse 5, "You shall love the LORD your God with all your heart and with all your soul and with all your might." Wagner argues, "In the act of confession are embedded obligations, which one, in and through confessing, accepts for oneself. Confessing faith in Yahweh means loving him and doing all that which is according to his will."[23]

Psalm 104 fits this analysis well. It begins (vv. 1–2),

> Bless the LORD, O my soul!
> O LORD my God, you are very great!
> You are clothed with splendor and majesty,
> covering yourself with light as with a garment,
> stretching out the heavens like a tent.

Then, in language reminiscent of Genesis 1, the psalm recounts in verse 14 God's creative acts, including his provision of food for humans:

20. Ibid., 57.

21. Ibid., 183.

22. Andreas Wagner, *Sprechakte und Sprechaktanalyse im Alten Testament: Untersuchungen im biblischen Hebräisch an der Nahtstelle zwischen Handlungsebene und Grammatik*, BZAW 253 (Berlin: de Gruyter, 1997), 215.

23. Ibid.

> You cause the grass to grow for the livestock
> and plants for man to cultivate,
> that he may bring forth food from the earth.

In verse 24 it exults,

> O LORD, how manifold are your works!
> In wisdom have you made them all;
> the earth is full of your creatures.

These recollections of God's work in creation motivate a strong commitment on the part of the psalmist as he concludes the psalm (vv. 31–35):

> May the glory of the LORD endure forever;
> may the LORD rejoice in his works,
> who looks on the earth and it trembles,
> who touches the mountains and they smoke!
> I will sing to the LORD as long as I live;
> I will sing praise to my God while I have being.
> May my meditation be pleasing to him,
> for I rejoice in the LORD.
> Let sinners be consumed from the earth,
> and let the wicked be no more!
> Bless the LORD, O my soul!
> Praise the LORD!

Evans is quite correct to insist, "In the biblical context, the utterance 'God is my Creator' is profoundly self-involving."[24]

His further point that the use of the present tense also has implications for future action is also important in reading the psalms ethically. Use of the present tense and the first person "tends to *commit* me to the pattern of behavior to which I am referring."[25]

Again, many passages from the Psalter could be cited in support of Evans. For example, Psalm 116 begins (v. 1),

24. Evans, *Logic of Self-Involvement*, 160.

25. Ibid., 119. Wagner (*Sprechakte und Sprechaktanalyse*, 98) notes that explicitly performative utterances in Hebrew are generally put in the first-person perfect.

> I love the LORD, because he has heard
>   my voice and my pleas for mercy.

Then, after an extended account of how God has answered his prayer, in verses 18–19 the psalmist promises,

> I will pay my vows to the LORD
>   in the presence of all his people,
> in the courts of the house of the LORD,
>   in your midst, O Jerusalem.
> Praise the LORD!

A similar pattern is discernible in Psalm 118. After affirming the constancy of God's love (vv. 1–4), the psalmist relates his experience of it (vv. 5–6):

> Out of my distress I called on the LORD;
>   the LORD answered me and set me free.
> The LORD is on my side; I will not fear.
>   What can man do to me?

In the body of the psalm he relates more fully what God has done for him, and then concludes (v. 28),

> You are my God, and I will give thanks to you;
>   you are my God; I will extol you.

In a recent article Karl Möller applies speech-act theory to Psalm 101. This apparently is a royal psalm in which the king declares how he will act and what sort of people he wants to serve him. In verses 2–3, 6–7, the king says,

> I will walk with integrity of heart
>   within my house;
> I will not set before my eyes
>   anything that is worthless. . . .
> He who walks in the way that is blameless
>   shall minister to me.
> No one who practices deceit
>   shall dwell in my house;

no one who utters lies
shall continue before my eyes.

The genre of this psalm has been the subject of much debate. Is it a vow, a charter, an oath, a royal program, a manifesto, or a pledge? Karl Möller thinks that it matters little: "What all these descriptions have in common is a clear tendency to think of Psalm 101 not only in self-involving but also in specifically commissive terms."[26]

Möller goes on to point out that anyone who then uses the psalm as a personal prayer thereby makes a commitment to its values. "The king does commit himself to a certain kind of future behavior. But so does anyone who sings or prays Psalm 101."[27] In singing or praying Psalm 101 today, we "follow the lead of Israel's ancient kings and psalmists in pledging ourselves, again and again, . . . to the kind of ethical behaviour that is the subject of Psalm 101.[28]

What Möller argues for in Psalm 101 seems to me to apply to most, if not all, of the Psalter. Praying the psalms is a performative, typically a commissive, act: saying these solemn words to God alters one's relationship in a way that mere listening does not. This is not a new insight; the apostle Paul saw confession of faith as altering one's status before God. In Romans 10:9–10 he writes, "Because, if you confess with your mouth that Jesus is Lord and believe in your heart that God raised him from the dead, you will be saved. For with the heart one believes and is justified, and with the mouth one confesses and is saved."

Paul's argument may be applied to the psalms. Throughout the Psalter one is confessing that the Lord is God, and, as the psalms often insist, this is supposed to be a confession that comes from a pure and sincere heart. And certainly it is salvation that the psalmist seeks: time and again he pleads to God to save him, to deliver him, to hear his prayer, and so on. Whether this always occurs or not is something that I do not seek to discuss now. I simply want to draw

26. Karl Möller, "Reading, Singing and Praying the Law: An Exploration of the Performative, Self-Involving, Commissive Language of Psalm 101," in *Reading the Law: Studies in Honour of Gordon J. Wenham*, ed. J. G. McConville and Karl Möller, LHBOTS 461 (London: T&T Clark, 2007), 134.

27. Ibid., 135.

28. Ibid., 137.

out some of the similarities between taking an oath, making a vow, confessing faith, and praying the psalms. I think that these parallels may help us to see how powerful the commitment is that the psalms demand of their user. In praying the psalms, one is actively committing oneself to following the God-approved life. This is different from just listening to laws or edifying stories. It is an action akin to reciting the creed or singing a hymn. It involves strong commitment, and this is why I think that the psalms have been so influential in molding Jewish and Christian ethics in the past, and why as scholars we should again study them for their ethical content.

5

The Concept of the Law in the Psalms

Introduction

In the previous chapters I have surveyed the use of the psalms in worship over the centuries, and I have argued that their liturgical use has given their ethical outlook a unique persuasiveness. To pray a psalm is to commit oneself to its values and standards in a way that is quite different from listening to a proverb, legal rule, or story. To pray a psalm may well involve more than praise or petition; it may commit the worshiper to act in certain ways. Praying psalms with such ethical content may therefore be compared to making a vow or taking an oath, which are public commitments made before human witnesses and before God.

We therefore now turn to a survey of psalmic ethics. As I explained in chapter 2, it is not my intention to investigate the meaning of individual psalms in a hypothetical *Sitz im Leben* or what the original authors meant, but rather to examine what the psalms mean in their final editorial position in the Hebrew canon.[1] It is not that I think

1. Here I agree with the exegetical stance taken by Jean-Luc Vesco, *Le psautier de David traduit et commenté*, 2 vols., LD 210, 211 (Paris: Cerf, 2006).

that this canonical sense necessarily differs from a psalm's original meaning or from its later Christian appropriation, but that the final or canonical sense is more approachable than its alternatives. It is also the sense that a reader reciting the psalms consecutively is likely instinctively to infer. This final-form approach licenses the modern exegete to call on other texts in the Psalter, especially those in adjacent psalms, to clarify what the editors of the Psalter meant in problem passages—a procedure that may be questioned if one holds that the texts in question are from different hands.

In this chapter, therefore, I will look at what the psalms have to say about the law and, in particular, their attitude toward the law as an idea and as an institution. The structure of the Psalter, which commends the law in the opening psalm and makes it the theme of the longest psalm, immediately draws attention to the law's importance. Later parts of the Old Testament often are accused of a dry legalism, and I will examine whether this is a fair representation of the Psalter's outlook. In the next chapter I will look at the way the psalms actually use some of the laws in the Pentateuch.

The Psalter Framed by Law

The importance of the law for the editors of the Psalter is seen immediately in Psalm 1:1–2:

> Blessed is the man who walks not in the counsel
>   of the wicked,
>   nor stands in the way of sinners,
>   nor sits in the seat of scoffers;
> but his delight is in the law of the LORD,
>   and on his law he meditates day and night.

Psalm 1 is the introduction not only to the Psalter but also to the third section of the Hebrew canon, the Writings.[2] It echoes God's instruction to Joshua recorded in Joshua 1:8: "This Book of the Law

2. The Writings comprise (in the order of the Hebrew Bible) Psalms, Job, Proverbs, Ruth, Song of Songs, Ecclesiastes, Lamentations, Esther, Daniel, Ezra, Nehemiah, and 1–2 Chronicles.

shall not depart from your mouth, but you shall meditate on it day and night, so that you may be careful to do according to all that is written in it. For then you will make your way prosperous, and then you will have good success."

Not only do both Joshua 1:8 and Psalm 1 commend meditating on the law day and night but also both offer the same reward, a "prosperous way." The verb *ṣālaḥ* ("prosper") is found in Psalm 1:3, "In all that he does, he prospers," and in Joshua 1:8. Similarly, the noun "way" (*derek*) occurs in Psalm 1:6, "For the Lord knows the way of the righteous," and in Joshua 1:8. Just as the book of Psalms opens the third part of the Hebrew canon, so the book of Joshua opens the second part, the Prophets. In this way, the second and third parts of the Old Testament canon both point back to the Torah (the Law), the first part of the canon, as foundational for a righteous and successful life.

The Psalter does not just begin with a psalm extolling the value of the law; it is itself divided into five books like the Pentateuch (Pss. 1–41; 42–72; 73–89; 90–106; 107–150). It thus seems probable that the law that the righteous should delight in is not just the law of Moses in the Pentateuch, but the law of David enshrined in the Psalter.[3]

It is striking that both the first book and the last book of the Psalter have at their center a psalm praising the law. Psalm 19 is found at the midpoint of Book 1, while Psalm 119 comes about halfway through Book 5. The two share many key terms and also have a similar structure.

Described by C. S. Lewis as "the greatest poem in the Psalter,"[4] Psalm 19 falls into three main parts. The first part (vv. 1–6) celebrates God's glory visible in creation, particularly the sun, whose "rising is from the end of the heavens, and its circuit to the end of them, and there is nothing hidden from its heat" (v. 6).

The second part (vv. 7–11) celebrates God's wisdom manifest in the law. Verse 7 states, "The law of the Lord is perfect, reviving the soul; the testimony of the Lord is sure, making wise the simple."

In fact, there are six clauses, each with a different term for the law ("law," "testimony," "precept," "commandment," "fear," "rules")

3. See Gerald H. Wilson, *The Editing of the Hebrew Psalter*, SBLDS 76 (Chico, CA: Scholars Press, 1985).

4. C. S. Lewis, *Reflections on the Psalms* (London: Collins, 1961), 56.

followed by the phrase "of the Lord." These same terms figure prominently in Psalm 119, where nearly every verse contains a word for the law. Interestingly, each line in Psalm 19:7–9 (vv. 8–10 in the Hebrew text) consists of five Hebrew words, which Jean-Luc Vesco thinks may be an allusion to the five books of the Pentateuch.[5]

The third and final section of Psalm 19 (vv. 12–14) is a prayer:

> Who can discern his errors?
> Declare me innocent from hidden faults.
> Keep back your servant also from presumptuous sins;
> let them not have dominion over me!
> Then I shall be blameless,
> and innocent of great transgression.
> Let the words of my mouth and the meditation of my heart
> be acceptable in your sight,
> O Lord, my rock and my redeemer.

These three very different sections make it hard to classify this psalm. Typically, commentators suggest that the first section about the sky is a hymn, whereas the second (including vv. 12–14), with its focus on the law, is a wisdom poem. It is frequently surmised that the two parts come from different hands, that perhaps an earlier hymn to creation has been supplemented by later poetry in praise of the law.

However, there are many links between the two parts.[6] This makes it likely that the two belong together. And although the subject matter of each of the two halves may seem totally different, in fact in ancient Near Eastern thought the sun and the law went closely together. For example, in Babylon the sun-god Shamash was the god of justice. Hammurabi's law stela is topped by a carving of Shamash giving the symbols of justice to the king. In Psalm 19 there is no suggestion that the sun is divine, but its power and its ability to shine light on dark places make it a vivid metaphor for the law. "There is nothing hidden from its heat" (v. 6).

5. Vesco, *Le psautier de David*, 209.

6. The closing verses pick up terms used earlier in the psalm: "hidden" (*sātar* [vv. 6, 12]), "speech, word" (*ʾōmer* [vv. 2, 3, 14]), "perfect, blameless" (*tmm* [vv. 7, 13]). For further connections, see Beat Weber, *Werkbuch Psalmen*, vol. 1 (Stuttgart: Kohlhammer, 2001), 112.

But those who recognize the coherence of the sun and the law in this psalm rarely utilize the last three verses to define the character of the psalm. However, Richard Clifford describes the issue exactly: the psalm "resembles a hymn in its praise of divine wisdom (vv. 1–11) and an individual petition (lament) in its plea for forgiveness and enlightenment (vv. 12–14)."[7] In this respect, Psalm 19 anticipates Psalm 119, which, as I will argue below, should be classified as an individual lament rather than as a wisdom or Torah psalm.

The importance of the law is underlined by the length and structure of Psalm 119. Not only is it the longest psalm but also it mentions the law, using a variety of terms, in nearly every verse. It is peppered with the refrain "teach me your statutes" (vv. 12, 26, 64, 68, 124, 135, 171) or "teach me your rules" (v. 108). The author's chief concern is to "keep your law" (vv. 34, 44, 55, 136) or at least not to forget it (vv. 61, 109, 153). Three times he declares his love for "your law" (vv. 97, 113, 163) or "your commandments" (vv. 47, 48, 127). In verse 97 the psalmist claims to have fulfilled the injunction in 1:2 ("and on his law he meditates day and night"), exclaiming, "Oh how I love your law! It is my meditation[8] all the day" (cf. v. 99).

It should be noted that neither of the Hebrew words translated as "meditate" or "meditation" refers to silent activities. The verb in Psalm 1:2, *hāgâ*, also refers to lions roaring (Isa. 31:4) and pigeons cooing (Isa. 59:11), to nations plotting (Ps. 2:1), and to the use of the tongue, mouth, and throat (Pss. 35:28; 37:30; 115:7). The other verb, *śîaḥ*, is defined as "loud, enthusiastic emotionally laden speech" (e.g., praise in Judg. 5:10; Ps. 145:5; lamentation in Ps. 55:17; taunting in Ps. 69:12) or as "meditating with thanks and praise" (Pss. 77:12; 119:15, 23, 27, 48, 78, 148).[9] When the psalmist speaks of "meditating" on the law, therefore, he is not just thinking about it in his head; rather, he

7. Richard J. Clifford, *Psalms 1–72*, AOTC (Nashville: Abingdon, 2002), 111. Cf. John Goldingay, "At the end, it has to come to a plea for redemption" (*Psalms: Psalms 1–41*, BCOTWP [Grand Rapids: Baker Academic, 2006], 299); and Erhard S. Gerstenberger, "We are dealing with a PERSONAL PRAYER built according to the old pattern of individual complaint" (*Psalms: Part 1, with an Introduction to Cultic Poetry*, FOTL 14 [Grand Rapids: Eerdmans, 1988], 102).

8. The Hebrew term translated "meditation" in 119:97, 99 (*śîḥâ*) differs from the more common term (*hāgâ*) in 1:2, but the LXX and ESV render it the same.

9. *HALOT* 1320.

is speaking out loud. He is not reading the text to himself, for several times he mentions doing it at night (Pss. 1:2; 63:6; 77:6), which would have been difficult before the invention of electric light. In line with my discussion in chapter 3, we probably should imagine him singing or reciting the psalm from memory.

Another device that the author of Psalm 119 uses to stress the importance, indeed the perfection, of the law is the acrostic; in fact, Psalm 119 is the longest acrostic poem in the Bible. It falls into twenty-two sections, each beginning with a different letter of the Hebrew alphabet. Thus, verses 1–8 begin with the first letter of the alphabet, *ʾaleph* (א), verses 9–16 with the second letter, *bet* (ב), and so on until the last eight verses (vv. 169–176), which begin with the last letter of the Hebrew alphabet, *taw* (ת). Psalm 112 does the same in miniature: its first full line begins with *ʾaleph* (*ʾašrê*, "blessed"), and its final word, *tōʾbēd* ("perish"), begins with *taw*. Psalm 1 is not an acrostic, but it too uses this device of making its first word begin with *ʾaleph* (*ʾašrê*) and its last word with *taw* (*tōʾbēd*).

The function of the acrostic in Hebrew poetry has been much discussed. Clearly, it is an aid to memorization, and it also displays the poet's ingenuity. But it is also helps to underline the message of a poem. By going through the whole alphabet systematically, it conveys the idea of totality or completeness.

"By using every letter of the alphabet the poet was trying to ensure that his treatment of a particular topic was complete. At the same time, the reader gained the impression that the poem he was reading covered every angle."[10] Thus, the book of Lamentations contains four acrostic poems bewailing the fall of Jerusalem. The use of the acrostic form emphasizes the totality of the disaster and the magnitude of the nation's grief. "The author . . . selected the external principle of the acrostic to correspond to the internal spirit and intention of the work. He wished to play upon the collective grief of the community in its every aspect, 'from *Aleph* to *Taw*,' so that the people might experience an emotional catharsis. He wanted to bring about a complete cleansing of the conscience through a total confession of sin."[11]

10. Wilfred G. E. Watson, *Classical Hebrew Poetry: A Guide to Its Techniques*, 2nd ed. (London: T&T Clark, 2005), 198.

11. Norman K. Gottwald, *Studies in the Book of Lamentations* (London: SCM, 1954), 30.

There is only one acrostic poem in the Wisdom literature: the hymn to the ideal wife in Proverbs 31:10–31. Here the acrostic seems to be chosen to accent her perfection. "What we have here is an A–Z of wisdom, a celebration of a true hero of the faith."[12]

A similar purpose is apparent in the Psalter's acrostics. For example, Psalm 111 celebrates the perfection of God's acts, while Psalm 112 celebrates the deeds and character of "the man who fears God," "the ideal wise person who might utter Psalm 112."[13] It is likely that a similar motive explains the longest acrostic in the Bible, Psalm 119. The acrostic pattern underlines the comprehensiveness and perfection of the law as well as the psalmist's yearning to live by it. "The acrostic form also expresses the perfection of *tôrat yhwh*: it is wholly divine (v. 89) and wonderful (v. 129). Nothing is missing: no part of *tôrâ* is incomplete."[14] It is often surmised that at one stage in the Psalter's growth Psalm 119 formed its climactic conclusion. This cannot be proved, but the very presence of this huge psalm indicates the importance of the law. This is reinforced by its connections with Psalm 1 and Psalm 19. Psalm 1, as the introduction to the Psalter, obviously highlights key concerns of the Psalter, while the brilliant Psalm 19, at the center of Book 1 of the Psalter, keeps the reader's eyes on the life-giving value of the law. This theme is central also to Psalm 119, to which we now turn to determine its views more exactly.

Psalm 119 often is classified as a wisdom poem praising the law's perfection. A closer analysis suggests that it is more: it is an individual lament in which the author prays to be delivered from his troubles so that he may keep the law with his whole heart. Psalm 119 often has been accused of a narrow, nitpicking legalism. It is alleged that the psalm advocates a pedantic concern with the minutiae of the law, not its uplifting spirit, that it is a forerunner of later rabbinic casuistry that flourished after the return from exile. This may well be the era in which the psalm was composed, but to read it as a paean to casuistry is far from the truth. It is permeated by a love for God and his

12. Craig G. Bartholomew, *Reading Proverbs with Integrity*, GBS 22 (Cambridge: Grove Books, 2001), 17.

13. Konrad Schaefer, *Psalms*, Berit Olam (Collegeville, MN: Liturgical Press, 2001), 278.

14. David Noel Freedman, *Psalm 119: The Exaltation of Torah*, BJS 6 (Winona Lake, IN: Eisenbrauns, 1999), 89.

revelation, which is seen as the path to true happiness and fulfillment. God's word gives life, as seen in verses 50, 93:

> This is my comfort in my affliction,
> that your promise gives me life.
>
> I will never forget your precepts,
> for by them you have given me life.

The psalm itself is an extended prayer that God will instruct the psalmist, so that he will love God with all his heart: "Give me understanding, that I may keep your law and observe it with my whole heart" (v. 34).

The central message of the poem is clear: the psalmist is waiting for divine intervention to free him. He counts on Yahweh for his hope of salvation. Fidelity to God ensures the hope of final victory. The word that God reveals allows the one who learns it and practices it to overcome all the crises of life while awaiting divine vindication. "The whole divine revelation [is] conceived as a rule of life which leads to salvation."[15]

At least in this psalm the law is not limited to the laws in the Pentateuch, or wisdom teaching or the book of Deuteronomy, but is the whole revelation of God, which is given for the salvation of mankind.[16] The psalmist's "one preoccupation is to know . . . the will of God better and put it into practice,"[17] so as to enjoy complete communion with God, day and night, as long as he lives. He yearns for the prophecy of Jeremiah 31:33, that God would write his law in the heart, to be fulfilled in him. "God's instruction is already his sun, already the complete love of his heart. . . . But he still feels he has not reached the height of the prophet's ideal, still he asks time and again for deeper divine enlightenment and more effective guidance, still he regards himself as a lost sheep, that Yahweh must first search for and then bring home."[18]

15. Vesco, *Le psautier de David*, 1130–31.

16. Alfons Deissler (*Psalm 119 [118] und seine Theologie: Ein Beitrag zur Erforschung der anthologischen Stilgattung im Alten Testament*, MTS 2, no. 1 [Munich: Karl Zink, 1955], 271–92) argues that Psalm 119 is particularly dependent on Deuteronomy, Jeremiah, Isaiah 40–66, Proverbs, and Job.

17. Vesco, *Le psautier de David*, 1143.

18. Deissler, *Psalm 119*, 308.

The terms that the psalmist uses in Psalm 119 to describe his attitudes witness to a deeply interior spirituality. Here are some of the most common terms that he uses to express his attitude: *šmr* "keep" (21×), *ḥyh* "live" (16×), *lmd* "learn" (13×), *ʾhb* "love" (10×), *byn* "understand" (10×), *nṣr* "preserve" (10×), *škḥ* "forget" (9×), *ydʿ* "know" (4×), *lēb* "heart" (15×), *ṣedeq* "righteousness" (12×), *ḥesed* "steadfast love" (7×), *ʾĕmûnâ* "faithfulness" (5×), *ʾĕmet* "truth" (4×). These terms are not unusual in the Bible, though their concentration in this one psalm is striking. But five times in Psalm 119 the psalmist uses a quite rare term, *šaʿăšuʿîm* ("delight"), to describe his attitude to revelation (vv. 24, 77, 92, 143, 174). For example, he says in verses 24, 77,

Your testimonies are my delight;
they are my counselors.

Let your mercy come to me, that I may live;
for your law is my delight.

The rare occurrences of *šaʿăšuʿîm* ("delight") outside this psalm bring out some of its nuances. In Isaiah 5:7 it refers to God's choicest vine, Judah, within the vineyard of Israel. In Jeremiah 31:20 it describes God's fondness for Ephraim, "my darling child." In Proverbs 8:30–31 it describes personified preexistent wisdom rejoicing before God as he creates the world:

Then I was beside him, like a master workman,
and I was daily his delight,
rejoicing before him always,
rejoicing in his inhabited world
and delighting in the children of man.

"Wisdom enjoys being with God and her position of honor. Her joy is especially intense as she watches God create."[19] So when the psalmist says, "Your law is my delight," he is affirming the intense pleasure that its study brings him.

19. Richard J. Clifford, *Proverbs: A Commentary*, OTL (Louisville: Westminster John Knox, 1999), 97.

But his relationship to the law is characterized not only by pleasure but also by love. A dozen times he mentions his love for the law. In verse 97 he exclaims, "Oh how I love your law! It is my meditation all the day" (cf. vv. 47, 48, 113, 119, 127, 132, 140, 159, 163, 165, 167).

These sentiments "express a deep affection which drives the psalmist to fulfill the commandments because they express God's will, which he loves more than everything."[20] These comments show that the psalmist has internalized the law in a way that anticipates a Christian understanding of the place of the law in ethics.[21] In the new covenant the Holy Spirit writes the law on the human heart (Jer. 31:33; Heb. 8:10; 10:16), so that the law is no longer "seen as something imposed on you from without,"[22] but rather as God's wisdom for our good.

Psalm 119 uses eight terms for the law.[23] These terms appear to be interchangeable, at least poetically. In all but two verses at least one of them is used.

Tôrâ (25×) is the most common term, always rendered "law," and usually having the Hebrew suffix for "your," referring to the Lord. The most obvious sense of "law" is the Pentateuch, especially the book of Deuteronomy, whose terminology pervades this psalm. But the associated verb *yārâ* (in the Hiphil) means "teach" (vv. 33, 102), and elsewhere the noun is used of wisdom, prophetic teaching, or priestly instruction (Prov. 13:14; Isa. 1:10; Hag. 2:11). Unlike the other terms in this psalm, it is used only in the singular, which suggests that it is a global term for the totality of God's revelation.

Dābār ("word" [24×]), the next most common term, is likewise very broad in its scope. Like *tôrâ*, it usually is suffixed in Hebrew with "your" and used in the singular. It may refer to divine commands, presumably in Scripture (vv. 9, 16, 17), but often it

20. Vesco, *Le psautier de David*, 1155.

21. Peter Bristow, *Christian Ethics and the Human Person: Truth and Relativism in Contemporary Moral Theology* (Oxford: Family Publications; Birmingham: Maryvale Institute, 2009), 59.

22. Ibid., 226.

23. For analyses of these terms in Psalm 119, see Will Soll, *Psalm 119: Matrix, Form, and Setting*, CBQMS 23 (Washington, DC: Catholic Biblical Association of America, 1991); Deissler, *Psalm 119*; Vesco, *Le psautier de David*; *TDOT*.

refers to God's promises, as in the refrain "I hope in your word" (vv. 81, 114, 147; cf. vv. 49, 74) or in the prayer "Give me life according to your word!" (vv. 25, 107). In verse 89, "Forever, O Lord, your word is firmly fixed in the heavens," "your word" appears to sum up all of God's revelation.

Mišpāṭ ("judgment, rule" [23×]) is the most transparent of these terms. It is the decision or sentence of a judge, *šōpēṭ*. Thus, the KJV's "judgment" is an exact and literal translation, but in modern English, divine judgment has quite negative connotations, which the Hebrew does not have in most passages. Rather, when God judges the wicked, usually he is seen as intervening to save the righteous. Occasionally *mišpāṭ* has this sense, but mostly God's judgments are viewed very positively as the benevolent rulings of the all-wise judge. So the RSV and NRSV substitute "ordinances" for "judgments," but this translation loses the connection with a judge. The ESV's "rules" does not hide this link so completely (e.g., vv. 7, 13, 20, 30), but in some contexts where it involves divine intervention to save the righteous or condemn the wicked, "judgment" still seems the best rendering (vv. 120, 149).

ʿĒdût ("testimonies") is used only in the plural (23×), and rarely (11×) with this sense outside Psalm 119. Extrabiblical usage and Psalm 25:10 ("for those who keep his covenant and his testimonies") make it likely that "testimonies" are the stipulations of the covenant set out in Deuteronomy. The English translation associates the term with the Hebrew *ʿûd* ("bear witness"), but it is not clear in what sense a divine direction is "testimony," unless it is that the testimony is seen as declaring God's will to the human conscience. For example, "When I think on my ways, I turn my feet to your testimonies" (Ps. 119:59).

Ḥuqqîm ("statutes" [22×]) is another favorite term for laws in the Pentateuch. It refers to the laws on sacrifice (e.g., Lev. 6:18, 22; 7:34) as well as ethical instruction (Deut. 4:5, 6, 8). Often these decrees are said to be eternal or unbreakable (e.g., Pss. 105:10; 148:6; cf. Prov. 8:29). So the psalmist prays that his loyalty to them will be as long lasting (119:33, 44).

Miṣwôt ("commandments" [22×]), is a noun derived from the verb *ṣiwwâ*, "command, order." It usually refers to particular instructions, but once, in Psalm 119:96, "your commandment is exceedingly broad," it is used in the singular to refer to the whole body of divine teaching, a sense often found in Deuteronomy (cf. Ps. 19:8).

Piqqûdîm ("precepts" [21×]) occurs only in Psalm 119 and in Psalm 19:8; 103:18; 111:7. The verbal root *pqd* is sometimes used of military orders, so there may be such overtones in the noun. Another sense of *pqd*, as "visit, intervene" (cf. Exod. 3:16; 1 Sam. 2:21), is apparent in Psalm 119:40, where the psalmist longs for God's intervention to save him from his oppressors. Its pairing with "covenant" (Ps. 103:18) and "the works of his hands" (Ps. 111:7) indicates that it may refer to a wide variety of divine words and deeds.

ʾImrâ ("word" [19×]) is another term that is rare outside Psalm 119. It can be used of human speech (e.g., Gen. 4:23), but mostly it refers to divine speech. It is derived from the verb *ʾāmar* ("say"), so it basically has a quite general meaning (e.g., Ps. 119:158, 172). But in the frequent phrase "according to your word" it clearly has the sense of "promise" and thus is most often translated that way.

This survey of terminology shows the breadth of Psalm 119's understanding of the law: it is not just ethical injunctions and rules, but rather the whole of God's revelation. "The divine instruction designated by this series of terms that Psalm 119 uses as synonyms is not the Mosaic law, or the Pentateuch, or the book of Deuteronomy, or the canon of Scripture fixed later, but the totality of revelation viewed as a guide . . . to salvation."[24] It covers all that helps to link God to his people, from the revelation in the created order (Ps. 19:1), to the patriarchal experience of salvation, to the laws given at Sinai, to the teaching of the sages, to the return to Zion. Contemplation on all these experiences of God's grace prompts a deep yearning for a closer walk with God.

24. Vesco, *Le psautier de David*, 1142.

Psalm 119 often is read as a wisdom poem celebrating the value of the law,[25] "a manual of pious and instructive thoughts, designed for popular improvement."[26] But although its ideas owe much to the Wisdom literature and even more to Deuteronomy, it is not just an anthology[27] of sayings praising God's revelation. It is a prayer. It is a "supplication from a situation of distress."[28] In a footnote, Sigmund Mowinckel characterizes it as an "individual psalm of lamentation."[29] In a long study, Will Soll demonstrates that Psalm 119 has the features that characterize an individual lament. Sixty verses contain a petition, as in verse 17: "Deal bountifully with your servant, that I may live and keep your word." Thirty-eight verses contain lament, as in verse 25: "My soul clings to the dust."

Psalm 119 has other features of a lament, including an address (vv. 1–3) and confessions of trust (vv. 52, 54, 56, 114). "The many protestations of love for God's law and fidelity to it constitute . . . part of Psalm 119's affinity to the individual lament genre. . . . Attached to a petition, these declarations of fidelity can serve as motivation for that petition to be answered. . . . Incorporated in a lament, they give that lament greater pathos, and thereby serve as further motivation for God to respond with deliverance."[30]

Regarding verse 157, "Many are my persecutors and my adversaries, but I do not swerve from your testimonies," Soll says that "verses of this kind more than any other provide Psalm 119 with its consistent tone."[31]

25. See Arnold A. Anderson, *The Book of Psalms*, 2 vols., NCB (Grand Rapids: Eerdmans, 1981), 806; Hans-Joachim Kraus, *Psalmen*, 7th ed., 2 vols. in 1, BKAT 15 (Neukirchen-Vluyn: Neukirchener Verlag, 2003), 1000; cf. Philip S. Johnston and David G. Firth, eds., *Interpreting the Psalms: Issues and Approaches* (Leicester, UK: Apollos, 2005), 299.

26. Joseph A. Alexander, *The Psalms Translated and Explained* (1873; repr., Grand Rapids: Baker, 1975), 482.

27. So Deissler, *Psalm 119*; followed by Kraus, *Psalmen*.

28. John H. Eaton, *The Psalms: A Historical and Spiritual Commentary with an Introduction and New Translation* (London: T&T Clark, 2003), 415. Klaus Seybold (*Die Psalmen*, HAT 15 [Tübingen: Mohr, 1996], 474) calls it a "Gebet."

29. Sigmund Mowinckel, *The Psalms in Israel's Worship*, trans. D. R. Ap-Thomas, 2 vols. in 1, BRS (Grand Rapids: Eerdmans, 2004), 2:78.

30. Soll, *Psalm 119*, 78–79.

31. Ibid., 79.

Finally, Psalm 119 contains assurances that the petitions will be heard (e.g., vv. 171–72).

Soll concludes, "The preceding analysis has shown that Psalm 119 contains all the features essential to the lament. . . . The petitions from Psalm 119 . . . are similar to many other petitions in the lament psalms. They are general in nature, and they express a desire for things such as life, vindication, and deliverance. What is distinctive in Psalm 119, of course, is the consistency with which Torah is brought to bear on all of the above petitions. As *promise*, Torah constitutes the ground of hope for God's deliverance."[32] Thus we read in verse 41, "Let your steadfast love come to me, O LORD, your salvation according to your promise."

Read as an individual lament, Soll argues, Psalm 119 has a coherent, developing train of thought from the first stanza to the last. It opens by affirming the blessedness of "those whose way is blameless, who walk in the law of the LORD" (v. 1). But the psalmist almost immediately confesses that he falls short of this ideal: "Oh that my ways may be steadfast in keeping your statutes!" (v. 5), and "How can a young man keep his way pure?" (v. 9).[33]

The strophes following contain a mixture of lament and petition. Among the psalmist's complaints are that princes plot against him, that his soul clings to the dust, and that the insolent smear him with lies. He prays that he will not be forsaken or abandoned to his oppressors, that God will answer his prayers and give him life. But these petitions are made the more pressing and poignant by his appeal to God's promises and his repeated assertions of his loyalty to God and his love of God's law. In verses 125–128 he says,

> I am your servant; give me understanding,
> that I may know your testimonies!
> It is time for the LORD to act,
> for your law has been broken.
> Therefore I love your commandments
> above gold, above fine gold.

32. Ibid., 82–83.

33. Soll (ibid., 60–61) argues the second half of verse 9 continues the question in the first; thus, it should read, "How can a young man keep his way pure to guard it according to your word?" (so also Alexander, *Psalms*, 483; Seybold, *Psalmen*, 461).

> Therefore I consider all your precepts to be right;
> I hate every false way.

If God cares for his servant, God should recognize his loyalty and save him from the threats to his life. This is the logic of these remarks. The psalmist's pledges of loyalty and love of the law show where his heart is. Nevertheless, running through all these protestations and underlying them is an awareness of his own failure to walk blamelessly and keep the law perfectly (vv. 1–2). He keeps on praying for God to give him life and teach him his statutes.

The final strophe (vv. 169–176) brings all these ideas together. He prays for deliverance (v. 170):

> Let my plea come before you;
> deliver me according to your word.

He affirms that with God teaching him, he will praise God properly (v. 171):

> My lips will pour forth praise,
> for you teach me your statutes.

He affirms again his need for help and underlines it with a reminder of his affection for God's law (vv. 173–175):

> Let your hand be ready to help me,
> for I have chosen your precepts.
> I long for your salvation, O Lord,
> and your law is my delight.
> Let my soul live and praise you,
> and let your rules help me.

And he closes with one more plea for God's grace to heal and restore him (v. 176):

> I have gone astray like a lost sheep; seek your servant,
> for I do not forget your commandments.

So this psalm is far from an exercise in self-righteousness. Rather, it is confession: the psalmist confesses the wonder and grace of God's self-revelation in the divine promises and demands and also his need of that grace, without which he cannot live up to those demands. "This note of urgent necessity that ends the psalm puts its author much closer to the publican in the gospel parable than to the Pharisee. Instead of affirming his own righteousness, the psalmist solicits the help of God and reaffirms his constant desire for conversion."[34]

This understanding of the psalm as a lament is important for its ethic. It is not a detached piece of wisdom instruction, like a chapter from the book of Proverbs, that has been taken over in Jewish and Christian worship and turned into prayer. It is intrinsically a prayer, and this has profound consequences for its ethical stance. As I have argued in chapter 4, prayer necessarily involves the worshiper in a more profound way than does listening to a law, proverb, story, or sermon. Praying commits the worshiper to the values and standards that he articulates in his prayer. Commissive and behabitive speech acts appear everywhere in Psalm 119. For example, in verses 7–8 the psalmist says,

> I will praise you with an upright heart,
> when I learn your righteous rules.
> I will keep your statutes;
> do not utterly forsake me!

The constant use of the first person, "I," expresses the commitment of the psalmist, as in verses 10–11:

> With my whole heart I seek you;
> let me not wander from your commandments!
> I have stored up your word in my heart,
> that I might not sin against you.

His repeated praise of the law and his declarations of affection for it underline his commitment to its teaching. In verses 89, 97–98, 105, he says,

> Forever, O LORD, your word
> is firmly fixed in the heavens.

34. Vesco, *Le psautier de David*, 1152.

Oh how I love your law!
It is my meditation all the day.
Your commandment makes me wiser than my enemies,
for it is ever with me.

Your word is a lamp to my feet
and a light to my path.

By themselves, these affirmations might give the impression that the psalmist is a self-righteous law fanatic, but the frequent petitions fundamentally change this perception. The psalmist, and all who pray this psalm with him, are aware of their shortcomings and their need for divine aid to live up to these standards. In the first stanza he prays, "Oh that my ways may be steadfast in keeping your statutes!" (v. 5). Such a prayer acknowledges that he may not keep the statutes.

The repeated petition "Teach me your statutes" also implies that as yet the psalmist neither knows them fully nor practices them as he ought. Verses 36–37 are even more explicit about the temptations that he faces and needs divine help to overcome:

Incline my heart to your testimonies,
and not to selfish gain!
Turn my eyes from looking at worthless things;
and give me life in your ways.

This type of prayer shows that the psalmist not only is passionate about the value of the law but also recognizes his own shortcomings. It shows humility and sincerity. John H. Eaton describes it as

> a sustained work of prayer and communion. . . . A person who has loved the Lord and treasured his guidance is now ill-used by powerful people and brought near to the borders of death. So the prayer for new life rises, supported by the great stream of affirmations about the Lord's word in promise, teaching and commandments—how the sufferer has loved and followed it and longs to know it better. These considerations are not urged in the spirit of one who is blameless. There is almost a contradiction between the claims to have kept the Lord's law and the readiness to admit inadequacy and erring from the path. If it is a contradiction, it is a common experience—years of

> devotion and loyalty, yet shot through with deviation, and perceived in deep moments to be quite inadequate.[35]

This combination of a passion for God and his word with an awareness of the psalmist's own weaknesses and liability to fail is often expressed elsewhere in the Psalter. The closest parallel is Psalm 19, another psalm that focuses on the glory of the law and shares much of the same terminology with Psalm 119. Of the law, Psalm 19:7–11 says,

> The law of the LORD is perfect,
> reviving the soul;
> the testimony of the LORD is sure,
> making wise the simple;
> the precepts of the LORD are right,
> rejoicing the heart;
> the commandment of the LORD is pure,
> enlightening the eyes;
> the fear of the LORD is clean,
> enduring forever;
> the rules of the LORD are true,
> and righteous altogether.
> More to be desired are they than gold,
> even much fine gold;
> sweeter also than honey
> and drippings of the honeycomb.
> Moreover, by them is your servant warned;
> in keeping them there is great reward.

But then abruptly the psalmist looks at himself and asks (vv. 12–13),

> Who can discern his errors?
> Declare me innocent from hidden faults.
> Keep back your servant also from presumptuous sins;
> let them not have dominion over me!
> Then I shall be blameless,
> and innocent of great transgression.

35. Eaton, *Psalms*, 421–22.

The bright light of the law, which verses 1–6 have compared to the brilliance of the sun, penetrates deep into the human soul, making it aware of its shortcomings. The same realism and humility is found in many other psalms.

> O Lord, hear my voice!
> Let your ears be attentive
> to the voice of my pleas for mercy!
> If you, O Lord, should mark iniquities,
> O Lord, who could stand? (Ps. 130:2–3)

> Do I not hate those who hate you, O Lord?
> And do I not loathe those who rise up against you?
> Search me, O God, and know my heart!
> Try me and know my thoughts!
> And see if there be any grievous way in me,
> and lead me in the way everlasting! (Ps. 139:21, 23–24)

> Do not let my heart incline to any evil,
> to busy myself with wicked deeds
> in company with men who work iniquity,
> and let me not eat of their delicacies! (Ps. 141:4)

This dual-track approach needs to be borne in mind as we examine the ethical content of the psalms. Very often the psalmists are speaking of ideals that they know they fall short of, but that does not inhibit them from asserting such ideals. This mixture of idealism and realism pervades the Psalter. The psalmists affirm both their love for God and his law and their hatred of sin. Although this means that the psalmists are righteous in comparison to the wicked, who ignore God and despise his law, it does not mean that the psalmists see themselves as perfect or righteous in an absolute sense. This approach to God and his revelation forms the foundation on which are based the detailed ethical judgments discussed in the following chapters.

6

Laws in the Psalter

In the preceding chapter I established the importance of the law in the Psalter. I noted that both the first psalm and the longest psalm focus on the law. The variety of terms for the law—"commandment," "word," "promise," "precepts"—points to the fact that law is understood to be much more than regulations and rules, such as are found in the Pentateuch. "Law" or "instruction" covers all God's revelation to Israel, whether it is found in the Pentateuch or other parts of the Bible.

I also noted that Psalms 1; 19; 119 breathe a passionate devotion to the law—"My eyes shed streams of tears, because people do not keep your law" (Ps. 119:136). But this devotion is coupled with frequent acknowledgments of failure to live up to the law's highest demands: "With my whole heart I seek you; let me not wander from your commandments!" (Ps. 119:10). These prayers for divine aid in keeping the law show that the psalmist has a sense of perspective and humility in the face of his own shortcomings. He should not be accused of pride or self-righteousness.

Although the psalms' understanding of "law" is much broader than the rules laid down in the Pentateuch and comprises all divine revelation, there is no doubt that the sense of "law," "commandments," "rules," or other synonyms for the law is, first, the revelation at Sinai and, second, the Mosaic sermons about the law in Deuteronomy. Psalm 119 is full of Deuteronomic phraseology, for example.[1] It therefore seems appropriate to begin an examination of the Psalter's dependence on the law with a survey of its explicitly ethical teaching before proceeding to review its use of the pentateuchal narratives for ethical instruction.

The Decalogue of the Psalter

At the heart of the Sinai revelation are the Ten Commandments. They are seen in both Exodus and Deuteronomy as uniquely inspired, "written with the finger of God" (Exod. 31:18), and the heart of the covenantal requirements. A comparison of the ethics of the psalms and the Pentateuch can well begin here.

But surprisingly, although the Sinaitic commandments are familiar to the psalmists, the lawgiving at Sinai is rarely mentioned. In the long psalms reciting Israel's history it is usually omitted. The plagues of Egypt are mentioned, as are the exodus, wilderness wanderings, and the conquest of Canaan, but the lawgiving is notable by its absence (Pss. 78; 105; 106; 107; 114). In fact, Sinai is explicitly named only in Psalm 68:8, 17, and Horeb in Psalm 106:19. However, although the lawgiving is not mentioned at the most appropriate place in the historical sequence, it obviously is presupposed. When psalms do depict God's appearance, there are clear echoes of the Sinai experience. In Psalm 18 "the allusions . . . to the Sinai theophany should not be overlooked."[2] Similarly, Psalm 68:2 mentions the smoke and fire

1. See Deuteronomy 6:1–7, which contains many terms key for Psalm 119. Alfons Deissler comments, "Diese und ihnen verwandte Texte des Dtn waren für unsern Verfasser gleichsam seine heimatlich geistige Luft. Er lebte in ihnen, ja sie lebten in ihm." ("These and related texts of Deuteronomy were for our author as it were his native spiritual air. He lived in them, indeed they lived in him.") (*Psalm 119 [118] und seine Theologie: Ein Beitrag zur Erforschung der anthologischen Stilgattung im Alten Testament*, MTS 2, no. 1 [Munich: Karl Zink, 1955], 271).

2. Hans-Joachim Kraus, *Psalms 1–59: A Commentary*, trans. Hilton C. Oswald (Minneapolis: Augsburg, 1988), 260. Cf. A. F. Kirkpatrick, *The Book of Psalms*, CBSC (Cambridge: Cambridge University Press, 1902), 89; W. H. Gispen, *Indirecte gegevens voor het bestaan van den Pentateuch in de Psalmen?* (Zutphen: Drukkerij Nauta, 1928), 58–70; John Goldingay, *Psalms: Psalms 1–41*, BCOTWP (Grand Rapids: Baker Academic, 2006), 260.

that accompanied the lawgiving, and Psalm 97 has a string of terms drawn from Exodus 19–20.[3] These psalms show that the accounts of the lawgiving found in Exodus and Deuteronomy were known to the psalmists, but for them the substance of the law rather than the phenomena that accompanied its revelation was the primary concern.

This is seen in a number of psalms that do not describe the lawgiving itself but focus on Israel's reaction to the law. Psalm 78 is essentially demonstrating how Israel has persistently neglected the law that they had been given and told to teach to their children. Verses 5–8 say,

> He established a testimony in Jacob
> and appointed a law in Israel,
> which he commanded our fathers
> to teach to their children,
> that the next generation might know them,
> the children yet unborn,
> and arise and tell them to their children,
> so that they should set their hope in God
> and not forget the works of God,
> but keep his commandments;
> and that they should not be like their fathers,
> a stubborn and rebellious generation,
> a generation whose heart was not steadfast,
> whose spirit was not faithful to God.

Similarly, though Psalm 105 says nothing about the lawgiving in its historical review, it ends (vv. 44–45),

> And he gave them the lands of the nations,
> and they took possession of the fruit of the peoples' toil,
> that they might keep his statutes
> and observe his laws.
> Praise the Lord!

Key terms from Exodus 19 cluster in Psalm 18:7–15: *qôl* "voice" (v. 13); *bārāq* "lightning" (v. 14); *yhwh yārad* "the Lord came down" (v. 9); *'ēš* "fire" (v. 12); *'ālâ 'āšān* "smoke went up" (v. 8); *'ărāpel* "thick darkness" (v. 9; cf. Exod. 20:21); "mountains trembled" (v. 7).

3. "Clouds," "thick darkness," "fire," "lightnings," "earth trembles" (97:2–4). "Here as elsewhere (18:9, 11, & c.) the Theophany of Sinai supplies the symbolism" (Kirkpatrick, *Book of Psalms*, 580). Cf. Marvin E. Tate, *Psalms 51–100*, WBC 20 (Dallas: Word, 1990), 519.

These reviews of Israel's past are thus designed to produce a sense of gratitude resulting in observance of the law (so Ps. 105) or to highlight Israel's treachery in failing to keep it (Ps. 78). I think that it is reasonable to say that the psalms certainly know the lawgiving at Sinai, even though they do not make much of it. This may be because for the psalms, Zion is the new Sinai, the holy mountain where God reveals himself. Note how Psalm 78 ends (vv. 68–69):

> He chose the tribe of Judah,
> Mount Zion, which he loves.
> He built his sanctuary like the high heavens,
> like the earth, which he has founded for ever.

And Psalm 99 begins (vv. 1–2),

> The Lord reigns; let the peoples tremble!
> He sits enthroned upon the cherubim; let the earth quake!
> The Lord is great in Zion;
> he is exalted over all the peoples.[4]

The much shorter history found in Psalm 81 is rather unusual. It not only quotes the prologue to the Ten Commandments, "I am the Lord your God, who brought you up[5] out of the land of Egypt" (v. 10), but also paraphrases the first two commandments (v. 9):

> There shall be no strange god among you;
> you shall not bow down to a foreign god.

Compare Exodus 20:3–5:

> You shall have no other gods before me.
> You shall not make for yourself a carved image, or any likeness of anything that is in heaven above, or that is in the earth beneath, or that is in the water under the earth.
> You shall not bow down to them or serve them.

4. See also Psalms 46–48.

5. Exodus has "brought out" (*yāṣāʾ* hiphil), whereas Psalm 81 has "brought up" (*ʿālâ* hiphil).

I have not noted any other close quotation of the first commandment. However, in the very act of prayer, one is acknowledging God's power and authority and one's commitment to him. As Donald Evans puts it, "To glorify God is to express a feeling-attitude; it is to rejoice or "glory in" the deeds of the Lord. To glory in something other than God (except as the expression of God's own glory) is idolatry."[6]

But if explicit quotation of the first commandment is rare, the stress on God's uniqueness and his supremacy over other gods is frequent. For example, "There is none like you among the gods, O Lord, nor are there any works like yours" (Ps. 86:8; cf. 86:10; 95:3; 96:4; 97:9).

Other affirmations of the first commandment are the declarations affirming one's complete dependence on the one God, such as Psalm 62:5–6:

> For God alone, O my soul, wait in silence,
> for my hope is from him.
> He only is my rock and my salvation,
> my fortress; I shall not be shaken.

The perversity of doing otherwise is declared by calling the skeptic a fool: "The fool says in his heart, 'There is no God' " (Ps. 14:1).

The second commandment, banning idolatry, is reaffirmed strongly too. Psalm 24:3 asks,

> "Who shall ascend the hill of the Lord?
> And who shall stand in his holy place?"

And verse 4 replies,

> He who has clean hands and a pure heart,
> who does not lift up his soul to what is false
> and does not swear deceitfully.

6. Donald M. Evans, *The Logic of Self-Involvement: A Philosophical Study of Everyday Language with Special Reference to the Christian Use of Language about God as a Creator*, LPT (London: SCM, 1963), 178.

"What is false" (*laššāwʾ*) usually is taken to be a reference to idolatry.[7] One may compare the prayer in Psalm 119:37: "Turn my eyes from looking at worthless things [*šāwʾ*]." However, the phraseology is closer to the third commandment:[8] "You shall not take the name of the LORD your God in vain [*laššāwʾ*], for the LORD will not hold him guiltless who takes his name in vain" (Exod. 20:7).

Certainly there is no mistaking the robust assault on idolatry in Psalm 115:2–8 (cf. Ps. 135:15–18):

> Why should the nations say,
> "Where is their God?"
> Our God is in the heavens;
> he does all that he pleases.
> Their idols are silver and gold,
> the work of human hands.
> They have mouths, but do not speak;
> eyes, but do not see.
> They have ears, but do not hear;
> noses, but do not smell.
> They have hands, but do not feel;
> feet, but do not walk;
> and they do not make a sound in their throat.
> Those who make them become like them;
> so do all who trust in them.

Psalm 31:6 sums up the attitude of the Psalter:

> I hate those who pay regard to worthless idols [*hablê-šāwʾ*],
> but I trust in the LORD.[9]

The third commandment, "You shall not take the name of the LORD your God in vain" (Exod. 20:7), is not directly quoted in the

7. So Kraus, *Psalms 1–59*, 314; Gianfranco Ravasi, *Il libro dei Salmi: Commento e attualizzazione*, Lettura pastorale della Bibbia (Bologna: Edizioni Dehoniane, 1981–85), 1:459; Jean-Luc Vesco, *Le psautier de David traduit et commenté*, 2 vols., LD 210, 211 (Paris: Cerf, 2006), 252.

8. So Klaus Seybold, *Die Psalmen*, HAT 15 (Tübingen: Mohr, 1996), 105; Goldingay, *Psalms 1–41*, 359.

9. See also Psalms 44:20; 81:9; 97:7; 106:36.

psalms, unless Psalm 24:4 is an allusion to it, but the proper use of God's name is frequently celebrated.[10] Psalm 8 is devoted to this topic and is sandwiched between two calls to sing praise to the name of the "Lord Most High" (Pss. 7:17; 9:2). Psalm 8 begins and ends with an act of praising God's name (vv. 1, 9):

> O Lord, our Lord,
> how majestic is your name in all the earth!

Other typical sentiments in the psalms include these:

> Ascribe to the Lord the glory due his name;
> bring an offering, and come into his courts! (Ps. 96:8)

> Let them praise your great and awesome name!
> Holy is he! (Ps. 99:3)

The psalms underline the importance of the proper use of God's name by illustrating how it ought to be used, not by banning its misuse. If God's name were honored in the way the psalms do, there would be no question of taking it in vain.

The only commandment that seems to be completely ignored by the psalms is "Remember the Sabbath day, to keep it holy" (Exod. 20:8). One psalm (Ps. 92) has the heading "A Song for the Sabbath," and Psalm 81:3 urges, "Blow the trumpet at the new moon, at the full moon, on our feast day." But nowhere else is there a mention of the obligation to remember or keep the Sabbath. This is perplexing, especially because Sabbath observance was important in the postexilic period, when the Psalter was edited (cf. Neh. 13:15–22). There is no obvious explanation for the Psalter's silence on this issue. It does not seem likely that the psalmists did not care about it. Could it be presupposed that the worshiper using the psalms is reciting them on the Sabbath? Is it that Sabbath observance was so fundamental that it could be taken for granted? We cannot be sure.

10. Of the 864 uses of "name" (*šēm*) in the Old Testament, 109 of them are in the Psalter (*THAT* 2:937).

We may also note that other festivals are not explicitly mentioned either. For example, the terms "Passover" and "unleavened bread" are not mentioned, though there is plenty about the exodus from Egypt in the Psalter, and at least from New Testament times Psalms 113–118 were recited at the Passover meal. Nor is the Feast of Weeks mentioned by name, though more than one psalm seems quite suitable for such a celebration. Finally, there is no mention of the Day of Atonement or of the Feast of Tabernacles, though the enthronement psalms often are linked to the latter (Pss. 93–99).[11] Even the very general terms *ḥag* ("feast day") and *môʿēd* ("season") are used rarely in the psalms (Pss. 75:2; 81:3; 102:13; 104:19; 118:27). This lack of specificity seems strange, given the great value placed on worship in the temple that is expressed in many psalms (e.g., Pss. 42–43; 84; 100).

"Honor your father and your mother, that your days may be long in the land that the LORD your God is giving you." Exodus 20:12 is another commandment that at first sight seems to be ignored in the psalms. However, the gift of children and the privilege of parenthood are very much celebrated in the Psalter, and there is plenty about the promise of land (e.g., Ps. 105:9–11). Just as the psalms celebrate the name of God rather than condemn its profanation, so too they affirm the family dimension of life.

For instance, God is the archetypal father; this in itself implies that earthly fathers should be honored:

> He shall cry to me, "You are my Father,
> my God, and the Rock of my salvation." (Ps. 89:26)

> As a father shows compassion to his children,
> so the LORD shows compassion to those who fear him.
> (Ps. 103:13)

God's blessing is shown in the gift of children: a big family is to be treasured.

11. Sigmund Mowinckel, *The Psalms in Israel's Worship*, trans. D. R. Ap-Thomas, 2 vols. in 1, BRS (Grand Rapids: Eerdmans, 2004), 1:118–30; cf. Hans-Joachim Kraus, *Psalmen*, 7th ed., 2 vols. in 1, BKAT 15 (Neukirchen-Vluyn: Neukirchener Verlag, 2003), 816; John H. Eaton, *The Psalms: A Historical and Spiritual Commentary with an Introduction and New Translation* (London: T&T Clark, 2003), 331.

> Behold, children are a heritage from the Lord,
> the fruit of the womb a reward.
> Like arrows in the hand of a warrior
> are the children of one's youth.
> Blessed is the man
> who fills his quiver with them!
> He shall not be put to shame
> when he speaks with his enemies in the gate.
> (Ps. 127:3–5)[12]

If the fourth and fifth commandments are relatively underplayed in the Psalter, the prohibition of murder is quite frequently alluded to, even if some remarks do not imply literal killing so much as depriving someone of livelihood. The verbal root used in the Decalogue for "kill, murder" (*rāṣaḥ*) occurs twice in the psalms: "They kill [*hārag*] the widow and the sojourner, and murder [*rāṣaḥ*] the fatherless" (Ps. 94:6), and again in Psalm 62:3.[13] The more general term "kill" (*hārag*) is used in Psalms 10:8; 44:22; 94:6.

Enemies are compared to savage lions or dogs rending their prey (Pss. 7:2; 17:12; 22:13, 16; 35:17), to attacking bulls (Ps. 22:12), and to an ambusher (Ps. 10:8) who watches for the righteous and seeks to put them to death (Ps. 37:32; cf. 54:3; 70:2). The wicked also "kill the widow and the sojourner, and murder the fatherless" (Ps. 94:6). It should be noted that these accusations are mostly embedded in laments, pleas to God to prevent or avenge such crimes.

Adultery is mentioned explicitly only once in the Psalter, in Psalm 50:16–19:

> But to the wicked God says:
> "What right have you to recite my statutes
> or take my covenant on your lips?

12. See also Psalm 128.

13. The Hebrew in Psalm 62:3 is passive (Pual): "all of you will be slain" (cf. KJV). But commentators often suggest emendation. Revocalization produces an active (Piel): "all of you attacking" (Tate, *Psalms 51–100*, 117–18); "murder" (Vesco, *Le psautier de David*, 547); "seek to murder" (Frank-Lothar Hossfeld and Erich Zenger, *Psalms 2: A Commentary on Psalms 51–100*, trans. Linda M. Maloney, ed. Klaus Baltzer, Hermeneia [Minneapolis: Fortress, 2005], 110); cf. ESV: "to batter him." The root *rāṣaḥ* occurs a third time in Psalms, in 42:10 (42:11 MT): "deadly wound" (ESV).

> For you hate discipline,
> and you cast my words behind you.
> If you see a thief, you are pleased with him,
> and you keep company with adulterers.
> You give your mouth free rein for evil,
> and your tongue frames deceit."

The context of the condemnation of adultery; a rejection of God's statutes, covenant, and "words" (the Hebrew term for the Decalogue is the "Ten Words" [Exod. 34:28]); and the string of offenses (theft, adultery, false witness) make it clear that the psalmist is consciously recalling the Ten Commandments here.

Although this is the only explicit reference to adultery in the Psalter, it stands next to Psalm 51, the most moving of all the penitential psalms, which is titled "To the choirmaster. A Psalm of David, when Nathan the prophet went to him, after he had gone in to Bathsheba." The first verse reads,

> Have mercy on me, O God,
> according to your steadfast love;
> according to your abundant mercy
> blot out my transgressions.

Whatever the origin of Psalm 51 and its heading may be, readings that take seriously the canonical sequence of the psalms and their headings cannot fail to observe what a powerful statement this psalm is about the sin of adultery. David's sin is not merely a sin against his neighbor, but against his creator: "Against you, you only, have I sinned and done what is evil in your sight" (v. 4a). According to the law, adulterers deserve to die (Lev. 20:10; Deut. 22:22), and David admits the justice of such a sentence: "So that you may be justified in your words and blameless in your judgment" (v. 4b).

But the psalms are not simply concerned with condemning adultery; as we have already noted, they seek to commend the value of families (e.g., Pss. 127; 128). There is also one psalm (Ps. 45) that usually is classified as a royal wedding psalm because it would have been very suitable for such an occasion. After an introduction (v. 1) "follow five strophes addressed to the king (vv. 2–9), then three to the queen (vv. 10–14), a Tyrian princess. The closing strophe (vv. 16–17) is again dedicated to the king."[14] In its present context in the Psalter the psalm is interpreted messianically. "Perhaps composed originally for a royal wedding, the poem has acquired a messianic sense."[15] But whether understood royally or messianically, "this psalm helps to place the ordinary relations of human life in a truer light as part of the divine order of the world."[16] If Psalm 45 sets out the glorious potential of marriage, Psalm 51 declares the tragedy of its failure.

Theft and coveting are also frequently denounced in the Psalter. We have already noted the string of theft, adultery, and lying in Psalm 50:18. But stealing, especially from the poor, is condemned often elsewhere:

> [The wicked] lurks in ambush like a lion in his thicket;
> he lurks that he may seize the poor;
> he seizes the poor when he draws him into his net. (Ps. 10:9)

> "Because the poor are plundered, because the needy groan,
> I will now arise," says the Lord;
> "I will place him in the safety for which he longs." (Ps. 12:5)[17]

But of all the sins forbidden in the Decalogue, it is the one named in the ninth commandment that receives the fullest treatment: "You shall not bear false witness against your neighbor" (Exod. 20:16). Verse after verse in the Psalter condemns the misuse of the tongue.

> O men, how long shall my honor be turned into shame?
> How long will you love vain words and seek after lies?"
> (Ps. 4:2)

> You destroy those who speak lies;
> the Lord abhors the bloodthirsty and deceitful man. (Ps. 5:6)

14. Seybold, *Psalmen*, 185.
15. Vesco, *Le psautier de David*, 415.
16. Kirkpatrick, *Book of Psalms*, 245.
17. See also Psalms 14:4; 22:18; 35:4, 10; 69:4.

For there is no truth in their mouth;
  their inmost self is destruction;
their throat is an open grave;
  they flatter with their tongue.
Make them bear their guilt, O God;
  let them fall by their own counsels;
because of the abundance of their transgressions cast them out,
  for they have rebelled against you. (Ps. 5:9–10)

His mouth is filled with cursing and deceit and oppression;
  under his tongue are mischief and iniquity. (Ps. 10:7)

Everyone utters lies to his neighbor;
  with flattering lips and a double heart they speak. (Ps. 12:2)

He who walks blamelessly and does what is right
  and speaks truth in his heart;
who does not slander with his tongue
  and does no evil to his neighbor,
  nor takes up a reproach against his friend;
in whose eyes a vile person is despised,
  but who honors those who fear the Lord;
who swears to his own hurt and does not change. (Ps. 15:2–4)

Give me not up to the will of my adversaries;
  for false witnesses have risen against me,
  and they breathe out violence. (Ps. 27:12)

Do not drag me off with the wicked,
  with the workers of evil,
who speak peace with their neighbors
  while evil is in their hearts. (Ps. 28:3)

Keep your tongue from evil
  and your lips from speaking deceit. (Ps. 34:13)

Malicious witnesses rise up;
  they ask me of things that I do not know. (Ps. 35:11)[18]

18. See also Psalms 35:20; 50:19–20; 52:2–5; 55:9–11, 21; 59:12; 64:3–5; 66:13–14; 69:4; 73:8–9; 101:5; 109:2; 120:2–3; 140:3; 144:11.

The abundance of passages on this topic is striking. Why should this topic be so important, whereas the Sabbath is so neglected? In this respect, the Psalter has close parallels with the book of Proverbs, which has much to say about the tongue, its vices and its virtues, and relatively little about worship. For example,

> The tongue of the wise commends knowledge,
> but the mouths of fools pour out folly. (Prov. 15:2).

> "Death and life are in the power of the tongue,
> and those who love it will eat its fruits." (Prov. 18:21)

But whereas Proverbs focuses on the immediate consequences of speech, the psalms tend to relate sins of speech more directly to God. This could be seen as a consequence of their use in prayer. These psalms show how the tongue ought to be used in the praise of God and for the encouragement of one's neighbor. Set against this sacred norm, the misuse of speech to mock God or destroy one's neighbor seems the more heinous. James puts it this way: "With [the tongue] we bless our Lord and Father, and with it we curse people who are made in the likeness of God. From the same mouth come blessing and cursing. My brothers, these things ought not to be so" (James 3:9–10).

Two terms for coveting are used in the Decalogue: *ḥāmad* ("covet") in Exodus 20:17; Deuteronomy 5:21a, and *ʾawâ* ("desire" *hitpael*) in Deuteronomy 5:21b. In Genesis 3:6 both are used negatively. The verbs are rare in the psalms, but the noun "desire" (*taʾăwâ*) is used several times. Whether the desire is good or bad depends on the desirer. The "desires" of the righteous are good and tend to be fulfilled by God (Pss. 10:17; 21:2), whereas "the desire of the wicked will perish" (Ps. 112:10; cf. 10:3; 78:29–30; 106:14). The righteous yearn for God's salvation, while the wicked are self-indulgent, seeking only to satisfy their own appetites.

To sum up: There is plenty of evidence that the psalmists know the Ten Commandments and place them at the heart of their ethical thinking. The demand to worship God alone is fundamental to the psalms, and the manward commandments are also thoroughly endorsed, whether it be respecting parents, marriage, life, or property. But two things stand out when we compare the Decalogue and the Psalter. The first is the psalms' lack of mentioning the Sabbath command or indeed any of the festival obligations, except worship in Jerusalem. The second is the strong emphasis on sins of speech, which the Psalter shares with the book of Proverbs and in the New Testament with the Epistle of James. But the psalms also reflect other ethical principles embodied in pentateuchal law. To some of these we now turn.

Other Laws and the Psalms

Violence

A major concern of the pentateuchal narratives and laws is violence. Cain murders his brother, Abel. Lamech boasts that he will exact seventy-sevenfold vengeance on anyone who attacks him. Violence committed by "all flesh" (i.e., both humans and animals)[19] is twice said to provoke the flood (Gen. 6:11, 13). Within the chosen line, Esau plans to murder Jacob, Joseph's brothers propose to kill him, and Simeon and Levi massacre the Shechemites. Violent crime and its punishment figure prominently in the laws. It is not just murder that is regulated, but other violent disputes as well (e.g., Exod. 21:12–36; Num. 35:9–34; Deut. 19–21). Both laws and narratives demonstrate divine disapproval of violence. God explains to Noah why he sent the flood: "I have determined to make an end of all flesh, for the earth is filled with violence through them. Behold, I will destroy them with the earth" (Gen. 6:13). In his farewell song Jacob damns his sons Simeon and Levi for their actions at Shechem (Gen. 34): "Simeon and Levi are brothers; weapons of violence are their swords. . . . Cursed be their anger, for it is fierce, and their wrath, for it is cruel!" (Gen. 49:5, 7).

The Psalter shares this rejection of violence. The Hebrew term that most closely corresponds to English "violence" is *ḥāmās*. It occurs more often in the Psalter than in any other Old Testament book

19. See Gordon J. Wenham, *Genesis 1–15*, WBC 1 (Waco: Word, 1987), 171.

(fourteen of the sixty total occurrences). The second time that the Psalter mentions violence it declares, "The Lord . . . hates the wicked and the one who loves violence" (Ps. 11:5). The violent are oppressors of the poor and the weak (Ps. 35:11). Violence is the fruit of an attitude of mind: "No, in your hearts you devise wrongs; your hands deal out violence on earth" (Ps. 58:2; cf. 73:6).

This attitude leads to slander (Ps. 140:11) and, worse, "malicious witness" (literally, "witness of violence" [Ps. 35:11]). This phrase is twice used in the Pentateuch of those who conspire to pervert the course of justice by giving false witness in court (Exod. 23:1; Deut. 19:16) against someone who is innocent. In this way violence, under the pretext of justice, will be done to the innocent. Psalm 27:12 puts it vividly: "false witnesses . . . breathe out violence."

An associated problem leading to injustice is bribery. There are many texts in the law condemning the taking of bribes. For example, Deuteronomy 16:19 says, "You shall not pervert justice. You shall not show partiality, and you shall not accept a bribe, for a bribe blinds the eyes of the wise and subverts the cause of the righteous" (cf. Exod. 23:8; Deut. 10:17; 27:25). The point is taken up in Psalm 15: the person "who does not take a bribe against the innocent . . . shall never be moved" (v. 5).

But the Psalter affirms that ultimately the violent will be punished and the righteous vindicated: "His mischief returns upon his own head, and on his own skull his violence descends" (Ps. 7:16). As God rescued his anointed king from the man of violence, the king in turn will deliver the weak and needy from oppression and violence (Pss. 18:48; 72:14; 140:1, 4, 11).

Genesis 4 portrays violence spiraling out of control, beginning in the persons of Cain and Lamech and culminating in the violence of all flesh that triggers the flood (Gen. 6:11, 13). After the flood Noah becomes the new father of the human race, as only he and his family have survived. But although Noah was righteous and blameless in his generation (Gen. 6:9), Genesis 8:21 affirms that "the intention of man's heart is evil from his youth." This "evil heart" prompted God to send the flood initially, according to Genesis 6:5: "The Lord saw that . . . every intention of the thoughts of his heart was only evil continually." So this question is posed: What is to prevent Noah's descendants from behaving like Adam's, wreaking multiple vengeance on their enemies, and the world being engulfed in violence again?

Retribution

The answer is given in Genesis 9:6: "Whoever sheds the blood of man, by man shall his blood be shed, for God made man in his own image." Instead of the sevenfold vengeance exacted by Cain or the seventy-sevenfold vengeance of Lamech (Gen. 4:24), this first casuistically formulated law in Scripture insists on proportionate punishment, life for life, not many lives for one life. This principle of proportionate punishment, known as talion (from Latin *talio*), is expressed in its simplest form three times in the Pentateuch.

"But if there is harm, then you shall pay life for life, eye for eye, tooth for tooth, hand for hand, foot for foot, burn for burn, wound for wound, stripe for stripe" (Exod. 21:23–25; similarly, Lev. 24:17–21; Deut. 19:19–21). This is the so-called *lex talionis*, which, although it has sometimes been decried, actually spells out a principle of universal justice: the punishment should fit the crime. "Contrary to the popular and quite mistaken use of the phrase to mean unlimited vengeance, this was a simple, and almost certainly metaphorical, way of decreeing proportionality in punishment. . . . It was a handy way of saying that the punishment must fit the crime."[20] This principle was enshrined in ancient Near Eastern law long before the Pentateuch was drafted.[21] In most cases the Pentateuch allows for compensation rather than literal talion. Thus, if a slave lost an eye or a tooth, he was given his freedom to compensate for his lost tooth or eye; or if an ox gored a person to death, the owner of the ox could negotiate a ransom with the bereaved family in order to avoid being executed (Exod. 21:26–32). It is thus best to see the talionic formula "eye for eye" as a vivid statement of principle rather than

20. Christopher J. H. Wright, *Old Testament Ethics for the People of God*, rev. ed. (Leicester, UK: Inter-Varsity, 2004), 310. Jonathan Burnside observes, "The *lex talionis* expresses the ideal of poetic justice, namely that the punishment should fit the crime" (*God, Justice, and Society: Aspects of Law and Legality in the Bible* [New York: Oxford University Press, 2011], 275).

21. For example, the Code of Hammurabi (ca. 1750 BC).

as a rule that must be applied literally. "The most obvious principle of justice is that the revenge should in some way be commensurate with the hurt caused. The talionic formula is but one expression of this principle."[22]

It was on the principle of fair retribution that judges were supposed to operate. The fundamental duty of kings is to judge their people justly and deliver the oppressed. In Psalm 72:1–2, 4 we read,

> Give the king your justice, O God,
> and your righteousness to the royal son!
> May he judge your people with righteousness,
> and your poor with justice! . . .
> May he defend the cause of the poor of the people,
> give deliverance to the children of the needy,
> and crush the oppressor!

Whereas modern readers see judging primarily as condemning the guilty, the Old Testament views judging primarily as an act vindicating the weak and exploited. A good judge is viewed as a savior of the innocent.[23] Unfortunately, this did not always happen then, just as it does not always happen today, and therefore the lament psalms are full of appeals to God to act as judge and save the oppressed psalmist. There are also many statements expressing faith that God will impose a fair punishment on those who have afflicted others.

Often the psalms state that what the wicked plan to do to others will be done to them. They will fall into the pit that they have dug for others; they will be caught in their own net, be shot by their own arrow, and so on (Pss. 7:15–16; 9:15; 35:7–8; 64:3–4, 7–8). Psalm 37:14–15 says,

> The wicked draw the sword and bend their bows
> to bring down the poor and needy,
> to slay those whose way is upright;

22. Raymond Westbrook, *Studies in Biblical and Cuneiform Law*, CahRB 26 (Paris: Gabalda, 1988), 46. For fuller discussion, see ibid., 39–88; also Eckart Otto, *Theologische Ethik des Alten Testaments*, TW 3, no. 2 (Stuttgart: Kohlhammer, 1994), 73–81.

23. In the book of Judges, the judges function as such not only by presiding in court but also by saving the nation through defeating their foes.

their sword shall enter their own heart,
and their bows shall be broken.

The principle is stated more generally in Psalm 18:25–26:

With the loyal you show yourself loyal;
with the blameless you show yourself blameless;
with the pure you show yourself pure;
and with the crooked you show yourself perverse. (NRSV)

Sometimes, as in Psalm 28:4 (cf. Pss. 10:2, 14–15; 59:12–13; 109:17–18), the principle is couched not as an assertion of faith but rather as a prayer that God will act in this way:

Give to them according to their work
and according to the evil of their deeds;
give to them according to the work of their hands;
render them their due reward.

The principle is turned into a blessing in Psalm 137:8:

O daughter of Babylon, doomed to be destroyed,
blessed shall he be who repays you
with what you have done to us!

Most often, though, the psalms are less specific. They do not demand or affirm exact retribution; instead, they simply express the conviction that God will reward those who do good and punish those who do not. This idea is set out in the very first psalm, which is programmatic for the whole Psalter: "For the LORD knows the way of the righteous, but the way of the wicked will perish" (Ps. 1:6).

Although God's intervention to punish the wicked is not made explicit here, in many passages it is, as in Psalm 5:4–6:

For you are not a God who delights in wickedness;
evil may not dwell with you.
The boastful shall not stand before your eyes;
you hate all evildoers.
You destroy those who speak lies;
the LORD abhors the bloodthirsty and deceitful man.

It is not just wicked individuals within Israel who are subject to God's judgment; many passages extend it to all nations. For example, Psalm 9:5 asserts, "You have rebuked the nations; you have made the wicked perish; you have blotted out their name forever and ever" (cf. Pss. 9:8, 15–20; 10:16; 33:10; 46:10; 59:8; 66:7; 79:1, 6, 10).

The punishment of the wicked does not serve only to put right the injustice that they have done, for its goal is their reformation. The psalmists may think it unlikely, for more often they speak of the destruction of the wicked than of their repentance. But just as the punishments of the law are both retributive and reformatory,[24] so the same idea is expressed in the psalms. In Psalm 83:16–18, for example, the psalmist prays,

> Fill their faces with shame,
>   that they may seek your name, O Lord.
> Let them be put to shame and dismayed forever;
>   let them perish in disgrace,
> that they may know that you alone,
>   whose name is the Lord,
>   are the Most High over all the earth.

Psalm 96:10 proclaims the universal reign of God as good news for the nations because he is the absolutely righteous judge, who will bring a reign of righteousness and peace: "Say among the nations, 'The Lord reigns! Yes, the world is established; it shall never be moved; he will judge the peoples with equity'" (cf. Pss. 96:11–13; 98:2; 113:4; 117:1).

The Poor and Exploited

The conviction that God will come as judge is, as Erich Zenger points out,[25] the ultimate hope of the weak and oppressed. The righ-

24. See J. L. Saalschütz, *Das Mosaische Recht*, 2nd ed. (Berlin: Carl Heymann, 1853), 441–43; followed by Gordon J. Wenham, *The Book of Leviticus*, NICOT (Grand Rapids: Eerdmans, 1979), 283–84; Cyril S. Rodd, *Glimpses of a Strange Land: Studies in Old Testament Ethics*, OTS (Edinburgh: T&T Clark, 2001), 137; and Wright, *Old Testament Ethics*, 309–10.

25. Erich Zenger, *A God of Vengeance? Understanding the Psalms of Divine Wrath*, trans. Linda M. Maloney (Louisville: Westminster John Knox, 1996), 63–80.

teous judge will rescue them from the hand of the rich and powerful. This central theme of the Psalter has its roots in the pentateuchal law.[26] All sections of the law contain exhortations and rules to help the poor. The Decalogue insists that slaves and sojourners be allowed to rest on the Sabbath (Exod. 20:10; Deut. 5:14). Exodus has laws protecting slaves (21:1–11, 26–27), sojourners, widows, orphans, and the poor (22:21–27; 23:6–9). The same potential victims of injustice are listed in Leviticus 19:9–15, 33–34. Leviticus also insists that at harvest the gleanings should be left for the poor (19:9–10; 23:22). It devotes a whole chapter to the Jubilee Year, which was designed to prevent lifelong debt and consequent slavery or landlessness (Lev. 25). Deuteronomy similarly is punctuated by the call to care for the slave, the sojourner, the Levite, the widow, and the orphan (5:14; 14:29; 16:11, 14; 24:17–21; 26:12–13; 27:19). Israelites are to care for such people because God "executes justice for the fatherless and the widow, and loves the sojourner, giving him food and clothing" (Deut. 10:18).

That God cares for the poor is a core belief of the psalmists as well. He is "Father of the fatherless and protector of widows" (Ps. 68:5). The psalmist declares, "All my bones shall say, 'O Lord, who is like you, delivering the poor from him who is too strong for him, the poor and needy from him who robs him?' " (Ps. 35:10).

Elsewhere God is said to hear the poor, watch over them, help them and raise them up, feed them, and stand beside them (Pss. 10:14, 17; 69:33; 107:41; 109:31; 113:7; 132:15; 146:9). Because the weak and poor are God's special concern, it is particularly heinous to attack and exploit them (Pss. 37:14; 94:6; 109:16). So when the psalmist says, "But I am poor and needy; hasten to me, O God! You are my help and my deliverer; O Lord, do not delay!" (Ps. 70:5; cf. 25:16, 18; 40:17; 86:1; 109:22), this is strong incentive for God to intervene on his behalf. The Lord is known to have a special concern for the poor. To describe oneself as poor and needy[27] is to appeal to God's

26. For a thorough review of the pentateuchal provisions for the poor, see David L. Baker, *Tight Fists or Open Hands? Wealth and Poverty in Old Testament Law* (Grand Rapids: Eerdmans, 2009).

27. The exact sense of the different terms for the poor is not clear, though all of them refer to people who are economically weak, vulnerable, and often exploited. In the Pentateuch the terms *'ebyôn* ("needy") and *'ānî* ("poor") draw attention to the poverty of these people. They need loans, gleanings, and prompt payment of wages (Exod. 22:25; 23:11; Lev.

character as the one who looks after the weak and afflicted. And when God eventually does step in to rescue them, the poor and needy will praise his name (Ps. 74:21; cf. 140:12–13).

Obviously, in praising God's concern for the poor, the psalmist or any later user of the psalms is, in effect, making a commitment to care for them. This is sometimes put more explicitly, as in Psalm 41:1–2:

> Blessed is the one who considers the poor!
> In the day of trouble the Lord delivers him;
> the Lord protects him and keeps him alive;
> he is called blessed in the land;
> you do not give him up to the will of his enemies.

The righteous person lends to the poor without charging them interest (Pss. 15:5; 37:21, 26; 112:5). Indeed, the righteous person gives freely to the poor (Ps. 112:9). This is the opposite of the wicked, who "hotly pursue the poor" (Ps. 10:2), plunder them (Ps. 12:5), and even kill them (Pss. 37:14; 109:16). One of the chief marks of the righteous king is his action on behalf of the poor.

> For he delivers the needy when he calls,
> the poor and him who has no helper.
> He has pity on the weak and the needy,
> and saves the lives of the needy.
> From oppression and violence he redeems their life,
> and precious is their blood in his sight." (Ps. 72:12–14)

19:10; 23:22; Deut. 15:4–11; 24:12–15). In the Psalter *ʾebyôn* retains this primary economic dimension, but *ʿānî* seems to have more the sense of "wretched, afflicted," like the cognate noun *ʿŏnî* ("affliction"). The "poor" are plundered and attacked (Pss. 10:2, 9; 12:5; 25:16; 37:14; 40:17), cry out to God (Pss. 22:24; 34:6), and are saved by him (Pss. 18:27; 22:24; 35:10). The heading of Psalm 102 is "A Prayer of one afflicted [*ʿānî*], when he is faint and pours out his complaint before the Lord." Usually, *ʿānî* is translated "poor" elsewhere in the psalms, but here in Psalm 102 it is not poverty so much as illness that has brought the psalmist close to death, and concern for the nation is the burden of his complaint to God. A third term, *ʿānāw*, variously translated as "afflicted," "meek," or "humble," is often seen as interchangeable with *ʿānî* ("poor"), but whereas *ʿānî* ("poor") and *ʾebyôn* ("needy") refer to someone's external circumstances, *ʿānāw* appears to focus on the person's attitude, so "humble" seems the best rendering. The term is not used in the pentateuchal law, but only in Numbers 12:3 to describe Moses's attitude (see Pss. 22:26; 25:9; 37:11; 69:32; 147:6). For further discussion, see *THAT* 1:23–25; 2:342–50; *TDOT* 1:27–41; 11:230–52.

Jean-Luc Vesco sums up the centrality of the poor in the Psalter this way: "The cry of the poor resounds from one end of the Psalter to the other. The first book paints them as victims of the wicked. The second book ends by affirming their hope in the awaited king who will come to deliver them from the violence to which they are subject (Ps. 72:12–14). And at the end of the third book the Messiah, the son of David, is counted among them (Ps. 89). The fourth book ties the fate of the poor to that of Zion and Israel (Ps. 102:14; 106:42). The fifth book at last affirms their liberation (Ps. 149:4)."[28]

28. Vesco, *Le psautier de David*, 154.

7

Narrative Law in the Psalter

My examination of the terms for law in chapter 5 led to the conclusion that the law that the psalmist was meditating on was wider than the rules and legislation contained in the books of Exodus through Deuteronomy, that the term "law" covered all divine revelation. This wider interest is particularly obvious in the long psalms relating the history of the nation, such as Psalm 78, which retells the national history from the covenant at Sinai to the establishment of the Davidic monarchy, and Psalm 89, which tells of the end of the Davidic dynasty. Psalm 104 focuses on God's acts in creation and providence, while Psalm 105 and Psalm 106 focus on Israel's experiences in Egypt and the wilderness. Many other psalms have briefer reflections on Israel's history, often making allusions to events that we cannot identify. These retellings of the past are not merely historiographic, written to record events; their purpose is to educate the user of the psalms in both theology and ethics. It is the aim of this chapter to examine some of the ways that accounts of Israel's past are used to make ethical points. We will look at what events are recalled explicitly and the lessons that are drawn from them. But a close examination of the psalms reveals many more echoes of the Pentateuch than are apparent on first reading. So before turning to the most obvious connections with the biblical narratives, we will look at the way some psalms almost incidentally allude to these narratives.

The dependence of the psalms on the Pentateuch was thoroughly investigated by W. H. Gispen in 1928.[1] His interest was in establishing whether the current form of the Pentateuch was known by the psalms and the implications that this would have for the age of the Pentateuch. This means that he focused on the most obvious parallels between the two works, but there are plenty of passages that he does not discuss in which a psalm seems to be drawing on earlier narrative tradition.

For example, Psalm 14 (// Ps. 53), with its very gloomy outlook about the pervasiveness of sin,[2] makes us think of the flood story, which says, "And God saw the earth, and behold, it was corrupt, for all flesh had corrupted their way on the earth" (Gen. 6:12). The ideas and terminology of Genesis are echoed in the Psalm 14:2–3:

> The LORD looks down from heaven on the children of man,
> to see if there are any who understand,
> who seek after God.
> They have all turned aside; together they have become corrupt;
> there is none who does good,
> not even one.

Not only is the general theme of Genesis 6–9, universal sinfulness, similar to these psalms but also some of the terminology used is identical. "Corrupt" (*hišḥît*) occurs in Genesis 6:12–13; Psalms 14:1; 53:1. "God sees" in Genesis 6:12; Psalms 14:2; 53:2. "God is with the *generation* of the *righteous*" (Ps. 14:5) echoes the description of Noah as "*righteous* before me in this *generation*" (Gen. 7:1). Within the flood story "his heart" is a key term. "The LORD saw

1. W. H. Gispen, *Indirecte gegevens voor het bestaan van den Pentateuch in de Psalmen?* (Zutphen: Drukkerij Nauta, 1928).

2. The duplication of this psalm may suggest that for the editors of the Psalter its message was particularly important.

that . . . every intention of the thoughts of *his heart* was only evil continually" (Gen. 6:5; cf. 6:6; 8:21). Psalm 14 unpacks this idea in its opening statement: "The fool says in *his heart*, 'There is no God' " (v. 1). With no fear of divine judgment, the wicked suppose that they can literally get away with murder (e.g., Pss. 10:2–13; 12:3–4). Psalm 14 and Psalm 53 put it more generally: "They are corrupt, they do abominable deeds" (14:1; 53:1).

Within Genesis the account of the destruction of Sodom and Gomorrah, towns that completely lacked any righteous inhabitants apart from Lot, resembles the flood story in theme, structure, and terminology.[3] Not only do Psalm 14 and Psalm 53 echo Genesis 6–9 but they also resemble Genesis 18–19. The question of whether there are any "righteous" in Sodom is the central issue in Abraham's intercession for the town in Genesis 18. But there is another parallel: the unusual expression "the LORD looks down" (*hišqîp* [Ps. 14:2 // Ps. 53:2]) echoes Genesis 18:16, where the Lord and the two angels look down on the corrupt town of Sodom. "I will go down to see whether they have done altogether according to the outcry that has come to me" (Gen. 18:21) seems to be taken up in the second part of Psalm 14:2: "The LORD looks down from heaven on the children of man, to see if there are any who understand, who seek after God."

The third story of universal judgment in Genesis is the tower of Babel (Gen. 11:1–9), and this too is echoed in Psalms 14; 53. Genesis 11:5 says, "And *the LORD* came down *to see* the city and the tower, which *the children of man* had built." Psalm 14:2 (// Ps. 53:2) uses three key terms from this verse: "*The LORD* looks down from heaven on *the children of man*, *to see* if there are any who understand."

It is thus apparent that Psalm 14 and Psalm 53 are a theological reflection on the three stories of universal judgment in the book of Genesis: the flood, the tower of Babel, and Sodom and Gomorrah.[4] These Genesis stories could be taken simply as a condemnation of those who lived in olden days (flood, Babel) or foreigners (Sodom), but the thrust of the psalm is to contemporize and universalize the

3. See Gordon J. Wenham, *Genesis 16–50*, WBC 2 (Dallas: Word, 1994), 42–43.

4. This is noted by A. F. Kirkpatrick, *The Book of Psalms*, CBSC (Cambridge: Cambridge University Press, 1902), 65–67; Beat Weber, *Werkbuch Psalmen*, vol. 1 (Stuttgart: Kohlhammer, 2001), 91.

issue: "They have all turned aside; together they have become corrupt; there is none that does good, not even one" (Ps. 14:3 [// Ps. 53:3]).

Yet another allusion to the Pentateuch has been noted by J. Clinton McCann.[5] He suggests that the psalm may also be reflecting on the episode of the golden calf (Exod. 32), when all Israel apostatized and was threatened with annihilation. He points to the use of the verbs *šāḥat* ("become corrupt") in 32:7 and *sûr* ("turn aside") in 32:8 (cf. Deut. 9:12), which reoccur in Psalm 14:1, 3 (// Ps. 53:1, 3), as an indication that the psalmist also has Exodus 32 in mind. This seems likely in view of the close theological parallels between Exodus 32–34 and the flood story,[6] and the importance given to the incident of the golden calf by both Deuteronomy and the Psalter: not only is it fully described in Psalm 106:19–23 but also phrases from Exodus 32–34 and allusions to these chapters occur in many psalms. By alluding to the golden calf, the psalmist shows that universal sinfulness is a problem not only outside Israel, but is one that afflicts Israel itself.

This becomes explicit in Psalm 14:4–6, where it speaks of those "eating up my people." Whether these are the rich oppressors of the poor within Israel or foreign nations is not clear. But past experience of God's judgments in the flood or Sodom or at Sinai makes it certain those who reject God will be in great terror (Pss. 14:5; 53:5). So the psalm concludes with a prayer: "Oh, that salvation for Israel would come out of Zion!" (Ps. 14:7).

Psalm 14 is a good example of a psalm that draws on biblical narrative to make an exceedingly significant evaluation of the human condition, the universal tendency to sin, to live in a way that effectively denies God's existence, so that the truly righteous are the exception rather than the rule. This ties in with what we have seen in some of the laments, notably Psalms 119; 139, where the psalmist, while setting for himself the highest standard of loyalty to the law, nevertheless is acutely aware of his own shortcomings.

The episode of the golden calf (Exod. 32–34; Deut. 9:6–10:11) brings together two major theological themes of the Pentateuch:

5. J. Clinton McCann, "Psalms," in vol. 4 of *New Interpreter's Bible*, ed. Leander E. Keck (Nashville: Abingdon, 1993), 730.

6. See R. W. L. Moberly, *At the Mountain of God: Story and Theology in Exodus 32–34*, JSOTSup 22 (Sheffield: JSOT Press, 1983), 91–92.

the incorrigible sinfulness of Israel and the infinite compassion of God. In Exodus the heinousness of this act of apostasy is underlined by various means. First, it is in flat contradiction to the first two commandments: "You shall have no other gods before me" and "You shall not make for yourself a carved image." Second, the narrative implies that Israel was making the golden calf while God was telling Moses how to make the tabernacle, which was designed to enable him to dwell permanently with Israel. Third, the strength of God's reaction, threatening to annihilate the whole nation and start afresh with the family of Moses, emphasizes the seriousness of the sin. Fourth, the smashing of the tablets inscribed with the commandments signals not only Moses's wrath but also the termination of the covenant. Finally, the long intercessions by Moses indicate the gravity of the situation and God's reluctance to reinstate the covenant.

But eventually, after Moses prays, the Lord does relent. He promises that he will accompany his people into the promised land, and the erection of the tabernacle proceeds. The tabernacle is designed to be the palace of God on earth. It is lavishly decorated, as befits Israel's heavenly king, but is also portable so that he can travel with them through the wilderness to Canaan. In word and symbol God thus declares his compassion toward Israel.

God's character as exhibited in this episode is summed up in Exodus 34:6–7, a passage often quoted or alluded to in the psalms.[7] "The Lord passed before him and proclaimed, 'The Lord, the Lord, a God merciful and gracious, slow to anger, and abounding in steadfast love and faithfulness, keeping steadfast love for thousands, forgiving iniquity and transgression and sin, but who will by no means clear the guilty, visiting the iniquity of the fathers on the children and the children's children, to the third and the fourth generation.'"

Although the creation and worship of the golden calf could be described as the primeval national sin, it is, of course, not the only

7. Note how Moses repeats this description of God's character in interceding for the nation after the spies' debacle (Num. 14:18–19). On other passages in the psalms, see Gordon J. Wenham, "The Golden Calf in the Psalms," in *A God of Faithfulness: Essays in Honour of J. Gordon McConville on His 60th Birthday*, ed. Jamie A. Grant, Alison Lo, and Gordon J. Wenham, LHBOTS 538 (London: T&T Clark, 2011), 169–81.

grave sin of the wilderness wanderings. The spies bring back an unnerving account of Canaan, and in response the people declare that they dare not enter it; this prompts another threat of annihilation, more intercessions by Moses, and a forty-year delay before they enter the land (Num. 13–14; Deut. 1:19–45). Even on the verge of entry there is a mass defection to the Baal of Peor, which is punished by a plague in which twenty-four thousand die (Num. 25).

The journey from Egypt to Canaan is repeatedly interrupted by the people complaining about the lack of food and water, which shows their lack of faith in God and in the leader he has appointed. Newly ordained priests die immediately after their ordination because of their failure to follow instructions exactly (Lev. 10). Even Moses himself forfeits his hope of entering Canaan because he failed to do precisely what God had told him (Num. 20:2–13).[8] The narratives of the Pentateuch thus make a very strong appeal to the reader to obey God's teaching. The laws and directives of Exodus are to be obeyed not only because they are the word of God but also because of the catastrophic effects of ignoring this word. The three reflective sermons by Moses, which constitute the book of Deuteronomy, make the connection between disobedience and curse explicit. In the first he says, "Your eyes have seen what the LORD did at Baal-peor, for the LORD your God destroyed from among you all the men who followed the Baal of Peor" (Deut. 4:3). In the second he says, "Even at Horeb you provoked the LORD to wrath, and the LORD was so angry with you that he was ready to destroy you" (Deut. 9:8). In the third and final sermon he suggests that Israel may still not have learned its lesson: "But to this day the LORD has not given you a heart to understand or eyes to see or ears to hear" (Deut. 29:4).

This last verse "highlights Israel's failure to meet Yahweh's demands. Despite Israel experiencing, seeing and hearing the acts and commands of God, it has failed to apply this properly and to take the extra step of acknowledgement, faith and obedience. . . . Yet,

8. See Johnson Lim Teng Kok, *The Sin of Moses and the Staff of God: A Narrative Approach*, SSN 35 (Assen: Van Gorcum, 1997); Dennis T. Olson, *Numbers*, IBC (Louisville: John Knox Press, 1996), 126–28; cf. Horst Seebass, *Numeri*, BKAT 4 (Neukirchen: Neukirchener Verlag, 2002), 2:281–86.

without denying human responsibility, 29:4 has a glimmer of hope for it attributes to Yahweh the possibility of giving what is lacking."[9]

In retelling the pentateuchal stories, the psalmists make similar points, sometimes implicitly, sometimes explicitly. They recall time and again the nation's propensity to rebel and disobey and the consequences of this behavior, but they also point out the depth of divine forgiveness. Despite Israel's sins the covenant holds, and Israel still may call for and expect to receive God's gracious care. This care is summed up in the term *ḥesed* ("steadfast love").[10] Three long psalms retell the pentateuchal story: Psalm 104 celebrates creation, Psalm 105 the exodus, and Psalm 106 Israel's repeated rebelliousness in the wilderness. In Psalm 106 the recounting of Israel's misdeeds is prefaced by this comment: "Both we and our fathers have sinned; we have committed iniquity; we have done wickedness" (v. 6). Then, after a long recital of their rebellions in the wilderness (vv. 7–33), which continued after their entry into Canaan (vv. 34–43), comes this observation (vv. 43–45):

> Many times he delivered them,
> but they were rebellious in their purposes
> and were brought low through their iniquity.
> Nevertheless, he looked upon their distress,
> when he heard their cry.
> For their sake he remembered his covenant,
> and relented according to the abundance of his
> steadfast love.

This last phrase, "abundance of his steadfast love" (*rōb ḥasdô*), is an allusion to Exodus 34:7 and, within the context of the Psalter, a link to Psalm 103:8, "The Lord is merciful and gracious, slow to anger and abounding in steadfast love," which is a much fuller quotation of Exodus 34:7. Psalm 103 serves as an introduction to the three pentateuchal psalms (Pss. 104–106). By beginning and ending this group of psalms with a quote from Exodus 34, the psalmists show where

9. Paul A. Barker, *The Triumph of Grace in Deuteronomy: Faithless Israel, Faithful Yahweh in Deuteronomy*, PBM (Carlisle: Paternoster, 2004), 129.

10. *TDOT* 5:44–64; *THAT* 1:600–621. See Edgar Kellenberger, *Ḥäsäd wä'ämät als Ausdruck einer Glaubenserfahrung: Gottes Offen-Werden und Bleiben als Voraussetzung des Lebens*, ATANT 69 (Zurich: Theologischer Verlag, 1982).

their hope ultimately rests: the character of God. Thus, Psalm 106 concludes both itself and Book 4 of Psalms with this plea: "Save us, O Lord our God, and gather us from among the nations, that we may give thanks to your holy name and glory in your praise" (v. 47).

Psalm 136 reviews the whole of pentateuchal history from creation to the conquest of Transjordan, the defeat of Sihon and Og (vv. 19–21), and sees each step of the way as another demonstration that God's "steadfast love endures forever."

Book 3 of Psalms (Pss. 72–89) ends in despair that the Lord apparently has reneged on his promise to David: "Lord, where is your steadfast love of old, which by your faithfulness you swore to David?" (Ps. 89:49).

Book 4 of Psalms is an answer to this despair. Its message is twofold. First, the Lord indeed reigns; despite present circumstances, he is still king and will ultimately save his people when he comes as judge (Pss. 93–100). But second, his character is such that despite their sinfulness, his abundant steadfast love will lead him to answer their prayers (Pss. 103–106). This message is reinforced by the first psalm of Book 5, with its refrains "Then they cried to the Lord in their trouble, and he delivered them from their distress" and "Let them thank the Lord for his steadfast love, for his wondrous works to the children of man!" (Ps. 107:6, 8; cf. vv. 13, 15, 19, 21, 28, 31).

Both the prose and poetic accounts of the wilderness wanderings are paradigmatic in that they see Israel's past through the lens of divine provision, Israel's faithless rebellion, and divine forgiveness. The Psalter, like the book of Judges, traces this pattern into the period before the establishment of the monarchy.

Psalm 78:55–59 juxtaposes divine provision and divine anger:

> He drove out nations before them;
> he apportioned them for a possession
> and settled the tribes of Israel in their tents.
> Yet they tested and rebelled against the Most High God
> and did not keep his testimonies,
> but turned away and acted treacherously like their fathers;
> they twisted like a deceitful bow.
> For they provoked him to anger with their high places;
> they moved him to jealousy with their idols.

When God heard, he was full of wrath,
and he utterly rejected Israel.

Psalm 106 portrays Israel's sinfulness even more luridly (vv. 35–38):

They mixed with the nations
and learned to do as they did.
They served their idols,
which became a snare to them.
They sacrificed their sons
and their daughters to the demons;
they poured out innocent blood,
the blood of their sons and daughters,
whom they sacrificed to the idols of Canaan,
and the land was polluted with blood.

But this psalm also notes God's grace when Israel repents (vv. 44–45):

Nevertheless, he looked upon their distress,
when he heard their cry.
For their sake he remembered his covenant,
and relented according to the abundance of his
steadfast love.

God's readiness to forgive them in the past is the basis of the psalmist's prayer that he rescue them from the exile, which the text implies is the consequence of their sin (Ps. 106:47).

But the past is not entirely a record of Israel's disobedience. There are psalms that put a more positive spin on Israel's activity and give other grounds for hope (e.g., Pss. 44:1–3; 78:54–55; 135:12; 136:21–22). The land is God's gift to Israel, and this is often explicitly or implicitly stated. But interestingly, despite the space given to the patriarchal promises in Genesis, they are explicitly recalled only once in the Psalter. Psalm 105 contains many quotations of and allusions to the Pentateuch.[11] Verses 8–11 cite the patriarchal promise in a form that is closest to Genesis 15:7; 17:7–8:

11. See Gispen, *Indirecte gegevens*, 220–55.

> He remembers his covenant forever,
> the word that he commanded, for a thousand generations,
> the covenant that he made with Abraham,
> his sworn promise to Isaac,
> which he confirmed to Jacob as a statute,
> to Israel as an everlasting covenant,
> saying, "To you I will give the land of Canaan
> as your portion for an inheritance."

The psalm then continues to recount God's protection of the patriarchs in their various encounters with kings (vv. 14–15):

> He allowed no one to oppress them;
> he rebuked kings on their account,
> saying, "Touch not my anointed ones,
> do my prophets no harm!"

Here the terminology ("touch," "prophet") shows that the primary reference is to Abraham and Isaac's encounters with Abimelech, king of Gerar, the one occasion when a patriarch is called a "prophet" in Genesis (Gen. 20:6–7; 26:11). Abimelech is described in Genesis as king of the Philistines, and it may be deliberate that Psalm 105 focuses on these episodes within Canaan as instances of God's protection of the patriarchs. These episodes within the land may have seemed more relevant to later Israelites, who lived in the land themselves.

But why did God give the land to Israel and protect their forefathers? Psalm 105 concludes (vv. 44–45):

> And he gave them the lands of the nations,
> and they took possession of the fruit of the peoples' toil,
> that they might keep his statutes
> and observe his laws.
> Praise the LORD!

The goal of history was not the occupation of Canaan, but rather living by the law within that land.

We have noted that the whole pentateuchal story seems to be presupposed by Psalm 136 or the sequence of Psalms 104–106. So we should ask how the teaching about creation contributes to the Psalter's ethics. The longest psalm devoted to the topic is Psalm 104, the first of three psalms reviewing the Pentateuch. These psalms are prefaced and concluded by reference to Exodus 34:6, "The Lord, the Lord, a God merciful and gracious, slow to anger, and abounding in steadfast love and faithfulness," the definition of God's character disclosed to Moses after the sin of the golden calf (Pss. 103:8; 106:45).[12] In fact, Psalm 103 and Psalm 104 seem to go together as a pair: both begin and end with the call "Bless the Lord, O my soul" and they are the only two psalms that have this structure. Whereas Psalm 103 praises God for his steadfast love demonstrated in the forgiveness of sins, Psalm 104 praises him as the creator, who sustains all that he has made. Psalm 103 celebrates God's mercy to Israel, and Psalm 104 celebrates his mercy to all his creatures.[13]

Although the lyrical, exuberant tone of Psalm 104 is rather different from the tidy schema of Genesis 1, the message and vocabulary show the dependence of the psalm on Genesis. The connections with Genesis 1 are most obvious,[14] but there are clear connections with Genesis 2–3 as well.[15] Although the psalmist evidently knows Genesis and clearly affirms God's creative acts, he gives a different slant to it. Whereas Genesis looks at the origins of creation, Psalm 104 describes God's ongoing benevolent sustaining of the world. Like Genesis 1,

12. Kirkpatrick comments that in Psalm 103, "He made known his ways to Moses" in verse 7a "is a reminiscence of Moses' prayer, 'make known to me, I pray, thy ways'" (Exod. 33:13), and verse 8 "is quoted from the revelation of Jehovah's character which was the answer to that prayer" (Exod. 34:6) (*Book of Psalms*, 602).

13. See Jean-Luc Vesco, *Le psautier de David traduit et commenté*, 2 vols., LD 210, 211 (Paris: Cerf, 2006), 954.

14. Note the sequence: "light" (Ps. 104:1–2; Gen. 1:3–5); "firmament" and upper waters (Ps. 104:3–4; Gen. 1:6–8); "earth and waters" (Ps. 104:5–9; Gen. 1:9–10); vegetation for human and beast (Ps. 104:10–18; Gen. 1:11–13); "day and night" (Ps. 104:19–23; Gen. 1:14–19); marine creatures (Ps. 104:25–26; Gen. 1:20–22); the gift of food (Ps. 104:27–28; Gen. 1:25–30). Terms common to Psalm 104 and Genesis 1 include "create" (Ps. 104:30; Gen. 1:1); "seasons" (Ps. 104:19; Gen. 1:14); "beast, living creature" (Ps. 104:11, 20; Gen. 1:20–21, 24); "birds of the heavens" (Ps. 104:12; Gen. 1:26, 28, 30); "plants" (Ps. 104:14; Gen. 1:11–12, 29–30); "place" fixed by God (Ps. 104:8; Gen. 1:9); "deep" (Ps. 104:6; Gen. 1:2); "man" (Ps. 104:23; Gen. 1:26–27); "make, work" (Ps. 104:24–31; Gen. 1:7, 16, 25, 26).

15. "Grow, spring up" (Ps. 104:14; Gen. 2:5, 9); "plant" (Ps. 104:14; Gen. 2:5; 3:18); "bread" (Ps. 104:14–15; Gen. 3:19); "work" (Ps. 104:14, 23; Gen. 2:5, 15; 3:23); "ground" (Ps. 104:30; Gen. 2:5–7, 19; 3:17, 19, 23); "return to dust" (Ps. 104:29; Gen. 3:19). For further discussion, see Gispen, *Indirecte gegevens*, 214–20.

Psalm 104 affirms that "everything that God had made was very good" (Gen. 1:31); this is the focus of the psalm. Some phraseology in the psalm seems to be drawn from Genesis 2–3, but the teaching of these chapters about human sin and its consequences is merely alluded to: "When you hide your face, they are dismayed; when you take away their breath, they die and return to their dust" (Ps. 104:29). Here death is seen as God's sovereign decision, not as punishment of sin. But having deliberately ignored the issue for the rest of the psalm, the psalmist closes with a petition: "Let sinners be consumed from the earth, and let the wicked be no more!" (Ps. 104:35).

This shows that although the psalmist does not want to dwell on the issue of sin, which is central to Genesis 3–11, he is aware of it. As we have already observed, Psalm 103 serves as an introduction to Psalms 104–106. It has a particularly close relationship with Psalm 104, with the same opening and closing exhortation to "my soul" as well as many other links.[16] "Together the pair praise God, the savior who forgives and the creator who provides."[17] Psalm 103 focuses on God's mercy toward the sinful. If it is read as a psalm of David, as the title suggests, it is a powerful confession of God's mercy toward him, showing that it has not changed since the days when Israel made and worshiped the golden calf.[18] Given this emphasis on human sin and divine forgiveness in Psalm 103, it would have been superfluous to reiterate it in Psalm 104's reflections on creation. And this may well be the case with the other ethical concerns that are apparent in Genesis 1–2, such as the Sabbath, marriage, human dominion, which are not highlighted in Psalm 104. These seem to be taken for granted in the psalm.[19]

Instead, the main emphasis of Psalm 104 is God's provision of food and water for all his creatures. According to Genesis 1:29–30, God gave the plants to mankind "and to every beast of the earth and to every bird of the heavens and to everything that creeps on the earth."

16. See Vesco, *Le psautier de David*, 953.

17. Konrad Schaefer, *Psalms*, Berit Olam (Collegeville, MN: Liturgical Press, 2001), 256–57.

18. See the allusions to it in Psalm 103:7–8.

19. Note the reference to "seasons," resting and working in verses 19–23, the teeming seas in verse 25.

According to Genesis 2, God planted an abundantly watered garden full of "every tree that is pleasant to the sight and good for food" (Gen. 2:9). In Psalm 104 water is seen as God's gift:

> You make springs gush forth in the valleys;
> they flow between the hills;
> they give drink to every beast of the field. . . .
> From your lofty abode you water the mountains.
> (vv. 10–11, 13)

The water makes vegetation thrive:

> You cause the grass to grow for the livestock
> and plants for man to cultivate,
> that he may bring forth food from the earth
> and wine to gladden the heart of man,
> oil to make his face shine
> and bread to strengthen man's heart.
> The trees of the Lord are watered abundantly,
> the cedars of Lebanon that he planted. (vv. 14–16)

Even the lions are fed by God:

> The young lions roar for their prey,
> seeking their food from God. (v. 21)

So too are the sea creatures (vv. 25–26). In fact, every creature depends on God for food and life:

> These all look to you,
> to give them their food in due season.
> When you give it to them, they gather it up;
> when you open your hand, they are filled with good things.
> When you hide your face, they are dismayed;
> when you take away their breath, they die
> and return to their dust. (vv. 27–29)

For the psalmist, all creation is a demonstration of God's wisdom, power, and benevolence:

> O Lord, how manifold are your works!
> In wisdom have you made them all;
> the earth is full of your creatures. (v. 24)

His reflections on the world as God made it demonstrate the greatness of his God:

> O Lord my God, you are very great!
> You are clothed with splendor and majesty. (v. 1)

That is why he summons himself at the beginning and the end with the words "Bless the Lord, O my soul!" (Ps. 104:1, 35) and concludes by calling on everyone to "Praise the Lord." This is the first time in the Psalter that "hallelujah" has rung out. "For man, to live is to praise. The glory of God, which will never pass away, is to give life so that YHWH may be praised without ceasing by humans for his providences."[20] Thus, the apparently descriptive language of this psalm involves the worshiper in declaring his commitment and gratitude to his creator. Although the psalm does not repeat the specific ethical teaching of Genesis, its recitation is a declaration of loyalty whereby the singer acknowledges God's goodness and wisdom and, by implication, his intention to love God with all his heart and soul.[21]

Psalm 104 affirms that God's character is evidenced in the natural world. His glory is expressed in the created order. Other psalms make this point even more explicitly. God's voice is to be heard in the thunder (Ps. 29), in earthquake and volcano (Ps. 18:7–8), and in the heavenly bodies:

> The heavens declare the glory of God,
> and the sky above proclaims his handiwork.

20. Vesco, *Le psautier de David*, 969.

21. "In the biblical context, if I say, 'God is my Creator,' I acknowledge my status as God's servant and possession, I acknowledge my role as God's obedient steward and worshipper, I acknowledge God's gift of existence, and I acknowledge God's self-commitment to me" (Donald M. Evans, *The Logic of Self-Involvement: A Philosophical Study of Everyday Language with Special Reference to the Christian Use of Language about God as a Creator*, LPT [London: SCM, 1963], 158). It is this intense commitment that explains the closing prayer, "Let sinners be consumed from the earth, and let the wicked be no more!" (Ps. 104:35), for they refuse to respect God and his authority. Compare the closing petition of the Lord's Prayer: "Deliver us from evil."

Day to day pours out speech,
and night to night reveals knowledge. (Ps. 19:1–2)

The recognition of God's power and wisdom in creation prompts two distinct reactions, awe and confidence:

By the word of the LORD the heavens were made,
and by the breath of his mouth all their host.
He gathers the waters of the sea as a heap;
he puts the deeps in storehouses.
Let all the earth fear the LORD;
let all the inhabitants of the world stand in awe of him!
(Ps. 33:6–8)

You rule the raging of the sea;
when its waves rise, you still them.
You crushed Rahab like a carcass;
you scattered your enemies with your mighty arm.
The heavens are yours; the earth also is yours;
the world and all that is in it, you have founded them.
(Ps. 89:9–11)

This conviction that God rules the mightiest natural forces prompts awe and faith. This is illustrated by Psalm 74, one of the most outspoken communal laments, bewailing the sacking of Jerusalem and the destruction of the temple. Psalm 74 begins,

O God, why do you cast us off forever?
Why does your anger smoke against the sheep of your pasture? . . .
Direct your steps to the perpetual ruins;
the enemy has destroyed everything in the sanctuary!
(vv. 1, 3)

It continues,

How long, O God, is the foe to scoff?
Is the enemy to revile your name forever? (v. 10)

But then the psalmist recalls God's work in creation as proof that he could intervene and change the situation:

> Yet God my King is from of old,
> working salvation in the midst of the earth.
> You divided the sea by your might;
> you broke the heads of the sea monsters on the waters.
> You crushed the heads of Leviathan;
> you gave him as food for the creatures of the wilderness.
> You split open springs and brooks;
> you dried up ever-flowing streams.
> Yours is the day, yours also the night;
> you have established the heavenly lights and the sun.
> You have fixed all the boundaries of the earth;
> you have made summer and winter. (vv. 12–17)

Then the lament resumes and the psalm concludes,

> Arise, O God, defend your cause;
> remember how the foolish scoff at you all the day!
> Do not forget the clamor of your foes,
> the uproar of those who rise against you, which goes up continually! (vv. 22–23)

One might have expected that the psalmist would base his appeal on God's interventions on behalf of Israel or on the promises to the patriarchs, but although the covenant is mentioned (v. 20) nothing is made of it. Is it because the exile has made people wonder whether the covenant is still effective? Or is it because God's power and wisdom are even more obvious in creation than in, say, the exodus, that the psalm recalls this rather than the exodus? One could compare the divine speeches in Job 38–41. The string of rhetorical questions demonstrates the superiority of God's wisdom and power over all human efforts:

> Where were you when I laid the foundation of the earth?
> Tell me, if you have understanding.
> Who determined its measurements—surely you know!
> Or who stretched the line upon it? . . .

Or who shut in the sea with doors
  when it burst out from the womb. (Job 38:4–5, 8)

These questions put Job's in perspective, so that he admits,

I know that you can do all things,
  and that no purpose of yours can be thwarted.
"Who is this that hides counsel without knowledge?"
Therefore I have uttered what I did not understand,
  things too wonderful for me, which I did not know.
  (Job 42:2–3)

For the writer of Job and the psalmists, the belief in God the creator trumps all doubts that may be entertained about his wisdom, power, and benevolence. It is a topic for awe and praise.

For the Lord is a great God,
  and a great King above all gods. . . .
The sea is his, for he made it,
  and his hands formed the dry land.
Oh come, let us worship and bow down;
  let us kneel before the Lord, our Maker! (Ps. 95:3, 5–6)

These declarations in the psalms about God's creative work involve the worshiper in submitting to and praising the creator. The discrepancy between divine and human wisdom, God's power and human power, is so great that Psalm 8 begins,

O Lord, our Lord,
  how majestic is your name in all the earth!
You have set your glory above the heavens. (v. 1)

It continues by making this contrast:

When I look at your heavens, the work of your fingers,
  the moon and the stars, which you have set in place,
what is man that you are mindful of him,
  and the son of man that you care for him? (vv. 3–4)

Yet the psalmist recalls Genesis 1, where man is made in the image of God, to act as God's representative, indeed his vicegerent, on earth.[22] Kings in the ancient Near East were believed to bear the god's image on earth and to rule on the god's behalf. Genesis takes this idea and applies it to every human being:

> So God created man in his own image,
> in the image of God he created him;
> male and female he created them. (Gen. 1:27)

Because mankind bears the image of God, humans are given dominion over the rest of creation: "And God blessed them. And God said to them, 'Be fruitful and multiply and fill the earth and subdue it and have dominion over the fish of the sea and over the birds of the heavens and over every living thing that moves on the earth'" (Gen. 1:28). Psalm 8 puts these ideas into poetry:

> Yet you have made him a little lower than the heavenly beings
> and crowned him with glory and honor.
> You have given him dominion over the works of your hands;
> you have put all things under his feet,
> all sheep and oxen,
> and also the beasts of the field,
> the birds of the heavens, and the fish of the sea,
> whatever passes along the paths of the seas. (vv. 5–8)

The wonder and privilege of the role of mankind in the divine schema prompts the psalmist to exclaim once again, "O LORD, our Lord, how majestic is your name in all the earth!" (v. 9). This exclamation sums up the Psalter's reflection on creation and its implications. "The psalm insists on underlining that it is thanks to God's gift that man has received his privileged position as ruler of the world."[23] Richard Clifford remarks,

> The Bible often focuses on the limits of life and the evil that humans do. Psalm 8 offers a somewhat different perspective: God's beautiful and

22. See Claus Westermann, *Genesis 1–11*, trans. John J. Scullion, CC (Minneapolis: Augsburg, 1984), 147–61; Gordon J. Wenham, *Genesis 1–15*, WBC 1 (Waco: Word, 1987), 27–33.

23. Vesco, *Le psautier de David*, 142.

> coherent world with human beings occupying a noble and important place. The grandeur of the universe enhances rather than diminishes their place and vocation. As servants of the Lord, they rule over land, air, and sea. The psalm invites people to wonder at this work of God.[24]

This overview of the psalms' use of the pentateuchal narratives is revealing. Its poetic reformulation of the Pentateuch's grand narrative surely justifies Martin Luther's observation that the Psalter is a mini-Bible. The psalms, like the historical books, draw out two main lessons: first, the national tendency to sin and the disasters that ensue, and second, the long-suffering mercy of God, whose steadfast love endures forever. The Psalter's realism about human nature could lead to utter despair. However, it is lightened by hope in God, who does not forget his people and whose power to save is proved not only by his past interventions on Israel's behalf but also by his sovereignty in creation and his conquest of the powers of chaos. It is this faith that underlies and integrates all the specific virtues that characterize the way of life of the righteous.

24. Richard J. Clifford, *Psalms 1–72*, AOTC (Nashville: Abingdon, 2002), 70–71.

8

Virtues and Vices in the Psalter

In chapter 4 I noted various devices whereby the reciter of the psalms is made to identify with certain outlooks and to shun others. For instance, the use of the first person, "I," involves the worshiper in making a commitment to the sentiments expressed. Another device is to paint an attractive portrait of the righteous and a negative picture of the wicked. In this chapter I will explore the character of these types more fully, first by clarifying the terminology used about them, and then by noting some of their virtues and vices. In this way I hope to define more closely the ethical ideals of the Psalter.

The Wicked

We begin with the term *rāšāʿ*, usually translated as "wicked" (82×), which is surprisingly more common than its opposite, *ṣaddîq*, "righteous" (52×); this constitutes about a third of the uses of *rāšāʿ* in the Old Testament (264×). The first and last thing that the Psalter wants to say about the *rāšāʿ* is that they are on the road to nowhere, or, more precisely, on the road to Sheol. According to Psalm 1:6, "the way of the wicked will perish," and when they are last mentioned, in Psalm 147:6, it is said that "the Lord . . . casts the wicked to the ground." Here, "ground" (*'ereṣ*) may indicate the underworld,[1] a destination made explicit in Psalm 9:17: "The wicked shall return to Sheol, all the nations that forget God" (cf. Ps. 31:17).

But the destiny of the wicked is apparent only to the eye of faith, for in many cases they seem to flourish. They sprout like grass (Ps. 92:7). They seem to have all they need, and they are full of self-confidence and pride. The psalmist describes the prosperity of the wicked in this way:

> For they have no pangs until death;
> their bodies are fat and sleek.
> They are not in trouble as others are;
> they are not stricken like the rest of mankind. (Ps. 73:4–5)

And it is not simply arrogance that characterizes the wicked; their greed drives them to lying and violence. They achieve their wealth by oppressing the poor:

> The wicked draw the sword and bend their bows
> to bring down the poor and needy,
> to slay those whose way is upright. (Ps. 37:14)

The wicked are like lions, one minute prowling around (Ps. 12:8), the next pouncing on the unwary:

> He lurks in ambush like a lion in his thicket;
> he lurks that he may seize the poor;
> he seizes the poor when he draws him into his net.
> The helpless are crushed, sink down,
> and fall by his might. (Ps. 10:9–10)

> They kill the widow and the sojourner,
> and murder the fatherless. (Ps. 94:6)

1. So Mitchell Dahood, *Psalms III: 101–150: Introduction, Translation, and Notes*, AB 17A (Garden City, NY: Doubleday, 1970), 345. See also *HALOT* 91; *TDOT* 1:399; *THAT* 1:230.

They are like hunters trapping their prey in nets or shooting arrows at them (Pss. 11:2; 140:5). They are mean: they borrow, but do not pay back (Ps. 37:21). The wicked do not simply exploit the poor; they also hate the righteous (Ps. 34:21). They plot against him (Ps. 37:12) and seek to kill him: "The wicked watches for the righteous and seeks to put him to death" (Ps. 37:32).

Yet despite their heartless cruelty, the wicked attend worship and offer sacrifice. They are hypocrites; they recite the law and affirm the covenant, and yet, God says to them,

> If you see a thief, you are pleased with him,
> and you keep company with adulterers.
> You give your mouth free rein for evil,
> and your tongue frames deceit. (Ps. 50:18–19)

According to Psalm 119, the wicked do not care about keeping the law; instead, they forsake it (vv. 53, 155).

In chapter 6 I noted that one of the sins most often condemned in the Psalter is misuse of the tongue, and the wicked are particularly guilty of this. They lie and slander the righteous (Ps. 31:18). In Psalm 109:2–3 the psalmist complains,

> For wicked and deceitful mouths are opened against me,
> speaking against me with lying tongues.
> They encircle me with words of hate,
> and attack me without cause.

The wicked are proud and boastful (Pss. 10:3; 94:3–4). They curse and renounce the Lord (Ps. 10:3). A combination of complacency and skepticism informs their actions. They are complacent and say to themselves, "I shall not be moved; throughout all generations I shall not meet adversity" (Ps. 10:6). The psalms draw attention to a fundamental attitude of the wicked in the oft-repeated phrase "he says in his heart": "He says in his heart, 'God has forgotten, he has hidden his face, he will never see it' " (Ps. 10:11; cf. 10:13). The wicked are seen as deists; that is, they deny the practical intervention of God in the world. To put it another way: they have no fear of God.

> Transgression speaks to the wicked deep in his heart;
> there is no fear of God before his eyes.
> For he flatters himself in his own eyes
> that his iniquity cannot be found out and hated.
> (Ps. 36:1–2)

This denial of God's concern about oppression and his intervention to stop it is, in the psalmists' eyes, a denial of God's existence. And the psalms draw the conclusion that the wicked are covert atheists. They do not publicly proclaim their unbelief, but this is what drives their callous behavior: "In the pride of his face the wicked does not seek him; all his thoughts are, 'There is no God' " (Ps. 10:4; cf. 14:1; 53:1).

The psalms see these attitudes as deep-seated. They come from the heart, the center of the personality. They are long-lasting, even congenital. Their character has been apparent from birth: "The wicked are estranged from the womb; they go astray from birth, speaking lies" (Ps. 58:3; cf. 51:5).

This judgment echoes Genesis 8:21, that "the intention of man's heart is evil from his youth." But later in life the wicked are still deaf to instruction; they are like poisonous snakes, especially the type that cannot be charmed, the "deaf adder":[2]

> They have venom like the venom of a serpent,
> like the deaf adder that stops its ear,
> so that it does not hear the voice of charmers
> or of the cunning enchanter. (Ps. 58:4–5)

So what will happen to the incorrigible? As we saw earlier (see chap. 6 above), the psalms uphold the talionic principle: people should suffer for their offenses in a way that corresponds to the suffering that they have inflicted on others. This principle often is applied to the wicked. They will fall into the pit that they have dug for others; the violence that they inflicted will boomerang on themselves (Ps. 7:15–16). The wicked will be caught in the snares and nets that they have set for others (Pss. 9:15–16; 141:9–10). They will be pierced by

2. Possibly the "horned viper" (*HALOT* 990).

the sword with which they attacked others (Ps. 37:14–15). Those who curse others will themselves be cursed (Ps. 109:17–18).

For the psalms, this retribution is not automatic or autonomous, but it represents the justice of God. God's justice is apparent when the wicked receive their deserts: "The Lord has made himself known; he has executed judgment; the wicked are snared in the work of their own hands" (Ps. 9:16). When the wicked suffer for their misdeeds, "Mankind will say, 'Surely there is a reward for the righteous; surely there is a God who judges on earth'" (Ps. 58:11).

Some of the so-called enthronement psalms, with their refrain "The Lord reigns," end with a call to rejoice "before the Lord, for he comes to judge the earth" (Ps. 98:9; cf. 94:23; 96:13; 97:3; 99:4). For the modern worshiper, the thought of God coming to judge is disturbing. But for the psalmists, it is a cheerful prospect because then righteousness will be rewarded and wickedness punished. Thus, the reign of God is one of the key themes of the Psalter. The Lord is in control. Psalm 2:4–6 mocks the kings of the earth who dare to rebel against his rule:

> He who sits in the heavens laughs;
> the Lord holds them in derision.
> Then he will speak to them in his wrath,
> and terrify them in his fury, saying,
> "As for me, I have set my King
> on Zion, my holy hill."

The Psalter ends with a reaffirmation of God's kingship and a celebration of the defeat of those who rebel against him. It climaxes with a call to all creation, "Praise the Lord" (Pss. 149–150). This conviction that the creator of the world is also its ruler and the redeemer of Israel is, of course, central to the psalms. But equally important is the belief that the Lord is a God of truth and justice, a God who abhors evil and oppression, who hates wickedness and violence. Ignoring this fact is the fundamental mistake of the wicked.

But divine justice does not always seem to operate, and it is the discrepancy between justice and reality that drives the lament psalms. For example, Psalm 10 begins (vv. 1–2),

> Why, O LORD, do you stand afar off?
> Why do you hide yourself in times of trouble?
> In arrogance the wicked hotly pursue the poor;
> let them be caught in the schemes that they have devised.

The laments are prayers that God would intervene, that he would stop standing afar off or hiding himself. And usually they conclude on a hopeful note, based on the assurance that God will save the oppressed, as Psalm 10 does (vv. 12–14):

> Arise, O LORD; O God, lift up your hand;
> forget not the afflicted.
> Why does the wicked renounce God
> and say in his heart, "You will not call to account"?
> But you do see, for you note mischief and vexation,
> that you may take it into your hands;
> to you the helpless commits himself;
> you have been the helper of the fatherless.

Indeed, the psalms assert that eventually the wicked will perish (Pss. 1:6; 37:10, 20; 68:2), they will be totally forgotten (Ps. 9:6), they will return to Sheol (Pss. 9:17; 31:17; 147:6), they will be slain (Ps. 34:21), their weapons and their arms will be broken (Ps. 37:15, 17), their children will be cut off[3] (Ps. 37:28), they will be destroyed in a moment (Pss. 73:19; 145:20), they will drink the cup of God's wrath (Ps. 75:8), their horns[4] will be cut off (Ps. 75:10), and they are doomed to eternal destruction (Pss. 92:7; 101:8). In other words, the reign of wickedness will come to an end. But this will not happen instantly. The righteous must keep praying for it. This is why petitions for an end to the activity of the wicked are nearly as frequent as promises of their destruction. Petitions and promises often are juxtaposed. For example, "Save me, O my God! . . . You break the teeth of the wicked" (Ps. 3:7; cf. 10:12–14; 58:6–11; 71:4–5; 140:7–8).

In many cases it is uncertain whether a verb should be translated as a petition or a prediction, as the Hebrew prefix conjugation (imperfect) sometimes can be rendered as a jussive. For example, the ESV

3. "Cut off" (ESV) refers to a mysterious premature death sent by God.

4. "Horns" (ESV) are a symbol of power.

of Psalm 68:1 reads, "God shall arise, his enemies shall be scattered; and those who hate him shall flee before him!"[5] (cf. NEB), whereas the RSV reads, "Let God arise, let his enemies be scattered; let those who hate him flee before him!"[6] (cf. NIV, NRSV, NLT).

In the language of faith, petition relies on promises to become reality; hence the different renderings in different translations. But whatever the best translation of a particular verse, it is evident that the psalms both pray for the defeat of the wicked and are confident of their eventual destruction. The implications for any user of the psalms are abundantly clear: avoid acting like the wicked and commit yourself to the way of righteousness.

Other Terms for the Wicked

If "wicked" is the most general term for those opposed to God and his ways, there are many other subordinate terms, which focus on different aspects of their behavior and lifestyle. Such persons are described as enemies or foes or adversaries,[7] both of God and the righteous, sometimes in the singular (Pss. 7:5; 74:10) but more often in the plural (Pss. 6:10; 37:20; 56:9; 89:51; 92:9). As enemies of God and of the righteous, they hate God, (Pss. 21:8; 81:15; 83:2; 139:21), his people (Ps. 34:21), and their associated qualities, such as discipline (Ps. 50:17), peace (Ps. 120:6), and Zion (Ps. 129:5). In the communal laments "enemies" describes foreign nations that attack Israel (e.g., Ps. 80:6), whereas in the individual laments "enemies" tend to be

5. So Alexander, Kirkpatrick, Hossfeld and Zenger, Seybold, Eaton, Kidner, Weiser, Kraus. Derek Kidner observes that Psalm 68 "has boldly turned the prayer [i.e., Num. 10:35] into praise, although most translations conceal the fact" (*Psalms 1–72: An Introduction and Commentary on Books I and II of the Psalms*, TOTC 15 [Leicester, UK: Inter-Varsity, 1973], 238). Joseph Alexander says that "the change of the imperative [*qûmâ*] into a future [*yāqûm*]" shows that "this verse has not an optative meaning (*let God arise*) but is declaratory of what certainly will be hereafter" (*The Psalms Translated and Explained* [1873; repr., Grand Rapids: Baker, 1975], 283).

6. So Anderson, Ravasi, Vesco, Weber.

7. In the Old Testament two main Hebrew terms, *ʾōyēb* (74× in Psalms out of 282× in OT) and *ṣar* (26 out of 70 usages), are most commonly translated "enemy" and "foe," respectively, but they are not consistently rendered, and a third English term, "adversary," sometimes is used as an alternative in the traditional translations.

individuals (cf. Job's friends) who oppose the psalmist or shun him because of his suffering (e.g., Ps. 41:5).

There are two other near synonyms of "wicked," *pōʿălê ʾāwen* and *mĕrēʿîm*, usually translated as "evildoers" or "workers of evil." Both terms are used always in the plural. The expression *pōʿălê ʾāwen* occurs sixteen times in the Psalter. These persons are accused of most of the same offenses as the "wicked." They prowl around, plan evil, boast, attack the weak, spread slander, and harass the righteous. Because of their hostility to the righteous, they are also enemies of God. Consequently, the weapons that they employ against others will be turned on them (Pss. 5:5–6; 6:8–10; 28:3–5; 53:4–5; 64:2–8; 141:9–10). The term *mĕrēʿîm* occurs nine times in the Psalter, and several times these persons are mentioned as operating as a group or in a gang (e.g., Pss. 22:16; 26:5), but otherwise there is little to distinguish them from evil workers, *pōʿălê ʾāwen*, with whom they are sometimes paired (Pss. 64:2; 94:16). Like the wicked, they eventually will be cut off (Ps. 37:9).

Other terms for the wicked have a more precise sense. The term *ḥaṭṭāʾîm* ("sinners") occurs six times in the Psalter, always in the plural (Pss. 1:1, 5; 25:8; 26:9; 51:13; 104:35). Paired with "men of blood" (murderers) and transgressors, as well as the wicked, they appear to be worse-than-average wicked. In Psalm 1:1 they come between the wicked and the scoffers, the hardened offender.[8] Outside the Psalter, the people of Sodom (Gen. 13:13), the Korahite rebels (Num. 16:38), and the Amalekites (1 Sam. 15:18) are called "sinners," and all are regarded as deserving death (cf. 1 Kings 1:21).

Another term for the wicked, *pōšĕʿîm*, usually translated "transgressors" (Pss. 37:38; 51:13), is the participle of the verb *pāšaʿ* ("rebel"). From the same root, the noun *pešaʿ* is regularly rendered "transgression," as in Psalm 5:10: "Because of the abundance of their transgressions cast them out, for they have rebelled against you." However, the terms cover a broad range of offenses other than rebellion, from Jacob's alleged treachery against Laban (Gen. 31:36), to breach of trust (Exod. 22:9), to disloyalty toward allies (Amos 1:3, 6, 9, 11). The

8. A *lēṣ* ("scoffer") "is a typical manifestation of what it means to be 'unwise' in one's plans, words, and actions—presumptuous, arrogant, and conceited" (*TDOT* 7:550).

noun might then be translated as "act of treachery, treason," and the verb as "act treacherously." In a religious context, the wicked are those who act treacherously against God and neighbor (Ps. 59:3), not least by being unfaithful to the covenant.

On the other hand, God is the one who forgives treachery (Exod. 34:7). Thus, Psalm 32 begins, "Blessed is the one whose transgression [treachery] is forgiven, whose sin is covered" (v. 1), and continues, "I said, 'I will confess my transgressions to the Lord,' and you forgave the iniquity of my sin" (v. 5).

The Vices of the Wicked

The wicked are characterized by misuse of the tongue. They are liars,[9] boastful (Pss. 5:5; 10:3; 12:3; 52:1; 75:4; 94:4), and two-faced, speaking nicely but thinking quite differently:

> They take pleasure in falsehood [*kāzāb*].
> They bless with their mouths,
> but inwardly they curse (Ps. 62:4).
>
> Everyone utters lies [*šāw'*] to his neighbor;
> with flattering lips and a double heart they speak.
> May the Lord cut off all flattering lips,
> the tongue that makes great boasts. (Ps. 12:2–3)

The hypocrisy of the wicked manifests itself not merely in their saying one thing and thinking another, but specifically in flattery, literally "a lip of smooth things." They say nice things to ingratiate themselves with others (cf. Prov. 5:3). They also boast: "makes great boasts" (Ps. 12:3) is literally "speaks great things." Elsewhere in the psalms "great things" refers to God's saving acts (Pss. 71:19;

9. Several different terms are used in the Psalter for lies and deceit: *šeqer* (22×), *šāw'* (15×), *kāzāb* (6×), *kaḥaš* (1×), *mirmâ* (14×), and *rĕmîyyâ* (6×). The Psalter's sharpest condemnation of liars is in Psalm 52:2–4: "Your tongue plots destruction, like a sharp razor, you worker of deceit [*rĕmîyyâ*]. / You love evil more than good, and lying (*šeqer*) more than speaking what is right. *Selah* / You love all words that devour, O deceitful [*mirmâ*] tongue." For attempts to pin down the precise nuance of these terms, see articles in *TDOT* and *THAT*.

106:21; 136:4), so here the wicked are guilty of praising their own achievements rather than God's. This is apparent in the other term frequently translated as "boast." The root *hll* is most frequently used of the praise of God (e.g., "hallelujah"), but it is used by the wicked to praise themselves (Pss. 52:1; 75:4) or their ill-gotten gains (Ps. 49:6). Their speech is characterized by "arrogance" (*ʿātāq*) (Pss. 31:18; 75:5; 94:4).

This arrogant speech reflects their inner attitude; they often are described as being proud. They imagine that they are self-sufficient, that their own skill or wealth makes reliance on God unnecessary. Whereas the righteous are characterized by a strong sense of dependence on God, the wicked think that they can manage on their own without God. Psalm 73:6–12 says,

> Therefore pride is their necklace;
> violence covers them as a garment.
> Their eyes swell out through fatness;
> their hearts overflow with follies.
> They scoff and speak with malice;
> loftily they threaten oppression.
> They set their mouths against the heavens,
> and their tongue struts through the earth.
> And they say, "How can God know?
> Is there knowledge in the Most High?"
> Behold, these are the wicked;
> always at ease, they increase in riches.

As Psalm 73 and others point out, the proud are deluded. Psalm 49:7–10 says,

> Truly no man can ransom another,
> or give to God the price of his life,
> for the ransom of their life is costly
> and can never suffice,
> that he should live on forever
> and never see the pit.
> For he sees that even the wise die;
> the fool and the stupid alike must perish
> and leave their wealth to others.

In this psalm the wicked are called "fool" (*kĕsîl*) and "stupid" (*baʿar*). These terms point to obtuseness and failure to understand (Pss. 73:22; 92:6–7; 94:8). It is not merely a question of low intelligence that these terms highlight,[10] but the lack of moral and spiritual discernment.[11] However, these fools seem unaware of their blindness. This sets them apart from the other "fool" (*nābāl*), whose behavior is chosen, even though he knows better: "The fool says in his heart, 'There is no God.' They are corrupt, they do abominable deeds, there is none who does good" (Ps. 14:1).

Interestingly, terms for fools are quite rare in the book of Psalms compared with the wisdom books, such as Proverbs, Job, and Ecclesiastes. Similarly, the word for "wise" (*ḥākām*) is very rare in the Psalter compared with the wisdom books. Whereas the latter are concerned to make listeners wise and righteous and help them to avoid folly and wickedness, the psalms are primarily interested in instructing the reciter how to be righteous.[12]

The Righteous

The opposite of the "wicked" person is the "righteous" (*ṣaddîq*) one.[13] In Psalms *ṣaddîq* (50×) is the standard term for the good person, whereas *ṭôb* (59×), usually translated "good," is rarely used in a moral sense. More often *ṭôb* means "fine," "fit for purpose," as in Genesis 1:31. Other terms are *yāšār*, "upright" (25×), and *tāmîm*, "perfect" (12×). Whereas the negative portrayal of the wicked aims to deter

10. For fuller analyses of the nuances of these terms, see *THAT* 1:836–38; 2.26–31; *TDOT* 7:264–69; 9:157–71.

11. For a portrait of the "fool" (*kĕsîl*), see Proverbs 26:1–12.

12. Statistics from *THAT*:

	Psalms	Job	Proverbs	Ecclesiastes
kĕsîl	3	0	49	18
ḥākām	2	8	47	21
ṣaddîq	52	7	66	8
rāšāʿ	82	26	78	7

13. Two poetic synonyms are *pōʿēl ṣedeq* (Ps. 15:2) and *ʿāśâ ṣedeq* (Ps. 119:121), meaning "do righteousness."

the reciter of the psalms from imitating them, the positive portrayal of the righteous encourages imitation.

The fundamental characteristic of the righteous is that they depend on God. "The fear of the LORD is the beginning of wisdom" (Ps. 111:10; cf. 112:1). Three different verbs are used to characterize this stance of dependence: *yārēʾ* ("fear"), *bāṭaḥ* ("trust"), and *ḥāsâ* ("take refuge"). All of these verbs are more frequent in the psalms than elsewhere in the Old Testament, and within the Psalter itself they tend to be found in psalms attributed to David.[14]

The term "take refuge" is first met in Psalm 2:12: "Blessed are all who take refuge in him." Psalm 2, like Psalm 1, is programmatic and sets out fundamental themes of the Psalter. Those who take refuge in God are here contrasted with the nations and their kings, who think they can unseat the divinely anointed king of Zion. "Take refuge" (*ḥāsâ*) might be more exactly translated as "hide oneself in or under," as in the phrase "take refuge under the shadow of your wings" (Ps. 36:7). Psalm 104:18 refers to rocks as a "refuge" for coneys or rock badgers. As a refuge, God is likened to a shield, a fortress, or a stronghold (Ps. 144:2). By taking refuge in God, the righteous can expect to be delivered from their enemies (Pss. 7:1; 17:7), escape shame (Pss. 25:20; 31:1), and enjoy God's abundant provision (Pss. 31:19; 34:8–9).

Another term expressing the psalmist's dependence on God is "trust," whose kinship to "take refuge" is obvious in Psalm 118:8–9.

> It is better to take refuge in the LORD
> than to trust in man.
> It is better to take refuge in the LORD
> than to trust in princes.

Whereas the psalms do not explicitly mention alternatives to taking refuge in God, there are many other things in which people may put their trust. Not only persons and princes but also sword and bow, wealth and riches, extortion and idols (Pss. 31:6; 44:6; 49:6; 52:7; 62:10; 115:8; 146:3). By contrast, the righteous are urged to trust in

14. "Take refuge" appears 25 times in Psalms out of 37 times in the Old Testament; "trust," 45 times out of 116 times; "fearers of God," 27 times out of 45 times.

God's steadfast love, his saving power, and his word (Pss. 13:5; 78:22; 119:42). But above all, the psalms urge the reader to "trust in the LORD." Often this is in the imperative or the first person, "I trust in the LORD," which makes the demand on the reciter of these psalms more explicit. If the psalmist, often identified as David, trusts in the Lord, so should later Israelites.

Obviously, crises are times when trust is needed. As Psalm 56 puts it, "When I am afraid, I put my trust in you," and, "In God I trust; I shall not be afraid. What can man do to me?" (vv. 3, 11). But trust in God should not merely characterize the difficult times; as Psalm 62:8 insists, "Trust in him at all times, O people." It is an ongoing, persistent reliance on God in all circumstances that the Psalter seeks to instill in those who use it.

The third key term that characterizes the lifestyle of the righteous is "fear of God." "Fearers of the LORD" or "those that fear the LORD/him" is a common expression in the Psalter (27×) but comparatively rare elsewhere in the Old Testament (18×). Famous God-fearers are Abraham (Gen. 22:12) and Job (Job 1:1, 8; 2:3). "Those who fear him" are worshipers, who take refuge in God, who have God's eye caring for them, who experience his steadfast love and compassion, who trust in him and love him (Pss. 22:23, 25; 31:19; 33:18; 103:11, 13; 145:19–20). The psalms look for the day when all the ends of the earth will come to fear the Lord (Pss. 67:7; 102:15). Fearing God is not just a question of worshiping him or having an emotional attachment to him, but of trusting him and obeying him, just as Abraham did on Mount Moriah (Gen. 22:1–12). This is seen in Psalm 34:11, where the psalmist offers to teach the fear of the Lord by pointing out what sins to avoid. In Psalm 119:63 fearing God is equated with keeping his precepts.

Indeed, many traits of the wicked find their counterpart in the character of the righteous. Psalm 37 says that "the wicked borrows but does not pay back, but the righteous is generous and gives" (v. 21) despite the fact that the righteous is often poorer than the wicked (v. 16). The wicked are ruthless (Ps. 37:35),[15] whereas the righteous are gracious and merciful (Ps. 112:4).

15. The adjective *ʿārîṣ* ("ruthless") comes from the verb *ʿāraṣ* ("terrify"). The ruthless are those who terrify their enemies.

Whereas the ultimate fate of the wicked is destruction, the righteous can look forward to vindication and honor: "All the horns of the wicked I will cut off, but the horns of the righteous shall be lifted up" (Ps. 75:10).

Anger characterizes the wicked: "The wicked man sees it and is angry; he gnashes his teeth and melts away" (Ps. 112:10); in contrast, the righteous frequently are encouraged to rejoice: "Shout for joy in the LORD, O you righteous! Praise befits the upright" (Ps. 33:1).

The speech of the wicked is characterized by boasting, lying, and broken promises, but the righteous "speaks truth in his heart," "does not slander with his tongue," and "swears to his own hurt and does not change" (Ps. 15:2–4). He rejoices in the Lord and his salvation: "Glad songs of salvation are in the tents of the righteous: 'The right hand of the LORD does valiantly'" (Pss. 118:15; cf. 32:11; 52:6; 58:10; 64:10; 68:3; 97:12; 140:13).

Many of the references to the righteous rejoicing are in the imperative or jussive, perhaps because they need to be encouraged to be joyful, since often they are victimized: "The wicked watches for the righteous and seeks to put him to death" (Ps. 37:32; cf. 31:18; 34:21; 37:12).

Nevertheless, though in the short term the wicked may spread "like a green laurel tree" (Ps. 37:35) and the righteous suffer, in the long term their roles will be reversed. It is the righteous who will flourish like a "palm tree, like a cedar in Lebanon" and thrive "in the courts of our God" (Ps. 92:12–13). It is the righteous who "shall inherit the land and dwell upon it forever" (Ps. 37:29). Their children will not beg for bread (Ps. 37:25), whereas the children of the wicked will "wander about and beg, seeking food far from the ruins they inhabit!" (Ps. 109:10). The righteous will have the last laugh when the wicked have their comeuppance, as Psalm 52:6–7 affirms:

> The righteous shall see and fear,
> and shall laugh at him, saying,
> "See the man who would not make
> God his refuge,
> but trusted in the abundance of his riches
> and sought refuge in his own destruction!"

Another device used in the psalms by which the reciter becomes identified with their outlook is the use of the first person, "I" or "we," "my" or "our." The singular is much more common, which encourages each worshiper to take ownership of the sentiments.[16] In this way an outlook on life, a whole attitude, is inculcated. From this perspective, it is not just ethical principles that are inculcated, though these are not overlooked: Psalm 119 is replete with declarations of the psalmist's desire to keep God's precepts, to meditate on his testimonies, and to be taught his statutes. But the Psalter puts into words a very personal relationship between worshiper and creator as well as instructing the worshiper how to relate to others.

There are different slants on these relationships within different sections of the Psalter. For example, the Davidic collections contain most references to the attacks of enemies (e.g., Pss. 3:1; 5:8; 18:3; 55:3; 69:4; 140:1–5; 143:3), as well as more declarations of innocence (e.g., Pss. 7:3–5; 17:1, 3; 59:3–4; 101:2), whereas confessions of sin are scattered throughout the Psalter (e.g., Pss. 32:5; 38:1–5; 41:4; 65:3; 90:8; 119:67, 176; 139:23–24). But these differences of emphasis hardly impinge on the user of the psalms; rather, the changing moods of the psalmists encourage the worshiper to reflect different aspects of his or her relationship to God. But there will always be the tendency for the worshiper to identify with the "I" of the Psalter.

The life of the righteous is frequently affected by the behavior of the wicked.

The righteous worshiper will at times feel attacked by enemies:

> For strangers have risen against me;
> ruthless men seek my life;
> they do not set God before themselves. (Ps. 54:3)

> O Lord, how many are my foes!
> Many are rising against me;
> many are saying of my soul,
> there is no salvation for him in God. (Ps. 3:1–2)

16. Dorothea Erbele-Küster comments, "Die Geschichte und Erfahrung des Ichs des Psalms verkörpert ein religiöses Ideal, dessen Erfahrungswirklichkeit für die Leser offen ist." ("The history and experience of the 'I' of the Psalms embodies a religious ideal whose reality may be experienced by the reader.") (*Lesen als Akt des Betens: Eine Rezeptionsästhetik der Psalmen*, WMANT 87 [Neukirchen-Vluyn: Neukirchener Verlag, 2001], 112).

As a result, the worshiper may feel deserted, cast down, and reduced to tears (Ps. 6:2–6), perhaps even expecting to die (Ps. 18:4–5). But time and again in the Psalter the psalmist prays to God, taking refuge in him and trusting him: "In you, O LORD, do I take refuge; let me never be put to shame!" (Ps. 71:1). And usually his prayer is answered; he is rescued and knows that God is with him (Ps. 34:4–7).

The psalms abound with thanksgivings and praise for God's grace and deliverance (e.g., Pss. 103–104). Often these prayers and thanksgivings take place in the context of public worship, as is clear from the mention of sacrifice and worship in the temple (e.g., Pss. 5:3; 27:6; 42:4; 54:6; 61:4).

Sometimes it is not apparent that prayer has been heard. Some psalms speak of being forgotten by God and of prayers going unanswered: "How long, O LORD? Will you forget me forever? How long will you hide your face from me?" (Ps. 13:1; cf. 22:1–2). Usually, such laments end on a note of confidence, such as "I will sing to the LORD, because he has dealt bountifully with me" (Ps. 13:6), but several end with no sure resolution.[17] And indeed, Psalm 88 is gloomy all the way through.

Confession of Sin and Protestations of Innocence

God's deafness to some prayers is one prompt to the confession of sin that many psalms include. For example, in Psalm 32:5 the psalmist says, "I acknowledged my sin to you, and I did not cover my iniquity; I said, 'I will confess my transgressions to the LORD,' and you forgave the iniquity of my sin" (cf. Pss. 38:1–5; 39:8–11; 51:1–12; 130:3–4). Sometimes the sin is seen as chronic: the psalmist has sinned from his youth (Ps. 25:7) or even from his conception (Ps. 51:5). God knows even our secret sins: "You have set our iniquities before you, our secret sins in the light of your presence" (Ps. 90:8). Indeed, the problems reach back further into national history: "Both we and our fathers have sinned; we have committed iniquity; we have done wickedness" (Ps. 106:6). And near the end of the Psalter comes one of the most

17. See Federico G. Villanueva, *The "Uncertainty of a Hearing": A Study of the Sudden Change of Mood in the Psalms of Lament*, VTSup 121 (Leiden: Brill, 2008).

sweeping confessions: "Enter not into judgment with your servant, for no one living is righteous before you" (Ps. 143:2).

Such comments, especially one such as "They have all turned aside; together they have become corrupt; there is none who does good, not even one" (Ps. 14:3; cf. 53:3), sit uneasily with the declarations of innocence in the psalms—for example, "Vindicate me, O LORD, for I have walked in my integrity, and I have trusted in the LORD without wavering" (Ps. 26:1; cf. 59:3–4). How should they be reconciled? Certain observations may help.

First, it should be noted that these declarations of innocence are found in those psalms where the psalmist, usually David, is complaining about attacks from enemies (e.g., Pss. 7; 17; 18; 26; 41; 59; 101). He is contrasting his behavior with theirs. They have attacked him without reason; he has done nothing to merit their enmity. The enemies have charged him with particular offenses, which he knows he has not committed. He is affirming his relative innocence compared with their obvious guilt. He is so convinced of his innocence that in Psalm 7:3–5 he invokes a curse on himself if it turns out to be true that he has provoked his enemies.

> O LORD my God, if I have done this,
>   if there is wrong in my hands,
> if I have repaid my friend with evil
>   or plundered my enemy without cause,
> let the enemy pursue my soul and overtake it,
>   and let him trample my life to the ground
>   and lay my glory in the dust.

Second, even the protestations of innocence about particular faults are sometimes accompanied by admissions of sinfulness in other areas. In Psalm 19:12–13 (cf. Ps. 18:23) the psalmist says,

> Who can discern his errors?
>   Declare me innocent from hidden faults.
> Keep back your servant also from presumptuous sins;
>   let them not have dominion over me!
> Then I shall be blameless,
>   and innocent of great transgression.

The same juxtaposition of admission of fault and protestation of innocence is apparent in Psalm 17:3, probably best rendered as "What I planned to do has not passed my mouth."[18] In other words, the sinful thoughts that the psalmist entertained have not been expressed aloud. He has nipped the sin in the bud. Thus, anyone who prays the psalm is making a commitment to do likewise. This use of the first person in worship makes it commissive.

Other Duties of the Righteous

Although some of the psalms are penitential (e.g., Pss. 32; 51; 130) and by implication invite their users to confess their sins, many more are hymns of praise or thanksgiving. They too invite the worshiper to offer praise. Another device whereby the psalms involve those who pray them is use of the imperative. The psalms are punctuated by commands, such as "Praise the LORD," but usually it is not explicit who is meant to heed the command. However, these commands must be addressed to fellow worshipers, and that is why the great majority of these commands are calls to sing, shout for joy, bless, give thanks, magnify, glorify, and praise the Lord. Sometimes the addressees are listed:

> O house of Israel, bless the LORD!
>   O house of Aaron, bless the LORD!
> O house of Levi, bless the LORD!
>   You who fear the LORD, bless the LORD!
>   (Ps. 135:19–20)

18. Compare the Targum: "You have tested me and you have not found corruption. I thought the evil, but it has not passed my mouth" (so Jean-Luc Vesco, *Le psautier de David traduit et commenté*, 2 vols., LD 210, 211 [Paris: Cerf, 2006], 191). Franz Delitzsch translates, "If I think evil, it doth not pass my mouth" (*Biblical Commentary on the Psalms*, trans. Francis Bolton [1871; repr., Grand Rapids: Eerdmans, 1968], 1:231). Delitzsch (pp. 235–36) comments, "The psalmist is able to testify of himself that he so keeps evil thoughts in subjection within him, even when they may arise, that they do not pass beyond his mouth, much less that he should put them into action." Vesco translates, "Ce que j'ai comploté de mal n'a pas passé ma bouche" (*Le psautier de David*, 188). Compare Klaus Seybold's rendering: "Was ich ersonnen haben soll, meinen Mund überschreitet es nicht" (*Die Psalmen*, HAT 15 [Tübingen: Mohr, 1996], 72).

Occasionally, however, these commands are addressed to those outside the circle of worshipers. Kings opposed to the Davidic house are directed,

> Now therefore, O kings, be wise;
> be warned, O rulers of the earth.
> Serve the Lord with fear,
> and rejoice with trembling.[19] (Ps. 2:10–11)

The universal scope of these commands is even clearer when the psalms say, "Oh sing to the Lord a new song; sing to the Lord, all the earth!" (Ps. 96:1) and "Praise the Lord, all nations! Extol him, all peoples!" (Ps. 117:1). The Psalter ends with its climactic call to praise: "Let everything that has breath praise the Lord! Praise the Lord!" (Ps. 150:6). These commands to praise God, though addressed to others, imply that the reciter of the psalm should do the same, as the beginning and conclusion of both Psalm 103 (vv. 1, 22) and Psalm 104 (vv. 1, 35) put it, "Bless the Lord, O my soul."

But scattered throughout the Psalter are commands that apply outside the worship situation as well as within it. "Trust in the Lord" (Pss. 4:5; 37:3; 62:8; 115:9–11). Do not trust in extortion, riches, or princes (Pss. 62:10; 146:3). Do not boast (Ps. 75:4–5) or worship foreign gods (Ps. 81:9). But more positively, they are called to "Love the Lord, all you his saints!" (Ps. 31:23) and to reflect on God's deeds (Ps. 66:5; cf. 46:8).

In the face of provocation they are told to "Be silent" (Pss. 4:4; 37:7) and wait for God to act (Ps. 37:7, 34).

But perhaps the most remarkable use of an imperative is God's call to the divine council[20] in Psalm 82:3–4:

> Give justice to the weak and the fatherless;
> maintain the right of the afflicted and the destitute.

19. This strange comment has provoked a variety of suggested emendations, most frequently "with trembling kiss his feet" (e.g., NRSV). But emendation is not required, as is argued by Craigie, Weber, Vesco, and Goldingay, among modern commentators. Alexander explains, "Exercise those mingled feelings which are suited to your present situation, in full view of God's wrath on one side, and his mercy on the other" (*Psalms*, 18). Compare A. F. Kirkpatrick's comment: "Joyfulness tempered with reverent awe befits those who approach One so gracious, yet so terrible" (*The Book of Psalms*, CBSC [Cambridge: Cambridge University Press, 1902], 11).

20. For another glimpse of this heavenly committee, see Job 1:6; 2:1.

> Rescue the weak and the needy;
> deliver them from the hand of the wicked.

If God commands the heavenly beings to exercise the virtues of justice and care for the needy, how much more should humans, made in his image, do the same.

The Imitation of God

This notion brings us to the idea of the imitation of God as a theme in the ethics of the Psalter. It is an idea found in many parts of the Bible, both Old and New Testaments, and here I cannot explore its ramifications elsewhere.[21] But I will investigate how the psalms view human behavior in the light of the divine. In what ways should humans imitate God, and in what ways should they differ in their response?

I begin with the similarities, which are set out with some clarity in the pair of Psalm 111 and Psalm 112. These psalms often are characterized as twins, so similar are they in structure and content. Both begin with "hallelujah," and both are then followed by eight verses of two lines and then two verses with three lines. Each line begins with a different letter of the alphabet, making two fully acrostic psalms. Psalm 111 closes with "The fear of the LORD is the beginning of wisdom," and Psalm 112 opens with "Blessed is the man who fears the LORD." In fact, Psalm 112 begins, after the "hallelujah," with the same words that begin Psalm 1 and ends with almost the same terms: "The way/desire of the wicked shall perish" (Pss. 1:6; 112:10). This makes this psalm a paradigmatic description of the person who fears the Lord and at the same time underlines the parallels between the character of God and the God-fearing person.

21. Recent discussions include John Barton, "Imitation of God in the Old Testament," in *The God of Israel*, ed. Robert P. Gordon, UCOP 64 (Cambridge: Cambridge University Press, 2007), 35–46; Eryl W. Davies, "Walking in God's Ways: The Concept of *Imitatio Dei* in the Old Testament," in *In Search of True Wisdom: Essays in Old Testament Interpretation in Honour of Ronald E. Clements*, ed. Edward Ball, JSOTSup 300 (Sheffield: Sheffield Academic Press, 1999), 99–115; Walter J. Houston, "The Character of YHWH and the Ethics of the Old Testament: Is *Imitatio Dei* Appropriate?" *JTS* 58 (2007): 1–25.

Psalm 111	Psalm 112
Praise the Lord!	Praise the Lord!
I will give thanks to the Lord with my whole heart,	Blessed is the man who fears the Lord,
in the company of the upright, in the congregation.	who greatly ***delights*** in his commandments!
[2] Great are the works of the Lord,	[2] His offspring will be mighty in the land;
studied by all who ***delight*** in them.	the generation of the upright will be blessed.
[3] Full of splendor and majesty is his work,	[3] Wealth and riches are in his house,
and his righteousness endures forever.	***and his righteousness endures forever.***
[4] He has caused his wondrous works to be ***remembered***;	[4] Light dawns in the darkness for the upright;
the Lord is ***gracious*** and ***merciful***.	he is ***gracious***, ***merciful***, and righteous.
[5] He provides food for those who fear him;	[5] It is well with the man who deals generously and lends;
he ***remembers his covenant forever***.	who conducts his affairs with justice.
[6] He has shown his people the power of his works,	[6] For the righteous will never be moved;
in giving them the inheritance of the nations.	he will be ***remembered forever***.
[7] The works of his hands are faithful and just;	[7] He is not afraid of bad news;
all his precepts are trustworthy;	his heart is firm, trusting in the Lord.
[8] they are ***established forever*** and ***ever***,	[8] His heart is ***steady***; he will not be afraid,
to be performed with faithfulness and uprightness.	until he looks in triumph on his adversaries.
[9] He sent redemption to his people;	[9] He has distributed freely; he has given to the poor;
he has commanded his covenant forever.	***his righteousness endures forever***;
Holy and awesome is his name!	his horn is exalted in honor.
[10] The fear of the Lord is the beginning of wisdom;	[10] The wicked man sees it and is angry;
all those who practice it have a good understanding. His praise ***endures forever***!	he gnashes his teeth and melts away; the desire of the wicked will perish!

The italic type shows the verbal parallels between the psalms. Both the righteousness of God and that of the righteous endure forever (Pss. 111:3; 112:3, 9). Both are gracious and merciful (Pss. 111:4; 112:4). While God remembers his covenant forever and makes his works to be remembered, the righteous will be remembered forever (Pss. 111:4, 5; 112:6). Like God's precepts, the heart of the righteous is established or steady (Pss. 111:8; 112:8). Apart from these close verbal parallels there are other parallel ideas. Whereas God "provides food for those who fear him," the righteous "has distributed freely; he has given to the poor" (Pss. 111:5: 112:9). The Lord has "sent redemption to his people," so that the righteous "looks in triumph on his adversaries" (Pss. 111:9; 112:8). "The trustfulness of the godly man in 112:7, 8 answers to the trustworthiness of Jehovah in 111:7, 8."[22]

"Psalm 112 insists on the fact that what characterizes God must be reflected in the one who fears him. . . . The justice and faithfulness of God are examples to imitate. Mercy, compassion and care for the poor remain the essential values. . . . These common features make the God-fearer a mirror of his God."[23]

Parallels between God's actions and those of the righteous pervade the Psalter. In fact, God is "the righteous" (Pss. 7:9; 116:5; 119:137; 129:4; 145:17), so naturally he blesses the righteous, establishes them, and loves them (Pss. 5:12; 7:9; 146:8). Similarly, God is "upright" (*yāšār*) (Pss. 25:8; 92:15; cf. 19:8; 33:4; 119:137), so his people are frequently described as the "upright in heart" (Pss. 7:10; 11:2; 32:11; 64:10; 94:15; 97:11; 125:4) or simply as the "upright" (Pss. 11:7; 33:1; 49:14; 107:42; 111:1; 112:2, 4; 140:13). The Lord is "holy" (*qādôš*) (Pss. 22:3; 71:22; 78:41; 89:18; 99:3, 5, 9) and a term for his people is "holy ones" or "saints" (Pss. 16:3; 34:9). But the term most used to describe God's character in the psalms is *ḥesed*[24] ("steadfast love" is a common modern

22. Kirkpatrick, *Book of Psalms*, 671.

23. Vesco, *Le psautier de David*, 1072–73.

24. The word *ḥesed* occurs more times in the Psalter than anywhere else in the Old Testament, 129 out of 249 uses. It is one of the key terms to describe God's character, especially in the quotations of Exodus 34:6–7 in Psalms 86:5, 15; 103:4, 8; 145:8. It is God's *ḥesed* that Moses tapped into when he pleaded with God to forgive Israel for making the golden calf, and to which the psalmists repeatedly appeal (e.g., Pss. 6:4; 13:5; 25:7; 31:16; 69:13; 119:159). At one level, it is a disposition or attitude of forgiving benevolence and unprompted kindness; at another level, it is an act embodying this outlook. It is that as-

translation, "mercy" in the KJV, "love" in the NIV). Psalm 136 concludes every verse with "for his steadfast love endures forever." God's people are meant to mirror his love for them in their love for him and for others, so they are called *ḥăsîdîm*,[25] "faithful ones" (Pss. 4:3; 12:1; 16:10; 18:25; 30:4; 31:23; 32:6; 37:28; 50:5; 52:9; 79:2; 85:8; 86:2; 89:19; 97:10; 116:15; 132:9, 16; 145:10; 148:14; 149:1, 5, 9).

Not only are the same adjectives used of God and the godly but also similar attitudes and actions are postulated. God does not delight in wickedness, hates evildoers, and destroys liars (Ps. 5:4–6). On the other hand, he loves righteous deeds, acts in faithfulness and righteousness, and loves justice (Ps. 33:4–5). But he laughs at the wicked (Ps. 37:13) and raises the poor from the dust (Ps. 113:7). The king, addressed as God, "loved righteousness and hated wickedness" (Ps. 45:6–7). The dweller on God's holy hill is one "in whose eyes a vile person is despised" (Ps. 15:4), while the king in Psalm 101:7 promises to root out from his household the deceitful and liars. Like God, the righteous care for the poor (Ps. 37:21), and intervention on behalf of the poor and needy should particularly characterize the rule of kings: "For he delivers the needy when he calls, the poor and him who has no helper" (Ps. 72:12).

These parallels between divine attitudes and human virtues make explicit what is implicit throughout the psalms, at least when they are used in prayer and worship. To describe God's attributes and praise them is to express a positive attitude to them, as Donald Evans has pointed out.[26] Behabitives (i.e., verbs such as "praise" and "thank") declare one's attitude and commitment to a certain pattern of behavior. So in a sense the obligation to imitate God is built into the grammar of prayer and praise.

---

pect of God's character that underlies his willingness to keep covenant with a disobedient people. Although human *ḥesed* wanes, God's *ḥesed* "endures forever" (Pss. 106:1; 136). See further *TDOT* 5:44–64; *THAT* 1:600–621; Edgar Kellenberger, *Ḥäsäd wä'ämät als Ausdruck einer Glaubenserfahrung: Gottes Offen-Werden und Bleiben als Voraussetzung des Lebens*, ATANT 69 (Zurich: Theologischer Verlag, 1982).

25. The ESV offers a variety of translations: "godly," "holy one," "merciful," "saints," "faithful ones." Kellenberger defines *ḥāsîd* as "the pious, who lives out of the Yahweh-given *ḥesed* relationship and therefore does particular acts of *ḥesed* (*Ḥäsäd wä'ämät*, 80). Similarly, Helmer Ringgren speaks of "a person who has or practises *ḥesed*" (*TDOT* 5:76).

26. See Donald M. Evans, *The Logic of Self-Involvement: A Philosophical Study of Everyday Language with Special Reference to the Christian Use of Language about God as a Creator*, LPT (London: SCM, 1963), 127, 174–84. See also chapter 4 above.

However, the psalms show an awareness that there are limits to human emulation of God. The king, because of his sovereign power, can do more than the ordinary layperson, but the psalms draw attention to areas where humans cannot replicate God's work. This is particularly clear when God's work as creator is described (Pss. 104–106), or in the exodus from Egypt (Ps. 114), or in his future role as universal judge (Ps. 96). Such power belongs to God (Ps. 62:11). And whereas God can rescue people from the jaws of death (Ps. 18:4–5, 16–17), the psalmist asks rhetorically, "What man can live and never see death? Who can deliver his soul from the power of Sheol?" (Ps. 89:48). Human weakness, as much as divine power, is fully acknowledged in the Psalter, and this sets limits to the scope for imitating God.

If the imitation of God provides an important motive for behavior, the consequences of certain actions as well as God's expressed will also provide motivation for action. It is often thought that biblical ethics are essentially deontological: an action is taken or avoided because God has commanded it. The Ten Commandments, with their brusque "Thou shalt not" or bald commands such as "Remember the Sabbath day," are the most obvious example of biblical deontology. On the other hand, the book of Proverbs is full of warnings based on the consequences of behavior, such as "A tranquil heart gives life to the flesh, but envy makes the bones rot" (Prov. 14:30).

However, in the Bible the difference between a deontological approach to ethics and a consequentialist one is not cut-and-dried. The lines are often blurred. For example, the Decalogue mentions a reward for honoring parents, "that your days may be long in the land" (Exod. 20:12), and Proverbs contains purely deontological commands, such as "O simple ones, learn prudence; O fools, learn sense" (Prov. 8:5).

Although modern ethicists make a clear distinction between deontology and consequentialism, in the biblical worldview the issue is not so sharply defined, since God is understood to be in control of consequences. The consequences of actions are God's rewards and punishments for behavior that he applauds or condemns. Nevertheless, it may be useful to ask where the psalms lie on the spectrum between deontology and consequentialism: is their ethic closer to the Ten Commandments or to the book of Proverbs?

The answer is that both aspects are discussed in the psalms. In some psalms the consequences of actions are highlighted, while in others the rules are seen as good simply because they are God's. For example, Psalm 19:8–9 states,

> The precepts of the Lord are right,
> rejoicing the heart;
> the commandment of the Lord is pure,
> enlightening the eyes;
> the fear of the Lord is clean,
> enduring forever;
> the rules of the Lord are true,
> and righteous altogether.

In Psalm 119 nearly all the comments on the law are of this ilk—for example, "Your testimonies are wonderful; therefore my soul keeps them" (v. 129) and "Righteous are you, O Lord, and right are your rules" (v. 137).

On the other hand, Psalm 1, often classed with Psalms 19; 119 as a Torah psalm, emphasizes the benefits of observing the law. Psalm 1:3 says of the person who is obedient to the law,

> He is like a tree
> planted by streams of water
> that yields its fruit in its season,
> and its leaf does not wither.
> In all that he does, he prospers.

Psalm 37, by contrast, stresses the consequences of wickedness in many lines:

> For the evildoers shall be cut off. . . .
> . . . the wicked will be no more; (vv. 9–10)

> Their sword shall enter their own heart,
> and their bows shall be broken. (v. 15)

> But the wicked will perish;
> . . . like smoke they vanish away. (v. 20)

However, this is far from pure consequentialism. The destruction of the wicked may at one level appear to be self-inflicted, but the psalmists also regard it as heaven-sent. Sometimes divine punishment is implied, and sometimes it is explicitly said to come from God. Psalm 1:6, "For the Lord knows the way of the righteous, but the way of the wicked will perish," states a general principle reiterated throughout the Psalter. The Lord is linked explicitly to the prosperity of the righteous and implicitly, by analogy, to the fate of the wicked. Psalm 73 is quite clear that the ultimate ruin of the wicked results from God's intervention:

> Truly you set them in slippery places;
> you make them fall to ruin.
> How they are destroyed in a moment,
> swept away utterly by terrors! (vv. 18–19)
>
> You put an end to everyone who is unfaithful to you. (v. 27)

On balance, it seems to me that the Psalter inclines to a deontological approach, in that its fundamental metaphors include those of God as king and judge. In that the Lord is king, his word goes and his rules must be obeyed. In that he is judge, he punishes the wicked and vindicates the innocent. Although reward and punishment may be viewed as consequences of behavior, the psalms see these consequences ultimately as imposed by God, the all-knowing and righteous judge. In Psalm 9 the psalmist declares,

> When my enemies turn back,
> they stumble and perish before your presence.
> For you have maintained my just cause;
> you have sat on the throne, giving righteous judgment.
> You have rebuked the nations; you have made the wicked perish;
> you have blotted out their name forever and ever. (vv. 3–5)
>
> But the Lord sits enthroned forever;
> he has established his throne for justice,
> and he judges the world with righteousness;
> he judges the peoples with uprightness. (vv. 7–8)

This vision of God as the universal judge to whom all nations and individuals are answerable is at once frightening and a source of hope. It is frightening because according to the psalms no one is wholly righteous: "there is none who does good, not even one" (Ps. 14:3). Indeed, it is often very difficult to recognize one's own failings, as when the psalmist asks rhetorically, "Who can discern his [own] errors?" (Ps. 19:12). Only God can declare someone innocent of hidden faults (cf. Ps. 139:23–24).

But at the same time, the coming reign of the just judge is the hope of all who have been unfairly treated, persecuted, and otherwise subjected to oppression. Oppressors may crush God's people, kill the widow and the sojourner, murder the fatherless, and imagine that God does not see (Ps. 94:5–7), but Psalm 94:23 affirms, "He will bring back on them their iniquity and wipe them out for their wickedness; the LORD our God will wipe them out." This is the hope that inspires the psalms to rejoice repeatedly at God's coming as judge (e.g., Pss. 96:10–13; 99:4; 100:1–3). As Psalm 98:7–9 proclaims,

> Let the sea roar, and all that fills it;
> the world and those who dwell in it!
> Let the rivers clap their hands;
> let the hills sing for joy together
> before the LORD, for he comes
> to judge the earth.
> He will judge the world with righteousness,
> and the peoples with equity.

Conclusion

In pursuit of my investigation of the ethics of the Psalter, this chapter has taken a glimpse at the portraits of the righteous and wicked that it offers. The unpleasant image of the wicked is meant to deter the reciter of the psalms from imitating them, whereas the reverse applies to the descriptions of the righteous, which are intended to encourage righteous behavior. This is underlined by the parallels drawn between God's attitudes and actions and those of the righteous. In a variety of ways, the righteous are expected to imitate God and represent him on earth.

Furthermore, we have seen that the psalms point to the consequences of behavior as well as the character of God himself as motivation for righteous living. Not only does wickedness lead to self-destruction and righteousness lead to contentment and success but also the apparent exceptions to this principle will one day be rectified by God, the all-knowing and completely just judge. The kingship psalms confidently and joyfully affirm God's future intervention as judge and savior. However, in many of the laments there are appeals for God's immediate intervention to rescue the psalmist from his plight. Since these psalms have attracted a disproportionate amount of scholarly attention, I devote the next chapter to them.

9

Appeals for Divine Intervention

In the preceding chapter I investigated the vices of the wicked and the virtues of the righteous as portrayed in the Psalter. Modern readers have little difficulty identifying with the latter. We appreciate virtues such as honesty, reliability, and kindness. We admire truthful speech and detest exploitation of the poor and the exercise of violence. But sometimes the righteous break out into savage prayers against the wicked, which seem to overshadow, if not negate, their other virtues. Their harsh words have provoked even harsher criticism from modern writers. This issue is the focus of the present chapter.

The most common type of psalm is the lament, a prayer that God will rescue the psalmist from some uncomfortable situation, typically illness, injustice, persecution, or physical assault. Usually, laments end with a joyful assurance that God will indeed hear the prayer (e.g., Pss. 6; 7; 13). In many of these laments it is not stated how God will answer the prayer. We are left to use our imagination as to how God will deal with the oppressors who are making life a misery for the psalmist. But sometimes the psalmist becomes much more explicit; he tells God what his oppressors deserve and what he should do to them—for example, "Break the arm of the wicked and evildoer; call his wickedness to account till you find none" (Ps. 10:15) or "Let him rain coals on the wicked; fire and sulfur and a scorching wind shall be the portion of their cup" (Ps. 11:6).

The clear echo of Genesis 19:24 in Psalm 11 shows that verse 6 could be paraphrased "Make them like Sodom and Gomorrah." Such explicitness sticks in the throats of many who pray the psalms and has attracted adverse criticism from more than one older commentator. C. S. Lewis, for example, calls them "terrible" and "contemptible,"[1] A. F. Kirkpatrick, "barbarous and revolting,"[2] and W. O. E. Oesterley, "vindictive" and "a disgrace to human nature."[3] But are these gut reactions to the outspokenness of the psalms fair? What light does reading the Psalter canonically shed on the issue, and do reader-response theory and speech-act theory clarify the ethic of these laments? In an attempt to clarify these issues, I will look at three of the harshest of the so-called imprecatory psalms: Psalms 35; 69; 109.

Psalm 35 is titled "Of David," which invites the canonical reader of the psalms to see in it a reflection of David's experiences; however, unlike some other titles (e.g., Pss. 3; 18; 34), it does not say which events lie behind it. This indefiniteness allows the singer of this psalm to identify with the psalmist in a wide variety of circumstances. However, its ascription to David gives it a normativeness, in that it encourages later singers to regard David's experience and prayer as a pattern for theirs.[4] It is not clear whether David is lamenting his betrayal by Absalom or Sheba or Joab, which the military imagery might suggest, or whether he has fallen ill and his enemies are gloating over his misfortune.

Whatever situation we posit for Psalm 35, the psalmist feels totally betrayed by his closest friends:

> But I, when they were sick—
> I wore sackcloth;
> I afflicted myself with fasting;

1. C. S. Lewis, *Reflections on the Psalms* (London: Collins, 1961), 24.

2. A. F. Kirkpatrick, *The Book of Psalms*, CBSC (Cambridge: Cambridge University Press, 1902), xciii.

3. W. O. E. Oesterley, *The Psalms: Translated with Text-Critical and Exegetical Notes* (London: SPCK, 1962), 458, 548.

4. See Dorothea Erbele-Küster, *Lesen als Akt des Betens: Eine Rezeptionsästhetik der Psalmen,* WMANT 87 (Neukirchen-Vluyn: Neukirchener Verlag, 2001), 66–68.

> I prayed with head bowed on my chest.
> I went about as though I grieved for my friend or my brother;
> as one who laments his mother,
> I bowed down in mourning. (vv. 13–14)

But without any reason, they have hunted him like a wild animal: they have dug a pit for him and tried to snare him in a net (vv. 7–8). They have made false accusations against him: "malicious witnesses" (literally, "witnesses of violence") have risen against him (v. 11; cf. Deut. 19:16). They have repaid him evil for good (v. 12). They rejoice at the calamities that have befallen him. They hate him without cause (vv. 15, 19, 21, 25–26).

All of this stands in sharp contrast to the preceding psalm, with its reassurances that God hears the prayers of the oppressed:

> The eyes of the Lord are toward the righteous
> and his ears toward their cry.
> The face of the Lord is against those who do evil,
> to cut off the memory of them from the earth.
> When the righteous cry for help, the Lord hears
> and delivers them out of all their troubles. (Ps. 34:15–17)

The last line of Psalm 34 is "None of those who take refuge in him will be condemned" (v. 22). Yet the experience of "David" in Psalm 35 seems to contradict his faith-filled praise in Psalm 34. It is the clash between the conviction that God cares for the righteous who trust in him and the predicament of the psalmist in Psalm 35 that makes his plea so poignant. He therefore appeals for God to act as he has done in the past: "Vindicate me, O Lord, my God, according to your righteousness" (Ps. 35:24).[5] He prays that God will act in accordance with his character of righteousness.[6]

5. This plea for vindication usually is supported by a comment on the psalmist's righteousness—for example, "The Lord judges the peoples; judge me, O Lord, according to my righteousness and according to the integrity that is in me" (Ps. 7:8); "Vindicate me, O Lord, for I have walked in my integrity" (Ps. 26:1). But in Psalm 35:24 the plea is that God will vindicate by his own righteousness, which implies an identification of the psalmist's interests with God's. Compare the more general appeals to God's justice in Psalm 10:17–18: "You will incline your ear to do justice to the fatherless and the oppressed, so that man who is of the earth may strike terror no more"; Psalm 82:3: "Give justice to the weak and the fatherless; maintain the right of the afflicted and the destitute."

6. On the term *ṣedeq*, see *THAT* 2:518–23; *TDOT* 12:239–64.

Psalm 34:6 mentions that God listened to the poor man "and saved him out of all his troubles." This is the essence of his prayer in Psalm 35: "All my bones shall say, 'O LORD, who is like you, delivering the poor from him who is too strong for him, the poor and needy from him who robs him?'" (v. 10). It is God's character as savior of the poor that the psalmist appeals to and wants to see vindicated, so that "those who delight in my righteousness [will] shout for joy and be glad and say evermore, 'Great is the LORD, who delights in the welfare of his servant!'" (v. 27).

These urgent appeals, then, are not merely for the vindication of the psalmist, but for the vindication of God's own power and character, so that "mankind will say, 'Surely there is a reward for the righteous; surely there is a God who judges on earth'" (Ps. 58:11).

Second, what the psalmist asks of God is the application of the talionic principle.[7] We bridle at the bluntness of the "eye for an eye" formula, but we applaud the principle of proportionate punishment. Psalm 35:11 alludes to Deuteronomy 19:16–17: "If a malicious witness arises to accuse a person of wrongdoing, then both parties to the dispute shall appear before the LORD, before the priests and the judges who are in office in those days." When the judges establish that the witness is lying, they are to impose on the false witness the penalty that the accused would have faced, had the false testimony been accepted: "Your eye shall not pity. It shall be life for life, eye for eye, tooth for tooth, hand for hand, foot for foot" (Deut. 19:21). This is a perfect example of the punishment fitting the crime. And this is what the psalmist is asking God, the just judge, to do for him. "Let the net that he hid ensnare him" (Ps. 35:8).[8]

False accusation is also the problem in the other two psalms under study here:

> More in number than the hairs of my head
> are those who hate me without cause;

7. For a fuller discussion of talion, see chapter 6 above.

8. David Firth comments, "The prayer is thus an expression of the *lex talionis*," the psalmist asks God to treat his enemies as they have treated him (*Surrendering Retribution in the Psalms: Responses to Violence in Individual Complaints*, PBM [Milton Keynes: Paternoster, 2005], 135).

> mighty are those who would destroy me,
> those who attack me with lies.
> What I did not steal
> must I now restore? (Ps. 69:4)
>
> For wicked and deceitful mouths are opened against me,
> speaking against me with lying tongues.
> They encircle me with words of hate,
> and attack me without cause. (Ps. 109:2–3)

It seems probable that the list of curses in Psalm 109:6–20 reflects the actions, or at least the accusations, of the psalmist's oppressors. In either case, his prayer is that they be punished in the way they have afflicted or intended to afflict him. The psalmist is asking for justice, not revenge. This will demonstrate to others that God hears prayer and intervenes on behalf of the poor and oppressed.

In these psalms there is no suggestion that the psalmist will personally intervene; vindication is left to God. Clearly, the intensity of the psalmist's prayer arises from his past relationships. Because he was so kind to his accusers, he now feels totally betrayed: "They repay me evil for good" (Ps. 35:12); "In return for my love they accuse me, but I give myself to prayer. So they reward me evil for good, and hatred for my love" (Ps. 109:4–5).

This situation seems to be presupposed in Psalm 69 as well (see v. 4). And just as in the case of Psalm 35, an intense lament psalm follows a joyful and positive one. All four psalms (Pss. 34–35; 68–69) are ascribed to David. Psalm 68 celebrates the Lord's triumph over his foes, his protection of the fatherless and widows, which will lead to the nations journeying to Jerusalem to acknowledge his sovereignty. But then in Psalm 69 the Davidic king, who should be sharing in the Lord's triumphs, suddenly appeals for divine aid in a critical situation: "Save me, O God! For the waters have come up to my neck" (v. 1). That is, the waters of chaos are about to overwhelm him, a metaphor that recurs in verses 14–19.[9]

9. See Frank-Lothar Hossfeld and Erich Zenger, *Psalms 2: A Commentary on Psalms 51–100*, trans. Linda M. Maloney, ed. Klaus Baltzer, Hermeneia (Minneapolis: Fortress, 2005), 172.

In other words, he feels close to death, and his enemies say that this is divine punishment for him. Like Job's comforters, they claim that the psalmist's suffering is sent by God, in this case because he is a thief. "What I did not steal must I now restore?" (v. 4). He admits that he may have sinned inadvertently or in ignorance: "O God, you know my folly; the wrongs I have done are not hidden from you" (v. 5). But it is not for this that he is being persecuted, but rather for his enthusiasm for God's cause: "For it is for your sake that I have borne reproach, that dishonor has covered my face. . . . For zeal for your house has consumed me" (vv. 7, 9).[10] So in reality, the mockery that he is suffering is directed at God: "The reproaches of those who reproach you have fallen on me" (v. 9).

Furthermore, he fears that if he succumbs to the pressure, others who have put their trust in God may lose their faith: "Let not those who hope in you be put to shame through me, O LORD God of hosts; let not those who seek you be brought to dishonor through me, O God of Israel" (v. 6). Frank-Lothar Hossfeld and Erich Zenger observe, "His sole concern is the credibility of his God. . . . The truth of *this* God is at stake. If the speaker of the psalm fails as a witness to these traditions about God, the groups who . . . orient themselves to him as their 'model,' and who join him in opposing the . . . 'ridiculing of God' will also be disappointed and shamed."[11] Thus, it is not merely his own discomfort that drives the psalmist's prayer, but the honor of God's name and the perseverance of those who trust in him.

It is, however, his own sufferings that shape his prayer. He says of his persecutors, "They gave me poison for food, and for my thirst they gave me sour wine to drink" (v. 21). So he prays that their dinners will be upset: "Let their own table before them become a snare; and when they are at peace, let it become a trap" (v. 22). His enemies want to destroy him (v. 4), so he prays, "May their camp be a desolation; let no one dwell in their tents" (v. 25). They want to brand him as a thief and therefore as unrighteous (v. 4), so he asks that that be their fate: "Let them be blotted out of the book of the living; let them not be enrolled among the righteous" (v. 28). David Firth remarks, "The prayer, for all its anger,

10. It is not clear what is being referred to by the phrase "zeal for your house," either in the life of David or in the history of the postexilic community.

11. Hossfeld and Zenger, *Psalms* 2, 180.

simply asks that the enemies receive from Yahweh exactly the same as they have inflicted. The prayer is thus an expression of the *lex talionis*, in that Yahweh is asked to place back upon the enemies the experiences that they had themselves generated for the psalmist."[12]

Finally, it should be noted that although the psalmist asks for his persecutors to be treated in the way that they have treated him, there is no suggestion that he himself will take revenge or even dictate a timetable for divine retribution. He leaves the timing to God. But when his prayers are answered, then God's goodness and righteousness will be vindicated, and the humble seekers after God will be glad: "For the Lord hears the needy and does not despise his own people who are prisoners" (v. 33). The psalmist "trusts that in the conflict between the powerful and the weak, the persecutors and the persecuted, the exploiters and the poor, YHWH will in principle take the part of the victims."[13]

The context and message of Psalm 109 are similar to those of Psalm 35 and Psalm 69. Like them, Psalm 109 follows very positive psalms celebrating God's steadfast love toward Israel (Pss. 107:1, 8, 15, 21, 31, 43; 108:4). Like them, it deals with the issue of false accusation by people the psalmist has treated kindly: "They encircle me with words of hate, and attack me without cause. In return for my love they accuse me" (Ps. 109:3–4).

In response, the psalmist gives himself to prayer. His prayer would appear to begin with verse 6 and run through to verse 29, but some commentators hold that verses 6–19 are actually the curses invoked against the psalmist.[14] In favor of this is use of the third person ("he," "him") in verses 6–19, as opposed to the first person ("I," "my," "me") before and after this section. On the other hand, one would not expect him to cite at such length curses directed against him. On this interpretation, the psalmist has been accused of some capital offense, which would lead not only to his own death but also to the destitution

12. Firth, *Surrendering Retribution*, 135.

13. Hossfeld and Zenger, *Psalms* 2, 183.

14. For example, Kraus, Seybold; also Erich Zenger, *A God of Vengeance? Understanding the Psalms of Divine Wrath*, trans. Linda M. Maloney (Louisville: Westminster John Knox, 1996), 59–61; so too the NRSV (note its insertion of "they say" at the beginning of v. 6). Commentators taking the contrary view include Eaton, Kirkpatrick, McCann, Kidner, Schaefer; also Firth, *Surrendering Retribution*, 37.

of his family, a situation illustrated by the story of Naboth. Accused of cursing God and the king, Naboth was stoned to death, and his vineyard was forfeited to the crown (1 Kings 21). Facing such a fate himself, the psalmist prays that what his accusers are planning to do for him will in fact be their fate. J. Clinton McCann remarks,

> The psalmist's request is in accordance with what most persons, then and now, would say is only fair—the punishment should fit the crime. . . . In particular, the enemy deserves no kindness (v. 12, or "steadfast love"), because he showed no kindness (v. 16). The enemy deserves to be impoverished (vv. 8–11), because he mistreated the poor and the needy (v. 16; see Ps. 10:2). The enemy deserves to be cursed, because he cursed others (vv. 17–19, 28–29; see Ps. 62:4). "In short, the enemy deserves to die (v. 8), because he pursued others to their death (vv. 16, 31).[15]

Once again, we should note that there is no suggestion that the psalmist is intent on personally taking revenge. Instead, he is committing that to God (cf. Rom. 12:19) by uttering these prayers. And it is not only the injustice done to him that drives him to prayer but also God's reputation, his "name," for being the God of justice and steadfast love, the God who intervenes on behalf of the poor and oppressed:

> But you, O GOD my Lord,
> deal on my behalf for your name's sake;
> because your steadfast love is good, deliver me!
> For I am poor and needy,
> and my heart is stricken within me. (vv. 21–22)
>
> Help me, O LORD my God!
> Save me according to your steadfast love!
> Let them know that this is your hand;
> you, O LORD, have done it! (vv. 26–27)

And as McCann points out, this does have ethical implications: "The psalmist affirms that God's steadfast love means judgment upon

15. J. Clinton McCann, "Psalms," in vol. 4 of *New Interpreter's Bible*, ed. Leander E. Keck (Nashville: Abingdon, 1993), 1126.

victimizers for the sake of the victims—the poor and the needy. Psalm 109 thus teaches us who God is, what God wills and does, and what God would have us do. To be instructed by Psalm 109 is to take our stand with God, which means we shall stand with the poor and the needy as well."[16] One may add that the very intensity of this psalm challenges its users to a strong commitment to the plight of the oppressed.

Reading Psalm 109 canonically suggests further perspectives. Its heading, "A Psalm of David," suggests that we should hear a royal voice in its words, while its position after Psalm 107, recalling God's steadfast love in delivering Israel when they cried to the Lord in their trouble, and after Psalm 108, praying for victory over Edom, suggests that Psalm 109 should not be read simply as an individual lament, but as a national lament. The king "appeals for the covenanted support of the Lord against adversaries set on war (v. 3) and assailing him with deadly words, the curses used in war and false accusations. His case before the Lord is that this hostility has no just basis: indeed it is unleashed against one who has shown them goodwill."[17] Jean-Luc Vesco observes that Psalm 109 may be read as an extension of the prayer in Psalm 108 for victory over Edom.[18] In this perspective, the imprecations against the psalmist's enemies are comparable to the oracles against the nations in Isaiah 13–23; Jeremiah 46–51.[19] In the context of the postexilic era, the psalm may be read as a prayer for God to rescue the exiles from those who have deprived them of life and homeland.

The most valuable study of these psalms is Erich Zenger's book *A God of Vengeance? Understanding the Psalms of Divine Wrath*. His work reaffirms some of the points made here. First, the psalmists see God's honor and reputation being at risk if the wicked get away with their misdeeds. Second, the psalmists ask only that justice be done. Third, the psalmists' persecutors should suffer in the way they have made others suffer. Fourth, in praying for retribution to fall on their

16. Ibid., 1127–28.

17. John H. Eaton, *The Psalms: A Historical and Spiritual Commentary with an Introduction and New Translation* (London: T&T Clark, 2003), 382.

18. Jean-Luc Vesco, *Le psautier de David traduit et commenté*, 2 vols., LD 210, 211 (Paris: Cerf, 2006), 1046.

19. Ibid., 1051.

enemies, the psalmists are surrendering their case to God instead of plotting to take vengeance on their own.

According to Zenger, these imprecatory psalms epitomize and focus the message of the Psalter, if not the whole Bible. The story is "a dramatic conflict between the righteous and wicked—or in other terms, between the powerless poor and the too-powerful rich—but also between Israel, the people of God, and the idolatrous nations of the earth. That this conflict is ultimately to be decided by the 'God of vengeance' who fights on the side of the righteous/poor/Israel is the *basso ostinato* that (sometimes *piano*, sometimes *fortissimo*) joins together all the individual psalms and psalm songs."[20]

Zenger argues that much criticism of these psalms is essentially Marcionite—that is, the idea that the Old Testament portrays an essentially Jewish God of wrath and judgment, whereas the New Testament reveals the Christian God of love and mercy. Zenger points out that the passion in these psalms is based on a conviction of God's steadfast love (*ḥesed*) for his people: how can God let the righteous suffer this way at the hands of the wicked? Psalm 137's appeal to God to intervene "is rooted . . . in the recollection of the love of YHWH for Zion/Jerusalem/Israel experienced in history."[21] Anticipating the discussion in the next chapter, we note that the idea that God is judge runs through the New Testament, from the parables of Jesus to the book of Revelation. The second coming, when Christ will judge the living and the dead, is the great hope of the early church.

Within the Psalter, Zenger observes, disbelief in divine judgment is one of the marks that distinguish the wicked from the righteous. The wicked ridicule the idea that God will intervene on behalf of the poor and oppressed.[22]

> In the pride of his face the wicked does not seek him;
> all his thoughts are, "There is no God." . . .
> He says in his heart, "God has forgotten,
> he has hidden his face, he will never see it." (Ps. 10:4, 11; cf. 14:1; 73:11)

20. Zenger, *God of Vengeance?* 12.
21. Ibid., 50.
22. Ibid., 66.

On the other hand,

> The righteous will rejoice when he sees the vengeance; . . .
> Mankind will say, "Surely there is a reward for the righteous;
> surely there is a God who judges on earth." (Ps. 58:10–11)

These psalms view attacks on the people of God as attacks on God himself. If the righteous are routed, the wicked will conclude that God does not care, is powerless, or even may not exist. "In this, [these psalms] are a passionate conviction that this situation contradicts what they believe and hope about the reality of God. Thus these psalms are intended to be a challenge, a calling forth of God, to fight against chaos."[23]

Zenger further remarks, "As poetic prayers, the psalms of vengeance are a passionate clinging to God when everything really speaks *against* God. For that reason they can rightly be called *psalms of zeal*, to the extent that in them passion for God is aflame in the midst of the ashes of doubt about God and despair over human beings. These psalms are the expression of a longing that evil, and evil people, may not have the last word in history, for this world and its history belong to God."[24]

From the perspective of speech-act theory, we could describe these psalms as commissive, probably the most intensely commissive in the Psalter, as they identify their speaker so totally with the interests of God. As Zenger says, "They affirm God by surrendering the last word *to God*."[25] Thus, "the psalms of enmity are the most concentrated form of prayer: They reach out to God when everything seems to speak against God. Where *everything* speaks *against* God, those who pray them attribute *everything to* God."[26]

And this commitment has at least three ethical implications for those who pray the psalms. First, by praying them, worshipers express deep sympathy with the feelings of those who suffer. "With their concrete expressions of fear and pain, they bring that pain to the center

23. Ibid., 74.
24. Ibid., 79.
25. Ibid.
26. Ibid., 88.

of ordinary religious and social life. They are the expression of that sensitivity to suffering that is constitutive for biblical piety, and for any way of life that is shaped by the Bible."[27]

Second, by bringing the needs of the poor and oppressed to God in prayer, the worshiper's concern for their plight is enhanced. Prayed by the poor and oppressed, the psalms express faith that God is indeed concerned for their plight. "The appeal and the trust of those praying, in fact, depend essentially on the presupposition that God is *personally* touched by injustice, and is even called into question by it—and that God must bring about justice 'for the sake of God's own name.' "[28]

McCann writes, "In the face of monstrous evil, the worst possible response is to feel *nothing*. What *must* be felt is grief, rage, outrage. In their absence, evil becomes an acceptable commonplace. To forget is to submit to evil, to wither and die; to remember is to resist, be faithful, and live again."[29] "As we pray and reflect upon Psalm 137," McCann adds, "we remember and are retaught the pain of exile, the horror of war, the terror of despair and death, the loneliness of a cross."[30]

Third, these psalms teach their users to reflect on their own complicity in and responsibility for violence and oppression. Psalm 139, after expressing the psalmist's hatred of the wicked, "Oh that you would slay the wicked, O God! O men of blood, depart from me!" (v. 19), ends this way:

> Search me, O God, and know my heart!
> Try me and know my thoughts!
> And see if there be any grievous way in me,
> and lead me in the way everlasting! (vv. 23–24)

Zenger suggests that many who pray the psalms may themselves be guilty of violence and oppression. "Those who pray them are inevitably faced with the question of *their own* complicity in the web of violence."[31]

27. Ibid., 75.

28. Ibid., 71.

29. J. Clinton McCann, *A Theological Introduction to the Book of Psalms* (Nashville: Abingdon, 1993), 119.

30. Ibid., 121.

31. Zenger, *God of Vengeance?* 76.

To sum up: These appeals for divine intervention, often called "imprecatory psalms," are much more than curses parading as prayers. They are undergirded by the conviction that God is both sovereign and just, indeed that he cares about the injustice suffered by the poor and downtrodden. The psalmists cry out that God will treat the wrongdoers as they have treated others. In situations where faith in God's goodness seems to be disproved, the psalmists reassert that faith and place their trust in God to vindicate them rather than take revenge themselves.

Those who pray these psalms today may be taken aback by their directness, but could that reflect our own sheltered existence and the blandness of the piety that we were raised in and have continued in? These psalms shatter our illusions and make us face life in the raw and make us ask if we really believe in a sovereign, loving God. Zenger comments, "Any kind of trust in God or mysticism that is blind to social injustice or does not want to dirty its hands with such things is, in fact, a form of cynicism."[32] The cry of the poor, which resounds from one end of the Psalter to the other,[33] reaches its highest pitch in these psalms and challenges all who take them upon their own lips to identify with them and with their creator.

32. Ibid., 33.

33. See Vesco, *Le psautier de David*, 154.

10

The Ethic of the Psalms and the New Testament

In chapter 2 I looked at the evidence for the use of the psalms in Jewish and Christian worship. I noted various passages in the New Testament that mention the liturgical use of the psalms. In subsequent chapters I argued that memorization of the psalms and their use in worship should have made them very influential. Reciting the psalms in worship committed the worshipers to their values in a very strong sense. We should therefore expect psalmic principles to be detectable in the writings of those who used them in prayer. To test this hypothesis, this chapter looks at the influence of the psalms in some passages of the New Testament dealing with ethical issues.

Psalms and Isaiah are the Old Testament books most quoted in the New Testament.[1] A recent study lists 140 passages in the New Testament that quote or clearly allude to one or more psalms. Or to

1. Among the Dead Sea Scrolls, manuscripts of Psalms are more numerous than those of any other biblical book (Daniel C. Harlow, "The Hebrew Bible in the Dead Sea Scrolls," in *Eerdmans Commentary on the Bible*, ed. James D. G. Dunn and John William Rogerson [Grand Rapids: Eerdmans, 2003], 943).

look from the other direction, 68 out of the 150 psalms are drawn on by the New Testament writers,[2] many of them several times. A recent commentary finds citations of and allusions to 121 psalms in the New Testament.[3] As is characteristic of modern scholarship, more attention has been paid to the impact of the psalms on the theology of the New Testament than to their impact on its ethics. This is regrettable because their ethical influence is profound. Too often, sharp contrasts are drawn between the ethic of the New Testament and that of the Old on the basis of comparing the law of the Old Testament with the ideals of the New. It is forgotten that the case law of the Old Testament ("If a person does A, the penalty is B") indicates the floor of behavior, not the ideal of loving God with all your heart and loving your neighbor as yourself.[4] To love one's neighbor means much more than not murdering him or not stealing from him. The penal case law lays down what should be done in the case of murder or theft, but it is a mistake to suppose that the Old Testament holds that merely to refrain from such acts makes one a paragon of virtue. It is particularly in the psalms and the biblical narratives that we get closest to the Old Testament's ethical ideals, at least if the viewpoint of the (implied) author is sought.[5] For this reason, the ethics of the psalms ought to be of great interest to readers of the New Testament. Not only do we find echoes of their vocabulary throughout the New Testament but also many of the emphases of the psalms are reinforced there. I therefore will only glance in passing at the appeal to the psalms to establish points of theology.

Luke's Gospel is notable for its ethical stance on various topics, including women and the poor. It opens with three songs, the Magnificat, the Benedictus, and the Nunc Dimittis, which are programmatic for his Gospel. "They are the overture which sets out motifs which will recur in

2. Steve Moyise and Maarten J. J. Menken, eds., *The Psalms in the New Testament* (London: T&T Clark, 2004), 247–50.

3. Jean-Luc Vesco, *Le psautier de David traduit et commenté*, 2 vols., LD 210, 211 (Paris: Cerf, 2006), 1379–92.

4. See Gordon J. Wenham, "The Gap between Law and Ethics in the Bible," *JJS* 48 (1997): 17–29.

5. See Gordon J. Wenham, *Story as Torah: Reading Old Testament Narrative Ethically* (Grand Rapids: Baker Academic, 2004).

the body of the composition."[6] The opening blessing of the Benedictus (Luke 1:68–79), "Blessed be the Lord God of Israel," echoes the closing blessing of three books of the Psalter (Pss. 41:13; 72:18; 106:48). Phrase after phrase reminds one of the psalms. "Visited," "redeemed," "horn of salvation," "covenant remembered," "saved from enemies," "holiness," "righteousness," "sit in darkness and in the shadow of death" are some of the terms that Zechariah uses (Luke 1:68–79).

If anything, Mary's vocabulary in the Magnificat (Luke 1:46–55) is even more psalmic. Her hymn of praise finds its closest parallel in Hannah's song in 1 Samuel 2:1–10, but here I will note the parallels with the Psalter. In the Magnificat's opening words, "my soul magnifies the Lord" and "holy is his name" are reminiscent of Psalm 34:1–3, where the psalmist seeks to "magnify the Lord" and "exalt his name." Mary's declaration that "his mercy [*eleos*] is for those who fear him from generation to generation" (Luke 1:50 NRSV) is a close paraphrase of the favorite refrain of the Psalter: "for his steadfast love [*ḥesed*] endures forever." The Greek word *eleos* is the usual LXX translation of Hebrew word *ḥesed*. Mary speaks of the mighty and the proud being brought down and the hungry fed (cf. Pss. 107:9; 146:7). Her mention of the promise to Abraham, "as he spoke to our fathers, to Abraham and his offspring forever" (Luke 1:55), sounds quite like its mention in Psalm 105:8–9.

But it is the general drift of her song that so resembles the psalms. She declares that what the psalmists hoped for,[7] justice for the poor and the humbling of the proud and arrogant, is now being realized:

> He has brought down the mighty from their thrones
> and exalted those of humble estate;
> he has filled the hungry with good things,
> and the rich he has sent empty away. (Luke 1:52–53)

God's concern for the poor is, of course, one of the distinctive themes of Luke's Gospel. Only he records Jesus's first sermon at Nazareth, which includes the lines from Isaiah 61:1:

6. Stephen Farris, *The Hymns of Luke's Infancy Narratives: Their Origin, Meaning and Significance*, JSNTSup 9 (Sheffield: JSOT Press, 1985), 151.

7. See chapters 6, 9, above.

> The Spirit of the Lord is upon me,
> because he has anointed me
> to proclaim good news to the poor.
> He has sent me to proclaim liberty to the captives
> and recovering of sight to the blind,
> to set at liberty those who are oppressed. (Luke 4:18)

In Luke's Gospel the first beatitude is "Blessed are you who are poor, for yours is the kingdom of heaven" (Luke 6:20), and its converse is "Woe to you who are rich, for you have received your consolation" (Luke 6:24; cf. 7:22; 14:12–13, 21). Luke includes a number of parables in which the poor are central or the rich put down, such as the parables of the rich fool (12:13–21), Dives and Lazarus (16:19–31), and the ten minas (19:11–27), as well as the story of Zacchaeus (19:1–10).

This bias toward the poor is not confined to Luke's Gospel, of course; the danger of wealth is often mentioned elsewhere in the New Testament. Perhaps one of the fiercest denunciations is made by James:

> Come now, you rich, weep and howl for the miseries that are coming upon you. Your riches have rotted and your garments are moth-eaten. Your gold and silver have corroded, and their corrosion will be evidence against you and will eat your flesh like fire. You have laid up treasure in the last days. (James 5:1–3)

Like the psalms, the New Testament sees generosity as the antidote to wealth. To encourage the Corinthians to give generously to the poor in Jerusalem (2 Cor. 9:9), Paul quotes Psalm 112:9:

> He has distributed freely; he has given to the poor;
> his righteousness endures forever;
> his horn is exalted in honor.

Mary speaks of the mighty and rich being put down or sent away empty while the hungry are filled (Luke 1:51–53). This allusion to judgment is more explicit in Jesus's parables (e.g., Luke 16:23; 19:27) and in James's remarks quoted above. But it has its roots in the psalms where the prayer of the persecuted is that God will vindicate them. As we saw in the psalms, divine judgment is seen as vindicating the righteous who have suffered at the hands of the wicked. It is God's saving intervention on behalf of his people. Mary declares that what the Old Testament prophets and psalmists yearned for, God's coming as saving judge, has now come to be.

The Suffering of the Righteous

Persecution or suffering for righteousness' sake is a recurrent theme in the New Testament. And as we have seen, it is also prominent in the psalms: time and again the righteous have to endure the mockery of irreligious enemies who claim that God does not care about the trials of the righteous. The evangelists see this pattern fulfilled in great detail in the passion of Christ, and they often allude to or quote from psalms that describe such suffering.

For the New Testament, the prophetic psalm par excellence that foreshadows the sufferings of the Christ is Psalm 22. There are explicit quotations from this psalm in the Passion Narratives: "Jesus cried out with a loud voice, saying, 'Eli, Eli, lema sabachthani?' that is, 'My God, my God, why have you forsaken me?'" (Matt. 27:46; cf. Mark 15:34) and "They divided my garments among them, and for my clothing they cast lots" (John 19:24).

In addition there is a profusion of unmarked citations and allusions. Rikk Watts points out "Psalm 22's pervasive influence on the crucifixion narrative: the division of Jesus' garments (v. 19 [18]; Mk 15:24), mockery and head-shaking (v. 8 [7]; 15:29), 'save yourself!' (v. 9 [8]; 15:30–31), reviling (v. 7 [6]; 15:32), and the cry of dereliction (a citation of v. 2 [1]; 15:34)."[8]

Furthermore, it is in Psalm 22 that the righteous sufferer experiences the greatest reversal of fortune. His prayers are answered, and "all the ends of the earth shall remember and turn to the Lord, and all the families of the nations shall worship before you" (Ps. 22:27). Or in the terminology of Psalm 118:22, "The stone that the builders rejected has become the cornerstone." All three Synoptic Gospels record Jesus citing this last text as a prediction of his ultimate vindication (Matt.

8. Rikk Watts, "The Psalms in Mark's Gospel," in Moyise and Menken, eds., *Psalms in the New Testament*, 42.

21:42; Mark 12:10; Luke 20:17). Peter likewise cites it in one of his early sermons (Acts 4:11) and in his first epistle (1 Pet. 2:7).

The expectation that Christ's disciples will suffer runs through the New Testament from Matthew to Revelation. This message is underlined by numerous quotations and allusions to righteous sufferers in the psalms. Nowhere is this seen more clearly than in Peter's first epistle. He draws on the Psalter to demonstrate that Jesus fulfills the prophecies of the psalmist David, who, according to the titles, is the author of many psalms. But as King David of the psalms stands for every righteous person in Israel, the New Testament also draws lessons directly from the psalms for the Christian believer. Most obviously, the righteous sufferer is exemplified not only in Christ but also in the life of his followers. This connection is made explicitly by Peter: "For to this you have been called, because Christ also suffered for you, leaving you an example, so that you might follow in his steps. He committed no sin, neither was deceit found in his mouth. When he was reviled, he did not revile in return; when he suffered, he did not threaten, but continued entrusting himself to him who judges justly" (1 Pet. 2:21–23).

The language here is most reminiscent of Isaiah 53,[9] but the character of the suffering servant of Isaiah is very similar to that of the righteous sufferer met so often in the psalms, particularly in the psalms of lament. Peter's image of the devil as a roaring lion seeking someone to devour (1 Pet. 5:8) could well be drawn from the quintessential lament of Psalm 22:13, 21.

The righteous sufferer also appears in thanksgiving psalms, where he praises God for deliverance from various trials. One of these is Psalm 34, and it has been argued that the whole of 1 Peter is essentially a sermon based on this psalm. This theory seems to push the evidence too hard, but there is no doubt about the relevance of this psalm to Peter's exposition. He quotes it at length in 1 Peter 3:10–12 (cf. Ps. 34:12–14):

> For "Whoever desires to love life
> and see good days,
> let him keep his tongue from evil
> and his lips from speaking deceit;

9. Wayne A. Grudem, *1 Peter*, TNTC (Leicester, UK: Inter-Varsity, 1988), 129.

> let him turn away from evil and do good;
> let him seek peace and pursue it.
> For the eyes of the Lord are on the righteous,
> and his ears are open to their prayer.
> But the face of the Lord is against those who do evil."

In the context of 1 Peter this quotation is used to encourage Christians to avoid irresponsible speech so as to not provoke persecution. Instead, their humility and gentleness should make others respect them. But if, nevertheless, they do suffer persecution, "it is better to suffer for doing good, if that should be God's will, than for doing evil" (1 Pet. 3:17). Then Peter again reminds his readers of the way Christ endured unjust suffering. "The message of that psalm [Ps. 34] that God will protect and vindicate the righteous sufferer has been warmly embraced by the author of 1 Peter in his presentation of both Christ as the archetypal 'suffering servant' of Isaiah and also the Christian church as called to the *imitatio Christi*."[10]

But in fact this explicit quotation of Psalm 34 is but the tip of an iceberg of allusions to the psalm in 1 Peter. For example, 1 Peter 2:1, "So put away all malice and all deceit and hypocrisy and envy and all slander," is an allusion to Psalm 34:13, "Keep your tongue from evil and your lips from speaking deceit." And 1 Peter 2:3, "if indeed you have tasted that the Lord is good," is based on Psalm 34:8, "Oh, taste and see that the Lord is good!" Sue Woan comments on the underlying hermeneutical assumption of 1 Peter, "The whole of 1 Pet. 1:13–2:10 is a delightful medley of metaphors and words of the author mingled with words and expressions culled from the Old Testament. . . . It is clear that the author has seen the (LORD) of the psalm as Christ. No explanation, argument or apology is given for this; it is natural and self-evident for the author and his church, and the overall effect is to provide from the scriptures an authoritative conclusion to the admonitions of 1 Pet. 2:1–2."[11]

But there is more to the use of Psalm 34 than this. Generally in 1 Peter, Old Testament quotations are retrospective; that is, they sum

10. Sue Woan, "The Psalms in 1 Peter," in Moyise and Menken, eds., *Psalms in the New Testament*, 227.

11. Ibid., 222.

up the preceding argument (e.g., 1 Pet. 1:24–25). But 1 Peter 3:10–12 is unusual in that it not only sums up the preceding argument but also introduces the next section. "It stands as a summary of the theme that has persisted throughout the letter to this point: the kind of behaviour expected from someone who has entered the 'new life' of the Christian. But it also seems to act as a springboard to the section that follows. . . . The section continues with a positive reference to the kind of speech Christians should be engaged in (3:15b), and the theme of Christian suffering, while at the same time behaving in a holy manner and doing good, pervades much of the rest of the letter."[12]

The influence of Psalm 34 is seen not only in 1 Peter 3 but also throughout the epistle. Woan finds allusions to Psalm 34:12 in 1:3, 8; 2:1; to Psalm 34:13 in 2:12, 14, 16, 20; and to Psalm 34:14 in 2:22–23; 3:9. It is not merely the coincidence of language (most apparent in the LXX), but the common sequence of ideas. "The *thematic progression* of 1:1–3:9 also mirrors very closely the format of 3:10–12 [Ps. 34:12–16], even when there is no verbal agreement."[13]

Not only do the opening chapters of 1 Peter anticipate the psalm quotation but also the material that follows the quotation echoes it. For example, key words in 3:13–17, "harm," "righteousness," "do good," "do evil," are drawn from 3:11–12.[14] If Psalm 34 is central to the thought of 1 Peter, then it seems that other slight overlaps in vocabulary are more than coincidental and are real allusions. In 1 Peter 1:14 the author speaks of "obedient children," which may recall Psalm 34:11: "Come, O children, listen to me; I will teach you the fear of the LORD." The next verse, 1 Peter 1:15, calls on the readers to be "holy" (*hagioi*), which, while most obviously drawn from Leviticus 11:44, is also the term used in the LXX of Psalm 34:9 (*hagioi*, "saints"). The injunction in 1 Peter 1:17 to "conduct yourselves with fear" could well reflect exhortations in the psalm: "Oh, fear the LORD, you his saints, for those who fear him have no lack!" (Ps. 34:9; cf. vv. 4, 8). Conversely, when Peter urges his reader not to fear anything that is frightening (1 Pet. 3:6), he could be echoing Psalm 34:4: "I sought the LORD, and he answered me and delivered me from all my fears."

12. Ibid., 223.
13. Ibid., 224.
14. This is clearer in the Greek than in the English translation.

The term "blessed" in 1 Peter 3:14; 4:14 could be derived from Psalm 34:8, and "do good" in 1 Peter 3:17 from Psalm 34:14.

So Woan concludes that all these parallels "show that the quotation from Psalm 34 at 3:10–12 is indeed pivotal to the thinking of the whole letter. This quotation not only stands at the climax of the letter; it not only concludes one section and introduces another; it also contains vocabulary and themes that pervade the entire letter."[15]

The message of 1 Peter that the righteous may expect to face persecution and suffering simply for being righteous is thus based both on the experience of Jesus and on the teaching of the Old Testament, most obviously Psalm 34. At the same time, the fulfillment of the prophetic predictions of suffering in that psalm in the life of Jesus confirms his identity as the Messiah. One could hardly wish for a higher endorsement of the Old Testament ethic than this.

Paul's Appeal to the Psalms

The apostle Paul is another writer who makes much use of the psalms to establish his ethic. To keep this study manageable I will confine it to Romans, which has more abundant quotation of the psalms than any of his other epistles. Paul quotes from the Old Testament some sixty times in Romans,[16] about one-fourth of which are drawn from the psalms. It is particularly to the psalms that he appeals to establish his doctrine of sin's universal reign. Not only quotations from the Old Testament but also allusions to it are fundamental to his argument. "The central theological vocabulary of the letter belongs to these allusions."[17]

Allusions to psalms have been detected already in his statement of the theme of the epistle: "For I am not ashamed of the gospel, for it is the power of God for salvation to everyone who believes, to the Jew first and also to the Greek. For in it the righteousness of God is revealed from faith for faith, as it is written, 'The righteous shall live by faith'" (Rom. 1:16–17). The explicit quotation comes from

15. Woan, "Psalms in 1 Peter," 226.
16. Mark A. Seifrid, "Romans," *CNTOT*, 607.
17. Ibid.

Habakkuk 2:4, but the mention of shame and righteousness is an allusion to Psalm 71:1–2:

> In you, O LORD, do I take refuge;
> let me never be put to shame!
> In your righteousness deliver me and rescue me;
> incline your ear to me, and save me!

Another lament psalm that Paul could be alluding to is Psalm 44, which mentions shame in verses 9, 15. But the highly positive tone of Paul's opening statement echoes even more clearly Psalm 98, with its declaration of salvation and God's righteousness to all the nations: "The LORD has made known his salvation; he has revealed his righteousness in the sight of the nations" (v. 2). But in Psalm 98, as in many others, the corollary to God's salvation is judgment on the wicked, a cause for rejoicing for those who have suffered at their hand. Verses 8–9 proclaim,

> Let the rivers clap their hands;
> let the hills sing for joy together
> before the LORD, for he comes
> to judge the earth.
> He will judge the world with righteousness,
> and the peoples with equity.

So, similarly, Paul moves in Romans 1:18 to declare that "the wrath of God is revealed from heaven against all ungodliness and unrighteousness of men, who by their unrighteousness suppress the truth." And this begins a section that continues to Romans 3:20 demonstrating the universal reign of sin, that all humans, both gentiles and Jews, have sinned and deserve divine condemnation. In denouncing the folly of gentile idolatry, Paul alludes in Romans 1:23 to Psalm 106:20: "They exchanged the glory of God for the image of an ox that eats grass." The psalm was referring to the golden calf, but Paul extends its condemnation to all idolatry.

After making his sweeping condemnation of gentile sins, a condemnation that any Jew would agree with, Paul challenges those who condemn others to realize that God's judgment may apply to them as well. In Romans 2:6 Paul makes his point by alluding to Psalm 62:12: "For you will render to a man according to his work." He argues that Jews are equally guilty with gentiles of breaking the law, but this does not revoke the privilege of being a Jew. Their unfaithfulness does not nullify the faithfulness of God.

Then in Romans 3:4 there follows a reference to Psalm 51:4: "so that you may be justified in your words and blameless in your judgment." This is apt because both the psalm and Paul's argument are concerned with human guilt and divine righteousness. Both are arguing that because of human sinfulness God is justified in judging people. Paul drives this point home with a string of quotations from six psalms, "the lengthiest citation of Scripture in all his letters."[18] Romans 3:10–18 reads,

> As it is written:
> "None is righteous, no, not one;
>   no one understands;
>   no one seeks for God.
> All have turned aside; together they have become worthless;
>   no one does good,
>   not even one." [= Ps. 14:1–3; 53:1–3]
> "Their throat is an open grave;
>   they use their tongues to deceive." [= Ps. 5:9]
> "The venom of asps is under their lips." [= Ps. 140:3]
>   "Their mouth is full of curses and bitterness." [= Ps. 10:7]
> "Their feet are swift to shed blood;
>   in their paths are ruin and misery,
> and the way of peace they have not known." [= Isa. 59:7–8]
>   "There is no fear of God before their eyes." [= Ps. 36:1]

In examining the psalms' use of the Decalogue, I noted their concentration on the sins of speech. Here Paul's focus is similar. Mark Seifrid notes, "The vice list in 1:29–31 is composed first and foremost of sins of the tongue. . . . Paul names the organs of speech (throat, tongue, lips, mouth) as the fundamental locus of human fallenness. As in the psalms that he cites, human sinfulness is simultaneously rooted in

18. Ibid., 616.

the 'being' of the fallen human ('their throat *is* an open grave') and expressed in culpable actions ('with their tongues *they* deceive')."[19]

Sylvia Keesmat notes that "the overwhelming condemnation of Romans 3:10–18 comes to a climax with two other quotations."[20] The first, "so that every mouth may be stopped" (Rom. 3:19), drawn from Psalm 63:11 ("for the mouths of liars will be stopped"), establishes "beyond any possible doubt" that "God is just in his judgment of the world."[21] The second, "no human being will be justified in his sight" (Rom. 3:20), drawn from Psalm 143:2 ("Enter not into judgment with your servant, for no one living is righteous before you"), is, paradoxically, the ground for human hope because Psalm 143 is an appeal for God's deliverance.

> Hear my prayer, O LORD;
> give ear to my pleas for mercy!
> In your faithfulness answer me, in your righteousness! (v. 1)
>
> Deliver me from my enemies, O LORD!
> I have fled to you for refuge! (v. 9)
>
> For your name's sake, O LORD, preserve my life!
> In your righteousness bring my soul out of trouble! (v. 11)

The LXX takes the verbs in verse 11 as futures, which lends itself to Paul's hopeful interpretation even more easily. And this hope that God's righteousness will bring salvation to mankind, despite their failure to live up to the law's demands, is grounded on the experience of Abraham (Rom. 4:1–8) and yet another passage from the psalms:

> Blessed is the one whose transgression is forgiven,
> whose sin is covered.
> Blessed is the man against whom the LORD counts no iniquity.
> (Ps. 32:1–2)

19. Ibid., 617.

20. Sylvia C. Keesmat, "The Psalms in Romans and Galatians," in Moyise and Menken, eds., *Psalms in the New Testament*, 147.

21. Richard B. Hays, *Echoes of Scripture in the Letters of Paul* (New Haven: Yale University Press, 1989), 50.

These opening chapters of Romans thus demonstrate the immense importance of the Psalter for Paul's understanding of sin, its nature, effects, and consequences. Although we tend to see these teachings as a branch of his theology, they are of fundamental importance to ethics as well and once again illustrate the impact that the Psalter had and has on the development of ethical debate.

After Romans 4, Paul appeals to the psalms more rarely. Nevertheless, some quotations pop up at significant points in the epistle. For example, in Romans 8 he addresses the issue of the suffering that Christians must endure while awaiting the revelation of God's final glory. Like the Gospels and 1 Peter, Paul sees the predicament of the church through the lenses of Christ's own suffering and the righteous sufferer in the psalms. In his great peroration, which begins, "If God is for us who can be against us?" (Rom. 8:31), we find a free citation of Psalm 118:6: "The Lord is on my side; I will not fear. What can man do to me?" Paul continues, "Who is to condemn? Christ Jesus is the one who died—more than that, who was raised—who is at the right hand of God, who indeed is interceding for us" (Rom. 8:34). This reference to Christ at the right hand of God is from Psalm 110:1, the psalm most frequently cited in the New Testament.

Finally, in Romans 8:36, Paul cites Psalm 44:22: "Yet for your sake we are killed all the day long; we are regarded as sheep to be slaughtered." For Paul, as for Peter, Christians are called to share in their Lord's sufferings, sufferings foreshadowed in those of the righteous sufferer in the psalms, whose voice is heard in so many of the lament psalms, such as Psalm 44. It is this understanding of persecution that undergirds many of Paul's injunctions about coping with suffering in Romans 12, such as "Be patient in tribulation" (v. 12), "Bless those who persecute you; bless and do not curse them" (v. 14), and "Repay no one evil for evil" (v. 17; cf. Prov. 20:22). In Romans 12:19 Paul writes, "Beloved, never avenge yourselves, but leave it to the wrath of God, for it is written, 'Vengeance is mine, I will repay, says the Lord.'" The quotation is from Deuteronomy 32:35, with a probable allusion to Psalm 94:1. Certainly Paul's injunctions capture the philosophy of the lament psalms, with their frequent appeals to God to avenge the injustice that the psalmist has suffered. But like the psalmists, Paul implies that the sufferer is not going to take vengeance into his own hands.[22]

Finally, the argument of Romans ends with four more quotations from the Old Testament, two of them from the psalms. This time Paul quotes the Old Testament to demonstrate the inclusion of the gentiles within the people of God. Romans opened by demonstrating the patent sinfulness of the gentiles (1:18–32); it closes with the gentiles praising God for his mercy (15:9, 11), quoting from two psalms:

> For this I will praise you, O LORD, among the nations,
> and sing to your name. (Ps. 18:49)
>
> Praise the LORD, all nations!
> Extol him, all peoples! (Ps. 117:1)

This brief survey of the use of the psalms in Romans has further illustrated the profound effect of the psalms on the ethical thinking of the New Testament writers. Paul uses the psalms to demonstrate the universality of sin and to define some of its characteristics. Like the psalms, he especially highlights the sins of the tongue as proof of the pervasiveness of sin. Also drawing on the psalms, he warns his readers that they must expect to suffer for their convictions, for this is the fate of the righteous in the psalms and in the gospel. And like the righteous sufferer, they must not retaliate—a principle explicit in Proverbs and implicit in Psalms. Paul's epistle to the Romans thus offers further support for my contention of the importance of the Psalter for early Christian ethical thought.

Hebrews

Hebrews is another book that relies on the psalms to establish both doctrine and ethics. Indeed, it is so permeated by quotations of the Old Testament that commentators cannot agree how many there

22. See discussion in chapter 9 above; see also David Firth, *Surrendering Retribution in the Psalms: Responses to Violence in Individual Complaints*, PBM (Milton Keynes: Paternoster, 2005), 35, 67.

are. George Guthrie, mediating between the extremes, suggests that Hebrews contains thirty-seven quotations of and forty allusions to the Old Testament.[23] "The author of Hebrews depends most heavily by far on Psalms. . . . Nineteen of the quotations and another fifteen allusions come from this portion of the OT."[24] Hebrews is essentially a homily urging its readers to be steadfast in the faith in the face of pressure to abandon it and revert to Judaism. The author's chief thrust, therefore, is to assert Christ's superiority to the angels and to Old Testament predecessors such as Melchizedek and Aaron.

To make his points, the author relies heavily on the psalms, especially Psalms 2; 8; 45; 95; 110. Psalm 110, with its reference to the eternal priesthood of Melchizedek (v. 4), demonstrates that the high priesthood of Christ is superior to Aaron's. Psalm 2:7, "The Lord said to me, 'You are my Son; today I have begotten you,'" again underlines his superiority to the angels (Heb. 1:5). And Psalm 8 is understood to foretell his suffering and glory (Heb. 2:5–11). The implications of these christological interpretations are both theological and moral: the readers of Hebrews must hold fast to faith in Christ and, if need be, put up with persecution. To this end, the author draws a parallel between the situation of Israel in the wilderness and the temptations facing his readers today. The Israelites broke faith with God and suffered for it; let not his first-century readers make the same mistake.

To make this point, Hebrews 3–4 presents a sustained exposition of Psalm 95:7–11:

> For he is our God,
> and we are the people of his pasture,
> and the sheep of his hand.
> Today, if you hear his voice,
> do not harden your hearts, as at Meribah,
> as on the day at Massah in the wilderness,
> when your fathers put me to the test
> and put me to the proof, though they had seen my work.

23. George H. Guthrie, "Hebrews," *CNTOT*, 919.
24. Ibid., 921.

> For forty years I loathed that generation
> and said, "They are a people who go astray in their heart,
> and they have not known my ways."
> Therefore I swore in my wrath,
> "They shall not enter my rest."

Significantly, Hebrews prefaces this psalm quotation with the remark "Therefore, as the Holy Spirit says" (3:7). The use of the present tense, "says," shows that this message was not addressed to the wilderness generation but rather to later times. Indeed, if one supposes that the psalm was written by David, it implies that even in his day Israel had not entered "my rest" (Heb. 4:1–10).

"Therefore, the author understood Psalm 95 as a perennially pertinent word from God to people. Rather than being primarily concerned with the wilderness generation, the author uses that generation as an exemplar on how people should not respond to God and his revelation."[25]

Hebrews develops a regular theme of the historical psalms (e.g., Pss. 78; 106; 107), Israel's propensity to forget and disobey God, by quoting Psalm 95:8–11. The thrust of the author's comments on this text is that his readers must not make the same mistakes that their ancestors made, by hardening their hearts and falling away from God. The exodus generation died in the wilderness because of their unbelief. They forfeited their right to enter the promised land and missed the promised rest. Let not this generation make the same mistake. "Let us therefore strive to enter that rest, so that no one may fall by the same sort of disobedience" (Heb. 4:11). "The negative tone of the psalm, therefore, is turned inside out. That the wilderness generation was not allowed to enter God's rest means that there is a rest to be entered by those who take the opposite path, that of belief and obedience."[26]

Hebrews urges its readers to keep the faith: "We share in Christ, if indeed we hold our original confidence firm to the end" (3:14). This emphasis on endurance in the face of problems is reiterated at many points (4:1, 11; 6:11–12; 9:28; 10:23–39). This call to persevere

25. Ibid., 955.
26. Ibid., 956.

climaxes in Hebrews 11, with its roll call of Old Testament heroes and the difficulties that they overcame. This catalog of triumphant saints is crowned by a reminder of the endurance of Christ, "who for the joy that was set before him endured the cross, despising the shame, and is seated at the right hand of God. Consider him who endured from sinners such hostility against himself, so that you may not grow weary or fainthearted" (12:2–3).

The Book of Revelation

The call to endure in the face of opposition is central to the message of the book of Revelation too. The last book of the Bible is saturated with citations and allusions to the Old Testament. "It is generally recognized that Revelation contains more Old Testament references than does any other NT book,"[27] though exactly how many is a matter of debate. After Isaiah (46×), Daniel (31×), and Ezekiel (29×), Psalms is quoted most often in Revelation, about twenty-seven times.[28] These quotations have been thoroughly studied by Steve Moyise, who categorizes them under four main headings.[29] First, quotations from the psalms announce judgment on the idolatrous nations by God. For example, "To him I will give authority over the nations, and he will rule them with a rod of iron, as when earthen pots are broken in pieces" (Rev. 2:26–27) is a quotation of Psalm 2:8–9 (cf. Rev. 12:5; 19:15). Second, a quotation from Psalm 86:8–10 in Revelation 15:3–4 proclaims that all the nations will eventually acknowledge God's sovereignty. Revelation 15:3–4 reads,

> Great and amazing are your deeds,
> O Lord God the Almighty!
> Just and true are your ways,
> O King of the nations!
> Who will not fear, O Lord,
> and glorify your name?

27. G. K. Beale and Sean M. McDonough, "Revelation," *CNTOT*, 1082.

28. Ibid. (following the count by H. B. Swete).

29. Steve Moyise, "The Psalms in the Book of Revelation," in Moyise and Menken, eds., *Psalms in the New Testament*, 244–45.

For you alone are holy.
All nations will come
and worship you,
for your righteous acts have been revealed.

Third, images of salvation are drawn from the psalms (Pss. 23; 69; 141; 144).[30] Fourth, Revelation draws on the psalms to describe attributes of God and his anointed (e.g., Rev. 1:5; 2:23; 19:11; cf. Pss. 89:27; 7:9; 96:13). Moyise sums up the hermeneutic of Revelation's use of the psalms: the author of Revelation "thinks that Psalm 2 speaks about the victory of Jesus the Messiah; Psalm 89 offers a description of him as firstborn, faithful witness and ruler of the kings of the earth; and Psalm 86 describes the eschatological conversion of the nations."[31]

But it is not only the phraseology and theology of the psalms that Revelation draws on: many of the songs of Revelation are similar in genre and flavor to the psalms, especially the laments. Moyise notes that "the language of the psalms is frequently echoed in the hymns and praises of Revelation."[32] For our study of the ethics of the psalms and their impact on the New Testament, the prayers and songs in Revelation provide some of the most intriguing material. For example, the martyrs' prayer in Revelation 6:10 echoes many a psalmic lament (e.g., Pss. 7; 11; 13). The souls under the altar "cried out with a loud voice, 'O Sovereign Lord, holy and true, how long before you will judge and avenge our blood on those who dwell on the earth?' " Many a lament includes the question "How long?" (Pss. 6:3; 13:1–2; 74:10; 79:5; 94:3), as the psalmists, seeing the wicked get away with their misdeeds, protest God's apparent indifference. Psalm 79:10, "Let the avenging of the outpoured blood of your servants be known among the nations before our eyes!" is paraphrased by the martyrs: "How long before you will judge and avenge our blood?"

30. Moyise (ibid., 244–45) lists the following images of the redeemed. They are "led to springs of living waters" (Ps. 23:1–2; Rev. 7:17); they are "not erased from the book of life" (Ps. 69:28; Rev. 3:5); "both small and great fear his name" (Ps. 115:13; Rev. 11:18; 19:5); they sing a new song (Ps 144:9; Rev. 5:9; 14:3); and their prayers rise like incense (Ps. 141:2; Rev. 8:3–4).

31. Ibid., 245.

32. Ibid., 240.

Moyise notes allusions to Psalms 2:1–2; 115:13 in Revelation 11:17–18:

> We give thanks to you, Lord God Almighty,
> who is and who was,
> for you have taken your great power
> and begun to reign.
> The nations raged,
> but your wrath came,
> and the time for the dead to be judged, . . .
> both small and great.

The mention of the nations raging and "those who fear your name, both small and great" connects the Revelation text with Psalms 2; 115.[33] But formally this passage has features that resemble thanksgiving and lament psalms, which praise God for intervening on behalf of his people (e.g., Pss. 34; 41; 92; 118; 138). And often in their positive sections such psalms recall God's defeat of evil (e.g., Pss. 9; 54; 58; 63; 79). These features certainly are present in Revelation 11.

I have already commented on the content of the song in Revelation 15:3–4. It should also be noted that it is explicitly modeled on the song of Moses (Exod. 15:1–18; Deut. 32). However, its content "comes not directly from Exod. 15, but rather from passages throughout the OT extolling God's character."[34] Verbally, it owes most to Psalm 86:9–10, and there is a strong echo of Psalm 111:2–4, which praises God for his great works: "Great and amazing are your deeds, O Lord God the Almighty" (Rev. 15:3).

In Revelation 16:5–6 we have a hymn from an angel:

> Just are you, O Holy One, who is and who was,
> for you brought these judgments.
> For they have shed the blood of saints and prophets,
> and you have given them blood to drink.
> It is what they deserve!

To which the altar replies, "Yes, Lord God the Almighty, true and just are your judgments!" (Rev. 16:7). The angel seems to be paraphrasing

33. Ibid., 232, 241.

34. Beale and McDonough, "Revelation," *CNTOT*, 1134.

Psalm 79:3, 10,[35] which speaks of God avenging the blood of his servants, whereas the altar's words are taken from Psalm 119:137: "Righteous art thou, O LORD, and upright are thy judgments" (KJV).[36]

But most striking are the chants of the heavenly voices in Revelation 18–19. They are pervaded by joy at the downfall of the oppressive rich. Revelation 18 is a paean over the fall of Babylon, famed for its wealth and immorality. It is the Magnificat, but in lurid colors. Revelation 18:3 says,

> For all nations have drunk
> the wine of the passion of her sexual immorality,
> and the kings of the earth have committed immorality with her,
> and the merchants of the earth have grown rich from the power of her luxurious living.

And in Revelation 18:20 saints, apostles, and prophets are commanded,

> Rejoice over her, O heaven,
> and you saints and apostles and prophets,
> for God has given judgment for you against her!

This call to rejoice that God has judged the archetypal city of sin, Babylon, echoes many psalms with their exhortations to rejoice that God will judge the wicked (e.g., Pss. 96:10–13; 97:7–9; 98:7–9; 99:4–5). As we saw earlier,[37] the righteous should welcome God's coming in judgment because it brings justice to situations of palpable injustice. His coming as judge will disprove the boasts of the wicked that God does not care about the suffering that they inflict on the weak and defenseless (cf. Pss. 10:13; 14:1). It is this sentiment that informs the call in the book of Revelation to rejoice over the fall of Babylon. Its fall is the triumph of good over evil. It is the vindication of God's righteous rule.

35. "They have poured out their blood like water all around Jerusalem" (Ps. 79:3); "Let the avenging of the outpoured blood of your servants be known among the nations before our eyes" (Ps. 79:10).

36. Moyise, "Psalms in the Book of Revelation," 244.

37. See chapter 9 above.

Then in Revelation 19 we hear the words of a great multitude in heaven. Their songs are the last in the book, and in various ways they follow the pattern of the psalms that close the Psalter (Pss. 146–150). Both sections include repeated cries of "hallelujah" (Pss. 146:1, 10; 147:1, 20; 148:1, 14; 149:1, 9; 150:1, 6; Rev. 19:1, 3, 4, 6). Both celebrate God's reign (Pss. 146:10; 147:15; 149:2; Rev. 19:1, 6, 16) and his vindication of his people (Pss. 146:7–8; 147:2, 6; 148:14; 149:4; Rev. 19:2, 7–8). Both summon God's servants to praise him (Pss. 146:1; 147:1, 7, 12; 148:1–13; 149:1–9; 150:1–6; Rev. 19:5), particularly for ending injustice and destroying evil (Pss. 146:7–9; 147:6; 149:6–9; Rev. 19:2, 11–21). In other words, the closing chapters of Revelation seem to be inspired by the same sentiments that close the Psalter. In Revelation 19:1–3 John reports,

> After this I heard what seemed to be the loud voice of a great
> multitude in heaven, crying out,
> "Hallelujah!
> Salvation and glory and power belong to our God,
> for his judgments are true and just;
> for he has judged the great prostitute
> who corrupted the earth with her immorality,
> and has avenged on her the blood of his servants."
> Once more they cried out,
> "Hallelujah!
> The smoke from her goes up forever and ever."

Their cries of "hallelujah" are prompted not merely by the fact that God has at last avenged the blood of his servants but also because "the Lord our God the Almighty reigns" (Rev. 19:6). In Revelation 19:15 one of the programmatic psalms, Psalm 2, is quoted: "You shall break them with a rod of iron" (v. 9). The affirmations of the so-called enthronement psalms, "The Lord reigns" (Pss. 93:1; 97:1; 99:1), are at last seen to be true. This reign culminates in the coming of the new Jerusalem to earth, so that God will at last dwell with man; "his servants . . . will see his face," and evil will be no more (Rev. 21:2–4; 22:3–4, 14–15). Then the longings and laments of the psalmists will finally be answered, and creation will be perfected.

Conclusion

This review of the New Testament use of the psalms in the formulation of a Christian ethic is by no means exhaustive. But it is, I think, sufficient to show that the Psalter had a strong influence on the New Testament writers, especially in the formulation of their ethic. I have selected just a few of the passages that explicitly cite the psalms in developing ethical teaching. From Mary's Magnificat to the book of Revelation, quotations of and allusions to the psalms abound. The apostle Paul's greatest epistle, Romans, bases its doctrine of sin on the Psalter, while many writers use the Psalter's image of the righteous sufferer not only as a prophecy of the sufferings of Christ but also as a picture of the trials that his followers must expect. But as the psalms affirm the ultimate vindication of the righteous, so the New Testament declares that the day of judgment has begun with the coming of the Christ. His resurrection is the guarantee of his followers' resurrection and the pledge of his return to complete the judgment and bring in the era of universal peace and justice, for which prophets and psalmists yearned and prayed.

Conclusion

This study has taken as its starting point current theories about the origin and use of the Psalter. Some of these theories may owe more to scholarly fashion than to indisputable historical proof. But there is no doubt that over the centuries the psalms have been prayed in public and private worship by both Jews and Christians, and this must have had a profound effect on the theology and ethics of the devout. Although the theological influence of the psalms has been recognized, less attention has been paid to their influence on ethics. In the preceding chapters I have attempted to begin to remedy this neglect.

Many commentaries on the psalms concentrate on determining the sense of the individual psalms in their supposed original settings, but I have adopted a canonical approach to reading them. I ask the question, "What did this particular psalm mean to the editor(s) of the Psalter who placed it here, sandwiched between two other psalms?" Often the answer to this question is little different from the usual critical interpretation. But whereas the form-critical approach discards the titles of the psalms as late and irrelevant in determining their original meaning, a final-form or canonical reading does otherwise. Whether historically valid or not, the titles give us insight into the way the postexilic editors understood the psalms.

More speculatively, I have argued that the Psalter is an anthology designed to be memorized and sung. Most commentators recognize the anthological nature of the Psalter. The grouping of the titles (e.g., psalms of David, Songs of Ascent) suggests that earlier collections of psalms have been brought together to form the present Psalter. It is less widely recognized that this collection was designed to be memorized. This probably is because most Western scholars operate with a literary model of textual transmission; that is, we read into the past the way we make and read books today. We ignore the fact that in ancient times scrolls and codices were rare and very expensive. Only the highly educated elite would have access to them. But this did not mean that the content of sacred texts was unknown to the wider public. Utilizing the work of Paul Griffiths and David Carr, who have shown that such texts were memorized by scribes or similarly well-trained officials to be recited at great festivals to the general public, I argue that the Psalter may well have been memorized and then said or sung in worship situations. Their poetic form would certainly help anyone memorizing the psalms.

Memorization of texts, especially if they are set to music, inevitably makes them more influential. They become part of the memorizer. Those who have learned a song sing it to themselves, and the song expresses their own feelings. In former years, before the mass distribution of pop songs, the psalms would have been some of the most familiar songs in Christian cultures and thereby molded the Christian conscience. And where they are still used in public worship, their influence remains quite significant, even if they are not memorized.

Donald Evans applied the insights of speech-act theory to utterances of worship. He argued that in prayer or praise to God worshipers are explicitly or implicitly committing themselves to God (commissive speech acts) or expressing explicitly or implicitly their attitude toward God and other people (behabitive). This applies to hymns, creeds, prayers, and, of course, psalms. By singing a hymn or reciting a psalm, a worshiper is taking personal ownership of the words of the text. When this is done in private, as in meditation, only God is witness to the worshiper's words. But when the text is sung or recited in public worship, other worshipers are aware of their fellows and whether they are joining in saying or singing the psalm or prayer. This public dimension thus creates a strong social pressure to conform to the beliefs or values of the text being recited. Not to recite the psalm or creed marks one as a nonconformist, a rebel against the system and its values. This makes the ethics embedded in liturgy—whether it be the Lord's Prayer, a psalm, or a worship song—particularly potent. In the act of reciting a psalm, a worshiper is making a public commitment to its sentiments. This may not always be a conscious commitment, as oft-repeated elements tend to sink into rote memory, so that worshipers need to be reminded of what they are affirming.

This affirmation ought to be an active commitment as opposed to the passive commitment involved in other forms of ethical instruction, such as preaching. If a preacher instructs the listeners to do something, they can just ignore it if they dislike it. The same is true of texts of Scripture. Someone who does not like a saying in the book of Proverbs, or a law of the Pentateuch, or the ethical implication of one of Jesus's parables can simply disregard it, and no one else will be the wiser. But it is quite different with a liturgical text. To pray a psalm is to address both God and fellow worshipers. Thus, either other worshipers will notice the silence of the person who does not pray it aloud, or God will take note of the hypocrisy of the person who prays it aloud but disagrees with it. Liturgy does not simply invite assent; it demands it. This is the main reason why the ethic of the Psalter has exercised such influence.

In the second half of the book, therefore, I attempted a sketch of the ethics of the Psalter. Much work still needs to be done to portray its character fully, but certain fundamentals are readily apparent. I follow those who see the Psalter as a second law, the law of David to be meditated on like the law of Moses, the Pentateuch. I traced some of the different emphases of the two laws. Markedly absent from the Psalter are instructions about observing the Sabbath or, indeed, any specific festival. The psalms, of course, often mention acts of worship, such as singing, praying, or sacrificing, and commend such action, but specific injunctions about Sabbath observance are lacking. Nor is there much explicit teaching about family life, though it clearly is regarded as a great blessing. When the ethical teaching of the Psalter is compared with the Decalogue, the former's emphasis on the use and misuse of the tongue is striking. This emphasis is shared with the book of Proverbs in the Old Testament and the Epistle of James in the New Testament.

But for the most part, the ethical emphases of the Psalter and the Pentateuch are similar. For example, both believe in fair and proportionate punishment. The formula of the *lex talionis* offers a handy rule to the biblical judge sitting in the gate of the city and deciding between litigants. But for those who fail to receive human justice, the talionic principle of fair and proportionate justice becomes the principle appealed to by the psalms of lament. The worshiper appeals to God, the all-knowing and just judge, to fulfill his role and mete out to the wrongdoer the same treatment that the wrongdoer has inflicted on the worshiper. Often, of course, it is the poorest and weakest members of society who suffer the most injustice and are least likely to find redress. So it is little surprise that the Pentateuch and the Psalter are at one in commending the needs of the poor.

In these ways, the law of David could be seen as a meditation on the law of Moses; however, the Psalter's interaction with the Pentateuch goes much deeper than the law codes. It also reflects on the teaching of the narratives in the Pentateuch and their ethical and theological implications. It retells many of the stories of Genesis through Deuteronomy in order to draw out their lessons for those who worship with the psalms. Psalm 104 reflects on the wonders of creation, Psalm 105 on the patriarchal promises, and Psalm 106 on the wilderness wanderings in some detail, while Psalm 78 covers the history of the nation from the exodus to David. Many other psalms make more passing reference to the formative events of the nation's past. Two themes recur in the retelling of the past: Israel's congenital tendency to sin, to disobey God's commands and thereby forfeit his blessing; and God's inexhaustible *ḥesed*, or "steadfast love," whereby he forgives and sustains his wayward people. For those suffering exile or its consequences, this message both explained their current predicament and gave hope for the future.

Finally, I looked at the use that the New Testament makes of the ethical teaching of the psalms. Often the law of the Old Testament is contrasted unfavorably with the ethic of the New Testament. The latter is often portrayed as more demanding on the one hand, for it requires one to respect the spirit of the law and not just the letter, and more charitable on the other hand, with a God of love replacing the Old Testament God of justice. Matching the different character of the "Gods" of the two Testaments, the ethic of the Testaments is likewise alleged to be different. This proposition seems intrinsically unlikely if the early church used the Psalter in its worship and regarded its teachings as authoritative. My sampling of some New Testament texts from Luke's Gospel to the book of Revelation showed the deep indebtedness of New Testament ethical teaching to the Psalter. Its concern for the poor, its analysis of human sin and suffering, its trust in divine mercy, and its yearning for justice—all are ways in which the New Testament endorses and deepens the ethical insights of the Psalter.

So although in many parts of the modern church the Psalter is used too little, its influence lives on in those who model their lives on the New Testament. The Psalter's theology and ethic inform many a passage of the Gospels and Epistles. But given the unique potency of prayers to mold attitudes and instruct the faithful, one must wonder whether neglect of the psalms has not impoverished the church's witness both to its own members and to the wider world. May this book encourage many to incorporate the psalms into their own prayer life and into the life of the wider church.

> Let everything that has breath praise the Lord!
> Praise the Lord! (Ps. 150:6)

Selected Bibliography

Commentaries

Alexander, Joseph A. *The Psalms Translated and Explained*. New York: C. Scribner and Co., 1873. Reprint, Grand Rapids: Baker, 1975.

Anderson, Arnold A. *The Book of Psalms*. 2 vols. NCB. Grand Rapids: Eerdmans, 1981.

Briggs, C. A. *A Critical and Exegetical Commentary on the Book of Psalms*. Vol. 1. ICC. Edinburgh: T&T Clark, 1906.

Clifford, Richard J. *Psalms 1–72*. AOTC. Nashville: Abingdon, 2002.

Craigie, Peter C. *Psalms 1–50*. 2nd ed. WBC 19. Nashville: Nelson, 2004.

Dahood, Mitchell. *Psalms III: 101–150: Introduction, Translation, and Notes*. AB 17A. Garden City, NY: Doubleday, 1970.

Delitzsch, Franz. *Biblical Commentary on the Psalms*. Translated by Francis Bolton. Vol. 1. 1871. Reprint, Grand Rapids: Eerdmans, n.d.

Eaton, John H. *The Psalms: A Historical and Spiritual Commentary with an Introduction and New Translation*. London: T&T Clark, 2003.

Gerstenberger, Erhard S. *Psalms: Part 1, with an Introduction to Cultic Poetry*. FOTL 14. Grand Rapids: Eerdmans, 1988.

Goldingay, John. *Psalms: Psalms 1–41*. BCOTWP. Grand Rapids: Baker Academic, 2006.

Hossfeld, Frank-Lothar, and Erich Zenger. *Psalmen 51–100*. HTKAT. Freiburg: Herder, 2000.

———. *Psalmen 101–150*. HTKAT. Freiburg: Herder, 2008.

———. *Psalms 2: A Commentary on Psalms 51–100*. Translated by Linda M. Maloney. Edited by Klaus Baltzer. Hermeneia. Minneapolis: Fortress, 2005.

Kidner, Derek. *Psalms 1–72: An Introduction and Commentary on Books I and II of the Psalms.* TOTC 15. Leicester, UK: Inter-Varsity, 1973.

———. *Psalms 73–150: An Introduction and Commentary on Books III–V of the Psalms.* TOTC 16. Leicester, UK: Inter-Varsity, 1975.

Kirkpatrick, A. F. *The Book of Psalms.* CBSC. Cambridge: Cambridge University Press, 1902.

Kraus, Hans-Joachim. *Psalmen.* 7th ed. 2 vols in 1. BKAT 15. Neukirchen-Vluyn: Neukirchener Verlag, 2003.

———. *Psalms 1–59: A Commentary.* Translated by Hilton C. Oswald. Minneapolis: Augsburg, 1988.

McCann, J. Clinton. "Psalms." In vol. 4 of *New Interpreter's Bible*, edited by Leander E. Keck, 639–1280. Nashville: Abingdon, 1993.

Oesterley, W. O. E. *The Psalms: Translated with Text-Critical and Exegetical Notes.* London: SPCK, 1962.

Ravasi, Gianfranco. *Il libro dei Salmi: Commento e attualizzazione.* 3 vols. Lettura pastorale della Bibbia. Bologna: Edizioni Dehoniane, 1981–85.

Schaefer, Konrad. *Psalms.* Berit Olam. Collegeville, MN: Liturgical Press, 2001.

Seybold, Klaus. *Die Psalmen.* HAT 15. Tübingen: Mohr, 1996.

Tate, Marvin E. *Psalms 51–100.* WBC 20. Dallas: Word, 1990.

Vesco, Jean-Luc. *Le psautier de David traduit et commenté.* 2 vols. LD 210, 211. Paris: Cerf, 2006.

Weber, Beat. *Werkbuch Psalmen.* Vol. 1. Stuttgart: Kohlhammer, 2001.

Weiser, Artur. *Die Psalmen.* 6th ed. 2 vols. ATD 14, 15. Göttingen: Vandenhoeck & Ruprecht, 1963.

Other Works

Alter, Robert. *The Art of Biblical Poetry.* New York: Basic Books, 1985.

Athanasius. *On the Incarnation: The Treatise "De Incarnatione Verbi Dei."* Translated by a religious of C.S.M.V. Rev. ed. Crestwood, NY: St. Vladimir's Seminary Press, 1993.

Austin, J. L. *How to Do Things with Words.* Edited by J. O. Urmson. Oxford: Clarendon, 1962.

Auwers, Jean-Marie. *La composition littéraire du psautier: Un état de la question.* CahRB 46. Paris: Gabalda, 2000.

Baker, David L. *Tight Fists or Open Hands? Wealth and Poverty in Old Testament Law.* Grand Rapids: Eerdmans, 2009.

Barton, John. "Imitation of God in the Old Testament." In *The God of Israel*, edited by Robert P. Gordon, 35–46. UCOP 64. Cambridge: Cambridge University Press, 2007.

———. *Understanding Old Testament Ethics: Approaches and Explorations.* Louisville: Westminster John Knox Press, 2003.

Beale, G. K., and D. A. Carson. *Commentary on the New Testament Use of the Old Testament.* Grand Rapids: Baker Academic, 2007.

Bock, Brian. *Singing the Ethos of God: On the Place of Christian Ethics in Scripture* (Grand Rapids: Eerdmans, 2007).

Briggs, Richard. *Words in Action: Speech Act Theory and Biblical Interpretation; Toward a Hermeneutic of Self-Involvement.* Edinburgh: T&T Clark, 2001.

Bristow, Peter. *Christian Ethics and the Human Person: Truth and Relativism in Contemporary Moral Theology.* Oxford: Family Publications; Birmingham, UK: Maryvale Institute, 2009.

Brown, William P. *Seeing the Psalms: A Theology of Metaphor.* Louisville: Westminster John Knox, 2002.

Burnside, Jonathan P. *God, Justice, and Society: Aspects of Law and Legality in the Bible.* New York: Oxford University Press, 2011.

Byassee, Jason. *Praise Seeking Understanding: Reading the Psalms with Augustine.* Grand Rapids: Eerdmans, 2007.

Calvin, John. *A Commentary on the Psalms of David.* 3 vols. Oxford: Thomas Tegg, 1840.

Carr, David M. *Writing on the Tablet of the Heart: Origins of Scripture and Literature.* New York: Oxford University Press, 2005.

Carroll R., M. Daniel, and Jacqueline E. Lapsley, eds. *Character Ethics and the Old Testament: Moral Dimensions of Scripture.* Louisville: Westminster John Knox, 2007.

Davies, Eryl W. "Walking in God's Ways: The Concept of *Imitatio Dei* in the Old Testament." In *In Search of True Wisdom: Essays in Old Testament Interpretation in Honour of Ronald E. Clements,* edited by Edward Ball, 99–115. JSOTSup 300. Sheffield: Sheffield Academic Press, 1999.

Deissler, Alfons. *Psalm 119 (118) und seine Theologie: Ein Beitrag zur Erforschung der anthologischen Stilgattung im Alten Testament*. MTS 2, no. 1. Munich: Karl Zink, 1955.

De Vos, Christiane. *Klage als Gotteslob aus der Tiefe: Der Mensch vor Gott in den individuellen Klagepsalmen*. FAT 2, no. 11. Tübingen: Mohr Siebeck, 2005.

Eaton, J. H. *Kingship and the Psalms*. SBT 32. London: SCM, 1976.

Erbele-Küster, Dorothea. *Lesen als Akt des Betens: Eine Rezeptionsästhetik der Psalmen*. WMANT 87. Neukirchen-Vluyn: Neukirchener Verlag, 2001.

Evans, Donald M. *The Logic of Self-Involvement: A Philosophical Study of Everyday Language with Special Reference to the Christian Use of Language about God as a Creator*. LPT. London: SCM, 1963.

Farris, Stephen. *The Hymns of Luke's Infancy Narratives: Their Origin, Meaning and Significance*. JSNTSup 9. Sheffield: JSOT Press, 1985.

Firth, David G. *Surrendering Retribution in the Psalms: Responses to Violence in Individual Complaints*. PBM. Milton Keynes: Paternoster, 2005.

Fokkelman, J. P. *Reading Biblical Poetry: An Introductory Guide*. Translated by Ineke Smit. Louisville: Westminster John Knox, 2001.

Ford, David F., and Daniel W. Hardy. *Living in Praise: Worshipping and Knowing God*. Rev. ed. London: Darton, Longman & Todd, 2005.

Freedman, David Noel. *Psalm 119: The Exaltation of Torah*. BibJS 6. Winona Lake, IN: Eisenbrauns, 1999.

Futato, Mark David. *Interpreting the Psalms: An Exegetical Handbook*. Grand Rapids: Kregel, 2007.

Gispen, W. H. *Indirecte gegevens voor het bestaan van den Pentateuch in de Psalmen?* Zutphen: Drukkerij Nauta, 1928.

Griffiths, Paul J. *Religious Reading: The Place of Reading in the Practice of Religion*. New York: Oxford University Press, 1999.

Harlow, Daniel C. "The Hebrew Bible in the Dead Sea Scrolls." In *Eerdmans Commentary on the Bible*, edited by James D. G. Dunn and John William Rogerson, 942–49. Grand Rapids: Eerdmans, 2003.

Hauerwas, Stanley, and Samuel Wells, eds. *The Blackwell Companion to Christian Ethics*. BCR. Oxford: Blackwell, 2004.

Holladay, William L. *The Psalms through Three Thousand Years: Prayerbook of a Cloud of Witnesses*. Minneapolis: Fortress, 1993.

Houston, Walter J. "The Character of YHWH and the Ethics of the Old Testament: Is *Imitatio Dei* Appropriate?" *JTS* 58 (2007): 1–25.

Johnston, Philip S., and David G. Firth, eds. *Interpreting the Psalms: Issues and Approaches*. Leicester, UK: Apollos, 2005.

Kellenberger, Edgar. *Ḥäsäd wä'ämät als Ausdruck einer Glaubenserfahrung: Gottes Offen-Werden und Bleiben als Voraussetzung des Lebens*. ATANT 69. Zurich: Theologischer Verlag, 1982.

Kleer, Martin. *Der liebliche Sänger der Psalmen Israels: Untersuchungen zu David als Dichter und Beter der Psalmen*. BBB 108. Bodenheim: Philo, 1996.

Kraus, Hans-Joachim. *Geschichte der historisch-kritischen Erforschung des Alten Testaments von der Reformation bis zur Gegenwart*. Neukirchen-Vluyn: Verlag der Buchhandlung des Erziehungsvereins, 1956.

———. *Theology of the Psalms*. Translated by Keith Crim. Minneapolis: Fortress, 1992.

Lewis, C. S. *Reflections on the Psalms*. London: Collins, 1961.

Lohfink, Norbert. *In the Shadow of Your Wings: New Readings of Great Texts from the Bible*. Translated by Linda M. Maloney. Collegeville, MN: Liturgical Press, 2003.

Lunn, Nicholas P. *Word-Order Variation in Biblical Hebrew Poetry: Differentiating Pragmatics and Poetics*. PBM. Milton Keynes: Paternoster, 2006.

Mays, James L. *The Lord Reigns: A Theological Handbook to the Psalms*. Louisville: Westminster John Knox, 1994.

McCann, J. Clinton, ed. *The Shape and Shaping of the Psalter*. JSOTSup 159. Sheffield: JSOT Press, 1993.

———. *A Theological Introduction to the Book of Psalms: The Psalms as Torah*. Nashville: Abingdon, 1993.

Miller, Patrick D. "The Beginning of the Psalter." In *The Shape and Shaping of the Psalter*, edited by J. Clinton McCann, 83–92. JSOTSup 159. Sheffield: JSOT Press, 1993.

———. *Interpreting the Psalms*. Philadelphia: Fortress, 1986.

Millgram, Abraham E. *Jewish Worship*. Philadelphia: Jewish Publication Society, 1971.

Moberly, R. Walter L. *At the Mountain of God: Story and Theology in Exodus 32–34*. JSOTSup 22. Sheffield: JSOT Press, 1983.

Möller, Karl. "Reading, Singing and Praying the Law: An Exploration of the Performative, Self-Involving, Commissive Language of Psalm 101." In *Reading the Law: Studies in Honour of Gordon J. Wenham*, edited by J. G. McConville and Karl Möller, 111–37. LHBOTS 461. London: T&T Clark, 2007.

Mowinckel, Sigmund. *The Psalms in Israel's Worship*. Translated by D. R. Ap-Thomas. 2 vols. in 1. BRS. Grand Rapids: Eerdmans, 2004.

Moyise, Steve, and Maarten J. J. Menken, eds. *The Psalms in the New Testament*. London: T&T Clark, 2004.

Nasuti, Harry P. "The Sacramental Function of the Psalms in Contemporary Scholarship and Liturgical Practice." In *Psalms and Practice: Worship, Virtue, and Authority*, edited by Stephen Breck Reid, 78–89. Collegeville, MN: Liturgical Press, 2001.

Otto, Eckart. *Theologische Ethik des Alten Testaments*. TW 3, no. 2. Stuttgart: Kohlhammer, 1994.

Ramsey, Paul. "Liturgy and Ethics." *Journal of Religious Ethics* 7, no. 2 (1979): 139–71.

Reid, Stephen Breck, ed. *Psalms and Practice: Worship, Virtue, and Authority*. Collegeville, MN: Liturgical Press, 2001.

Rodd, Cyril S. *Glimpses of a Strange Land: Studies in Old Testament Ethics*. OTS. Edinburgh: T&T Clark, 2001.

Saalschütz, J. L. *Das Mosaische Recht*. 2nd ed. Berlin: Carl Heymann, 1853.

Schökel, Luis Alonso. *A Manual of Hebrew Poetics*. SubBi 11. Rome: Pontificio Istituto Biblico, 1988.

Searle, J. R. *Expression and Meaning: Studies in the Theory of Speech Acts*. Cambridge: Cambridge University Press, 1979.

Soll, Will. *Psalm 119: Matrix, Form, and Setting*. CBQMS 23. Washington, DC: Catholic Biblical Association of America, 1991.

Vermes, Geza. *The Dead Sea Scrolls in English*. Harmondsworth: Penguin Books, 1962.

Villanueva, Federico G. *The "Uncertainty of a Hearing": A Study of the Sudden Change of Mood in the Psalms of Lament*. VTSup 121. Leiden: Brill, 2008.

Vos, C. J. A. *Theopoetry of the Psalms*. London: T&T Clark, 2005.

Wagner, Andreas. *Beten und Bekennen: Über Psalmen*. Neukirchen: Neukirchener Verlag, 2008.

———. *Sprechakte und Sprechaktanalyse im Alten Testament: Untersuchungen im biblischen Hebräisch an der Nahtstelle zwischen Handlungsebene und Grammatik*. BZAW 253. Berlin: de Gruyter, 1997.

Wallace, Howard N. *Words to God, Word from God: The Psalms in the Prayer and Preaching of the Church*. Aldershot: Ashgate, 2005.

Watson, Wilfred G. E. *Classical Hebrew Poetry: A Guide to Its Techniques*. 2nd ed. London: T&T Clark, 2005.

Wenham, Gordon J. "The Gap between Law and Ethics in the Bible." *JJS* 48 (1997): 17–29.

———. *Story as Torah: Reading Old Testament Narrative Ethically*. Grand Rapids: Baker Academic, 2004.

Westbrook, Raymond. *Studies in Biblical and Cuneiform Law*. CahRB 26. Paris: Gabalda, 1988.

Westermann, Claus. *The Praise of God in the Psalms*. Translated by Keith Crim. Richmond: John Knox, 1965.

Whybray, R. Norman. *The Good Life in the Old Testament*. Edinburgh: T&T Clark, 2002.

Wilson, Gerald H. *The Editing of the Hebrew Psalter*. SBLDS 76. Chico, CA: Scholars Press, 1985.

Wright, Christopher J. H. *Old Testament Ethics for the People of God*. Rev. ed. Leicester, UK: Inter-Varsity, 2004.

Zenger, Erich. *A God of Vengeance? Understanding the Psalms of Divine Wrath*. Translated by Linda M. Maloney. Louisville: Westminster John Knox, 1996.

———. "Was wird anders bei kanonischer Psalmenauslegung?" In *Ein Gott, eine Offenbarung: Beiträge zur biblischen Exegese, Theologie und Spiritualität*, edited by Friedrich V. Reiterer, 397–413. Würzburg: Echter, 1991.

Scripture Index

Hebrew Bible/Old Testament

Author Index

Subject Index